LITERARY JOURNALISM and the AESTHETICS of EXPERIENCE

ALSO BY JOHN C. HARTSOCK

A History of American Literary Journalism:
The Emergence of a Modern Narrative Form

Seasons of a Finger Lakes Winery

LITERARY JOURNALISM
and the
AESTHETICS
of EXPERIENCE

John C. Hartsock

University of Massachusetts Press

Amherst & Boston

Copyright © 2016 by University of Massachusetts Press
All rights reserved
Printed in the United States of America

ISBN 978-1-62534-174-7 (paper); 173-0 (hardcover)
Designed by Jack Harrison
Set in Adobe Minion Pro
Printed and bound by The Maple-Vail Book Manufacturing Group

Library of Congress Cataloging-in-Publication Data
Hartsock, John C., 1951–
Literary journalism and the aesthetics of experience / John C. Hartsock.
pages cm
Includes bibliographical references and index.
ISBN 978-1-62534-174-7 (pbk. : alk. paper) —
ISBN 978-1-62534-173-0 (hardcover : alk. paper)
1. Reportage literature—History and criticism. 2. Journalism and literature.
3. Creative nonfiction—History and criticism.
4. Reportage literature, American—History and criticism. I. Title.
PN3377.5.R45H38 2016
070.4'3—dc23
2015027972

British Library Cataloguing-in-Publication Data
A catalogue record for this book is available from the British Library.

Dedicated to my teachers

Contents

Acknowledgments

It would be impossible to undertake a volume like this without expressing gratitude—indeed a heartfelt gratitude—to the many who encouraged me in its creation. First, I must acknowledge the International Association for Literary Journalism Studies. The association has provided me a scholarly home since John Bak held the first organizing conference in Nancy, France, in 2006. To name just a few of the members, they include—in addition to John—David Abrahamson, Alice Donat Trindade, William Dow, Bill Reynolds, Isabel Soares, Nancy Roberts, Richard Keeble, Rob Alexander, Susan Greenberg, Isabelle Meuret, and Josh Roiland. And I emphasize that they are just some of my colleagues who I have come to value greatly for their insights. Of course, always there are Norm Sims, Tom Connery, and John J. Pauly, stalwarts of the scholarship and my early inspirations. Additionally, thanks to Kathy Roberts Forde for her continued support. I must also thank my cousin Paul Hartsock and his wife, Carol, in Santa Fe, New Mexico. I landed on their doorstep at a critical moment for the manuscript, and indeed was ready to abandon it, but was able to see my way through the mental fog at the Santa Fe Public Library, an oasis of calm necessary for getting new perspectives.

Then there is the editorial staff of the University of Massachusetts Press. They understood what I was attempting to do, and they provided welcome suggestions and a keen eye for detail, especially in the critical polishing process. These include senior editor Clark Dougan, managing editor Carol Betsch, copy editor Amanda Heller, and the press's former director, Bruce Wilcox. Always they helped me along gently with a project that was not always gentle to me.

My colleagues at SUNY Cortland who were always encouraging deserve my thanks, as well. They include my chair, Paul van der Veur, and Sam Kelley. I also thank my dean, Bruce Mattingly, who was always willing, when he could, to provide the material support necessary for this kind of undertaking. To them I can add Lan Ye and Fang Yang, who helped me through a difficult problem of Mandarin. It is this kind of generous spirit that makes it a genuine pleasure to have them as colleagues. I should also acknowledge the unwavering support of our SUNY Cortland library staff in finding rare and obscure works through interlibrary loan.

Then I must express my sincere appreciation to Dmitry Vladimirovich Kharitonov, an editor at the *New Literary Observer* in Moscow, for his helpful suggestions and insights regarding Russian language, literature, and culture.

Too, there are my anonymous reviewers, who were tremendously helpful with their suggestions and recommendations. So often one can become so engaged in one's own perspectives and develop a mental tunnel vision. My reviewers helped me to expand and broaden that vision in very important ways. For that, again my heartfelt thanks.

Finally, of course, there was the enduring patience of my family, without which this book could not have reached fruition.

LITERARY
JOURNALISM
and the
AESTHETICS
of EXPERIENCE

Introduction

ONE CANNOT HELP but be struck by the magnitude of the grisly destruction at Verdun in 1916. What comes to my mind are the black-and-white photos in the aftermath of the battle, photos of collections of bones—heavy femurs like kettledrum mallets, skulls laughing with a few teeth, one skull still topped with thick, tousled hair, as well as shards of bones unaccountable in their provenance. And they remind me of the idealized ambitions humans construct to impose on their lives, no matter the era: to have one's place in the sun, for example, as the Kaiser so earnestly desired (a consolation for his withered left arm?). They also remind us how much our idealizations can be reduced back from whence they came, the phenomenal world, the world of consequences, as a result of the negotiation between the testimony of our vital senses—the aesthetics of experience—and the murky ambitions of abstract consciousness.

Similarly, I would suggest, a narrative literary journalism is about the desire to recover the aesthetics of experience from such idealizations. This is what I explore in the pages that follow. Of course, in one sense such an ambition—recovering the aesthetics of experience—must fail, because, as Peter Dear has noted, "the singular experience could not be evident" or fully constituted in the mediation. He adds an important qualifier, however: "but it could provide evidence," in this case of what contributed to constituting the mediation.[1] Do the bones at Verdun give us much choice, however imperfect our mediations may prove?

I did not consciously have this in mind when I began this volume. Instead, it began as an attempt to try to answer some questions I have mused over since publication of my *History of American Literary Journalism: The Emergence of a Modern Narrative Form* in 2000. Those queries have a direct bearing, I believe, on what we mean by literary journalism as a narrative discourse. But

1

if they are the impetus for this volume, one consequence is that I detect the outlines of possible larger critical contexts from which to examine the genre. The result is a perspective drawn largely from the first three queries I start with, which I then find reflected to varying degrees in the remaining three. My organization follows from the order of my initial queries:

1. Why is a more traditional narrative model in the form of a narrative literary journalism desirable in journalism practice after a century in which it was largely (but not entirely) submerged beneath dominant professional practices?
2. What makes a narrative literary journalism's referentiality to phenomena different from that of other related genres, particularly conventional fictions on the one hand and dominant journalism practices on the other?
3. Given the emphasis on the referential to the phenomenal or material world, what are the consequences in a narra-descriptive journalism for the mediated social realities we create for ourselves as a community or as individuals?
4. Any comparative study must acknowledge the development of the similar European tradition of literary reportage, or reportage literature, given its widespread historical practice. How is the kind of narrative literary journalism I explore similar to and different from the literary reportage tradition?
5. How does a narrative literary journalism—fundamentally a narra-descriptive journalism drawn from the aesthetics of experience—differ from similar narra-descriptive memoir?
6. Granted that a narrative literary journalism is richly textured with literary tropes, why do many recent examples, often critically acclaimed, fall short?

The answers I provide to these are tentative, to be sure. But from the exploration, I hope deeper insights will emerge regarding a complex genre I believe should be central to both literary and journalistic study today.

Implicit in this volume, too, is an examination of the issue of the "reality boundary," articulated by Norman Sims, which exists between conventional fiction and a narrative literary journalism.[2] I would suggest that the boundary provides not so much a hard-and-fast divide, but rather a space of complex and dynamic relationships between both sides. Nor is the issue such that one genre is superior and the other inferior. Rather, they are simply different, and are prompted by different concerns, as I will explore.

Finally, I can only hope that this investigation will prompt additional insights into what a narrative literary journalism can contribute to discourse today. At a time when print media appear in decline, what place if any is there for a narrative literary journalism in a rapidly changing media world?

By a narrative literary journalism I mean in this instance a journalism that emphasizes narrative and descriptive modalities. This is why, for greater precision, I have come increasingly to characterize the genre as a narra-descriptive journalism, as I explain in chapter 1. It is a journalism, as I have suggested elsewhere, that works on a spectrum or continuum that, if taken to the extremes, results in either an increasingly alienated objectified world on the one hand or, on the other, a solipsistic subjectivity in the most personal of memoirs.[3]

My usage of the term "literary journalism" is historical, one that goes back at least to the first decade of the twentieth century in the United States.[4] In the 1960s and 1970s the genre was called the "New Journalism." Tom Wolfe provided what has perhaps proved the most widely used definition, describing it as a journalism that "reads like a novel" or "short story."[5] But as I will discuss, it is a very imprecise definition for a journalistic genre claiming to be literary. (Wolfe, incidentally, uses the term "literary journalist," although he echoed his compatriots in characterizing the genre as a "new journalism," largely unaware of a much more extensive earlier history than was acknowledged at the time; but in that regard he was not alone.)[6] Other times, the genre has been designated as narrative journalism, creative nonfiction, the nonfiction novel, literary nonfiction, literary reportage, reportage literature, the *ocherk* in Russian, *baogao wenxue* in Chinese, and *nuevo periodismo* in Colombia, among the many terms that have been applied, revealing, clearly, a heterogeneity to the subject.[7] Nor do I suggest that they are all necessarily an identical creature, as I tentatively explore in chapter 4, an initial exploration because the comparative study is still very much evolving. Rather, I have long posited a kind of quantum narrative or supra-narrative not entirely the same in time and space (or place) when we seek to encompass its measure.[8] Thus, we must be circumspect in the terms we apply. After all, literary journalism can have different meanings to different people and different meanings in different parts of the world.[9] I am not confident that there can ever be a single designating terminology for the form (but I could be wrong). This is why I have long characterized it as a narrative literary journalism and, more recently, as a "narra-descriptive journalism."

Moreover, there is a strong but not exclusive emphasis on cultural revelation to be detected in the genre. Again, it was Wolfe who probably more than anyone else identified this dimension when he characterized the 1960s version as a "social realism" that would reveal "the social tableau, manners and morals."[10] At the same time, and as the continuum or spectrum between objectification and solipsism suggests, the cultural is strongly inflected by and with a personal voice, as opposed to more traditional and mainstream models of journalism dominant throughout much of the twentieth century and into the twenty-first. This is because a narrative literary journalism embraces the more personal as revealing a different dimension to the cultural in the attempt to narrow the empathic distance between the protagonists in the discourse, the author, and the readers.[11]

Regarding the "aesthetics of experience," I first borrowed the phrase from the subtitle of Charles A. Laughlin's *Chinese Reportage: The Aesthetics of Historical Experience*.[12] The difference (but not necessarily an oppositional one) is that I do not see that the "aesthetics of experience" must necessarily be only historical. True, to some extent it must be because it examines what is past. But, as I explore later, a narrative literary journalism can also resist the impositions of history in its attempt to reclaim the contemporary. Nor, by the "aesthetics of experience," do I mean "the beautiful," as is often associated (erroneously) with the term by refined aesthetes who have hijacked it to their ends. In reality we are all aesthetes in our responses to experience, whether lowbrow or highbrow—and the gradations in between. Instead, my meaning comes closer to the original Greek, referring to a phenomenal experience that prompts a sensory response, a viewpoint revived in the concept of the aesthetics of the everyday. As Tom Leddy notes, when we engage in the everyday experience of life, such as taking a walk, "all of the senses are involved." The result, he adds, is a "sensuous or imaginative apprehension. . . . The properties appreciated in everyday aesthetics are neither wholly objective nor wholly subjective. They are properties of experienced things, not of physical objects abstracted from our experienced world,"[13] much the way, I might add, an objectified "objective" journalism attempts to abstract experience.

Joseph H. Kupfer further observes of the everyday aesthetic response to experience: "From an aesthetic promontory, we can see comprehensive reformulations of experience, reformulations that remain hidden when we think strictly within social, moral, political, or educational categories. The aesthetic runs through all of these domains of life and so seems an especially promising entrance into their interstices, interdependencies, and common problems. Because the aesthetic speaks with a radically different voice to the values cultivated in these various domains, it may uncover radically different approaches to their realization."[14] This gets to the heart of what a narrative literary journalism attempts to do, I propose, which is to engage in a revelation for the reader about our phenomenal world, one that is conjured imaginatively by means of sensate experience reflected in language, a conjuring that can disrupt taken-for-granted cultural and personal assumptions in the negotiations inherent in the "interstices, interdependencies, and common problems." As Kupfer also notes, "The varieties of aesthetic experience variously nurture a panoply of human values,"[15] which we, as individuals and a community, inevitably seek to share or reject in our assessments of those experiences. Clearly the varieties of aesthetic experience do not necessarily have to confirm existing shared (and abstract) values, and therein lies, I believe, a subversive nature to the genre, but one nonetheless different from conventional fictions and conventional journalisms.

As I did in my *History of American Literary Journalism*, I still subscribe to the view expressed by the critic Mark Edmundson that literature escapes critical closure because, as he says, it "resists being explained away."[16] He is only one in a long line who have taken up the theme that literature does not provide closed or global meanings as we find in the natural sciences, and as traditionally claimed by the social sciences in seeking to be sciences. Literature examines the ambiguities of human experience and acknowledges them as ambiguities, replete in the case of a narrative literary journalism with the tropes we associate—all too erroneously—with conventional fictions, and with a suggestiveness, as we will also see, derived from irony and paradox. And yet there are important differences from conventional fictions, which I also explore. Moreover, a narrative literary journalism defies some of the more conventional wisdoms in the journalism academy, where for so long it has been a cardinal rule that journalism should be clear, transparent, and unambiguous. The problem with such wisdom is, of course, that life is not always clear, transparent, and unambiguous. This is why a narrative literary journalism can prove to be a compelling and even profound discourse: it gives us the courage to confront the frailties of our cultural totalizations.

As I indicated, the origins of this volume lie in part in *A History of American Literary Journalism*. When it was first published, I could not fully appreciate that it marked not only the completion of one project but also the beginning of another in the form of this book. This is because, as I explored American narrative literary journalism during the writing of the earlier book, I realized that it raised more questions than I could answer. While the volume emphasized history, I sensed critical possibilities that helped to inform the work. As a result, I have been encouraged to expand on those issues not suited to the history (although I would not dispute that history can be its own kind of critical—and theoretical—construct). In doing so, I found myself drawn increasingly to issues surrounding the aesthetics of experience by virtue of one rather obvious fact: the genre cannot be understood in the absence of that kind of experience. Such an approach is necessary because some of the more traditional ways of explaining the genre—again, that it reads like a novel or short story, or, in a variation, its techniques are associated with "Great Literature" and its "timeless truths" (over which we all swoon)—are clearly inadequate.

Yet I too am guilty of having used Wolfe's imprecise definition that a narrative literary journalism reads like a novel or short story. It is imprecise for at least two reasons. First, there is a presumption in the claim that the origin of the species lies in the conventionally fictional novel and short story. Wolfe encourages that misperception by barely acknowledging earlier versions. To hear him tell it, one would think that not much existed before, which is not the case.[17] Unfortunately, the claim has been too often perpetuated since then as gospel. (But the claim would permit Wolfe to say he had done something "new" regarding the "New Journalism," even though he personally disdained the term.)[18] In reality, so much of what we commonly associate with traditional fiction was in fact long extant in nonfiction, or, as I prefer, narrative documentary forms, going back at least as far as classical Greece.[19] Indeed, it is not too much to suppose that it all goes back to the storyteller in her prehistoric cave chanting the story of the tribe's latest migration to her rapt audience. As I noted in the history, fiction borrowed many of its tropological tricks from early documentary forms and not the other way around. The reason why the perception persists that journalism borrowed them from fiction is cultural, I suspect. Undoubtedly, during the nineteenth and early twentieth centuries, the fictional novel and short story did represent the high point of the application of the tropes we associate with conventional fiction, and that is the memory most people (including Wolfe, I suspect) carry with them from their high school and university introduction to literature classes—certainly not from journalism classes, which for so long barely acknowledged traditional narrative as a legitimate journalistic form. In effect, those literature classes erased the memory of what came before by embracing only the conventionally fictional novel and short story.[20] This is why Wolfe's claims are understandable, but also erroneous.

The second reason why Wolfe's definition, as widely used as it has proved, is imprecise in defining what is perceived of as a journalism that is "literary" in the narrative sense is that few would dispute that there are examples of journalistic narrative out there that are the equivalent of the potboilers and bodice rippers we find in conventional fiction, yet they aspire to read like a novel or short story.

Regarding my audience, it can be explained in part by the following. My own background is that I was prepared in my studies largely through the literature academy. Yet I am a former print journalist, having spent a decade-plus in the business, and now teach in the communication academy. The literary preparation and professional practice (although I make no claim to being a "literary journalist," a term about which I am ambivalent) shape how I approach the material. I have often found the cross-pollination between literary study and the practice of journalism fascinating, rewarding, and providing insights I might not otherwise have gained if I had engaged in the study of only one or the other. I hope both sides will also find the crossing over of disciplines to be rewarding. But I bear in mind that such an audience is also a very disparate one, with at times very different critical values, and I do not expect to satisfy all. I hope rather to contribute to an ongoing dialogue among the disparate members.

Also, I must emphasize that I write as an American scholar. I say that in all humility, and certainly not triumph. This is because one thing I have learned in recent years as a scholar and editor is just how much literary values can shift and change between cultures. The only claim I can make is that, to crib from James Agee, my examination depends as much on who I am.[21] And I am, for better or worse, bound up in my culture. Still, if I am fortunate enough that scholars from other national traditions should benefit from my inquiry, that will be sufficient gratification.

In addition to the history I published in 2000, this volume draws on my publication over the years in journals such as *Genre: Forms of Discourse and Culture, Journal of Communication Inquiry, Critical Studies in Mass Communication, DoubleTake, Points of Entry*, and *Prose Studies*, as well as in the volumes *Literary Journalism across the Globe* and the forthcoming *Witnessing the Sixties*. The articles are where I initially tested ideas, and in reflecting over the years on the issues I examined, I have expanded on them as my own thinking has evolved. Indeed, I see my work as very much evolutionary because scholarship is a slow, patient, and at times tedious sifting of ideas. That is the only claim I can make.

Moreover, I have also been very much influenced by my role as founding editor of the journal *Literary Journalism Studies*. The position necessarily forced me to test and revise my own ideas, as well as introduced me to others. Finally, there has been the monumental (at least to me) critical work of such thinkers as Mikhail Bakhtin, Walter Benjamin, Friedrich Nietzsche, Wolfgang Iser, and Hans Robert Jauss, among others, which very much informs this book. Indeed, their critical perspectives have proved central in providing me with insights into what I believe is the distinctive nature, or part of the distinctive nature, of a narrative literary journalism. I find them as relevant and cogent today as I did more than twenty years ago, when I was introduced to them as a graduate student, and believe they still have much to offer. Hence my return to them at times as a point of departure for enlarging on my earlier preliminary assessments. To them I would add the Russian formalist critic Victor Shklovsky (a compatriot of Bakhtin's), whose insights I have come to better appreciate, especially when I read his *Sentimental Journey,* itself a work of narrative literary journalism.

My examination is, of course, wide-ranging. But the wide range shares in common one idea, that the aesthetics of phenomenal experience exercise a powerful influence over our imaginations, much as the images of bones at Verdun has for me.

1

Telling News Naturally

In the opening to Jon Franklin's Pulitzer Prize–winning 1978 article about death on an operating room table—an article that has taken on all but canonical status in discussions of narrative literary journalism in newspapers—Franklin selects his details with a discriminating and revealing precision: "In the cold hours of a winter morning, Dr. Thomas Barbee Ducker, University Hospital's senior brain surgeon, rises before dawn. His wife serves him waffles but no coffee. Coffee makes his hands shake."[1]

Clearly the "lead," as it is conventionally called in journalism, reveals the inauguration of a narrative story in the traditional sense of posing a complication that readers seek to unravel.[2] Among the obvious questions that arise, why is it important that Ducker's hands not shake this particular morning? Intuitively, the reader senses that he or she will be introduced to and explore the terrain of the problem, and arrive in the end at some kind of resolution, in this case the death of a patient during brain surgery. It may be an unpleasant resolution, but in storytelling happy endings are not guaranteed.

Such observations about the nature of narrative may seem obvious. But when we label something a "story" or "narrative," it is easy to overlook what we mean by it, as if its invocation implies some kind of automatic understanding we take for granted and are not inclined to question or examine. As the historian Hayden White has observed, "So natural is the impulse to narrate, so inevitable is the form of narrative for any report on the way things really happened, that narrativity could appear problematical only in a culture in which it was absent."[3] One detects a similar perspective in cognitive psychology: "Despite the ubiquity of narratives, calls for deeper understanding of their impact are rarely heard." Instead, we tend to "simply take narrative impact for granted."[4]

In taking the power of narrative for granted, we fail to acknowledge what a story in the traditional narrative sense attempts to do: show the account as

9

a process and as such as an organic part of the cognitive effort to help readers make sense of our complex and ambiguous world.[5] This is why it is important to understand what we mean by "story" in the narrative sense, if we are to understand what it offers in contrast to the more traditional journalistic models of the hard news account and the conventional feature article, which, at least in the American experience, for so long dominated print journalism throughout much of the twentieth century and into the present era.[6] They, too, can be identified as "stories." But they are very different kinds of "stories" in that they attempt to escape the meaning of "narrative," as I will explore.

I draw here from narratology and use one of the most basic of widely accepted definitions of *narrative*, meaning "a sequence of events."[7] While the accouterments of place and space have not necessarily been excluded, the emphasis is on a chronology or the passage of time. With such an emphasis, I explore why it was a mistake for journalism practice to have largely ignored more traditional narrative approaches in the past. An equally critical component is description (or what the *Norton Introduction to Literature* has long characterized as "setting").[8] In a narrative literary journalism, you cannot examine time without examining space and what inhabits it: place. These, then, are documentary accounts whose modalities are complementary, narrative and descriptive, or narra-descriptive as I prefer.

The rhetorical framing of the hard news model is constructed in what has traditionally been called the "inverted pyramid." Such a structure is altogether different from that of a narrative literary journalism because the inverted pyramid addresses the "news" in a continuously digressing manner, starting from the conclusion of a sequence of events. Fundamentally, the inverted pyramid model of journalism tends to be expository in its ultimate intention in that it summarizes the conclusion of the story in what is often called the "summary lead," and then provides the information in descending order of importance as determined by journalistic convention.[9] This is not to suggest that the descending order of importance is the same for each journalist—or editor. But in writing according to the inverted pyramid, the emphasis is placed on a deprioritization of value as the model descends to its tentative and diffident conclusion, for the concluding information is deemed of least value. Unlike classical exposition, the inverted pyramid model never arrives at a conclusion, because historically in the newsroom the model provided a convenient means for fitting copy according to space requirements in long newspaper columns. It could be cut from the bottom up if necessary, thus eliminating what the reporter and editor perceived as the least important information.[10] It also gives the reader the opportunity to read what has been determined by the journalist to be the most salient and important information at the top or beginning of the story. In the ideal this is, as noted, the conclusion to the event reported. To cite a hypothetical: "Mount Krakatoa blew up on Wednesday. . . . Estimates on casualties remain unclear. . . . The explosion came after an increase in volcanic activity during the last six months. . . . Volcanologists said initial tremors began to be felt last July in the village of . . . ," and so on, the information descending in order of perceived unimportance. In a reversal of our expectations when it comes to traditional narrative—the sequence of events—the concluding act of the event as it happened is located at the beginning of the article.

Given that the inverted pyramid with its summary lead came to all but represent in the twentieth century the rhetorical embodiment of what constitutes "objective" journalism—short, concise, relatively neutral in tone and intent, and structured in presentation from the most important to the least important information—the contrast with a traditional narrative model could hardly be more striking. In a sense, the inverted pyramid represents a reversal of the complication-resolution litmus test of traditional narrative because of the emphasis in the lead on the resolution—the "breaking news"— before the story examines the complication that led to the resolution.[11] Like most exposition, it may have narrative elements ("Mount Krakatoa blew up on Wednesday" is narrative in the sense of being one part of a chronology or sequence of events), but the configuration of the report reflects the rhetorical intention to isolate information from the sequence and to deprioritize it as it proceeds. Such continuing anachronic displacement reveals a pattern that does not return to the chronological as analepsis (the flashback) or prolepsis (the flash forward) would do, which are readily decipherable as a part of a chronology within traditional narrative. Instead, the displacement of the inverted pyramid moves toward an analytical ambition that extracts information from the sequence of time. Chronology is deemphasized (although it can never entirely disappear or be escaped), while analytical exposition of seemingly discrete elements is emphasized. And chronological time is what traditional narrative is about. Even analepsis and prolepsis do this in that they return us to the original sequence of events; not so the "inverted pyramid" of time and space displaced.

There is a variation in hard or spot news when the inaugurating complication is identified in the lead as a form of analepsis or flashback. But inevitably it is subordinated to the resolution that dominates the beginning of the account. For example, "Citing shoddy construction practices, police charged a local contractor with involuntary homicide on Monday." The complication in the form of a participial phrase, "Citing shoddy construction practices," is subordinated as an adjective to the resolution, "police charged a local contractor with involuntary homicide on Monday," because the latter is the immediate event in the phenomenal world prompting the news article at the contemporary moment. Certainly there is the echo of a narrative here, but the intention of the journalist is to analytically extract information in isolation from the traditional narrative process. In effect, the intent is largely expository.

Thus the issue is one of how the discourse is framed rhetorically with the modal emphasis on explication in a series of digressions as the reporter keeps circling around the information, extracting this fact, then that, and laying them out in what he or she perceives as the decreasing order of importance (with the editor providing corrections). The result is that the report slowly dissolves, growing fainter and fainter in its claim to having narrative value. Another effect of the displacement of chronology is a kind of rhetorical hash in a constant shifting between brief segments of narrative stitched together by an overriding expository ambition. In one sense, even the expository ambition fails if we recall what has echoed down through generations of freshman composition classes with origins in classical oratorical instruction: "Tell them what you're going to tell them [forecast], tell them [elaboration], then tell them again [summary/conclusion]." In the inverted pyramid, the classical formula is to some extent truncated because at the least the final element—summary/conclusion—is deleted and the reader is left without an ending. And as noted, the elaboration is not chronological. It piles one digression atop the other independent of chronology.

The relationship of a narrative literary journalism to conventional feature writing is more complex, in that feature writing can be viewed as a form reflecting a narrative outline—approximate at best—in the basic rhetorical framing, since features can and often have the "beginning [that] arouses expectations for the 'middle and end,'" to quote the reader-response critic Hans Robert Jauss, who of course cribs from Aristotle's prescription for trag- edy in the *Poetics*: "A whole is what has a beginning and middle and end."[12] (I modify this prescription slightly in the next chapter.) The boundary between conventional feature writing and narrative literary journalism is by no means always clear (nor is it between conventional feature writing and hard news when a feature lead or introduction is attached to the latter). Yet again there are basic distinguishing characteristics. One important difference is that in conventional feature writing, descriptive scene construction usually serves the purpose of illustrating an expository—and thus abstract—claim.

For example, Diana K. Sugg's Pulitzer Prize–winning story "Cruelest Mys- tery: Death before Life" opens with the kind of descriptive color generally associated with the narrative forms of the short story or novel with a pro- vocative scene of a mother cradling in her arms her stillborn infant. Hence we have a complication in which the reader will seek a resolution: Why is the mother cradling her dead infant? But the scene illustrates the abstract point that follows, or what journalists conventionally call the "nut graf," which provides the feature article's focus and establishes the journalistic contract with the reader: "Heber would never know what killed her child. In a time when surgeons can operate on fetuses, when parents can select the sex of their offspring, when physicians can screen embryos for genetic diseases, medicine has no answer for stillbirths. They are one of the last, great mysteries of obstetrics."[13]

Having thus provided a focus, the article could still embark on a traditionally descriptive narrative or story. True to the feature article form, however, Sugg engages instead in a largely expository examination of the issue. There are three further descriptive scenes in the article. The lead descriptive section consists of three paragraphs, the second descriptive section three, the third descriptive section seven, and the final descriptive section three. Sixteen paragraphs, then, are descriptive in their modality, this out of an article sixty-one paragraphs in length. Such scenes are, as a result, cursory at best, and fundamentally illustrative of abstract exposition framed overall as a kind of quasi- or ersatz narrative that reflects vaguely, but only vaguely, Jauss's "beginning [that] arouses expectations for the 'middle and end,'" in which the expository discourse nonetheless dominates and prevails. In effect, more conventional and formulaic feature reporting often works by means of a kind of rhetorical bait and switch when it opens with scenic description that would suggest to the reader that the article will mimic modal attributes of more traditional storytelling, only to digress into a dominating expository modality. In Sugg's case there is a kind of narrative "ghost" to be found in the four brief descriptive sections woven into the article, which hint suggestively at a traditional story model. But it is only the outline of a ghost.[14]

Integral to a narrative literary journalism is Tom Wolfe's idea of "scene-by-scene" construction and what the preposition "by" suggests about location, affinity, and relationship in the construction of the narrative with scenic attributes.[15] This does not preclude such narratives from containing elements of exposition. They can and often do. A classic example is George Orwell's chapter on the different leftist groups vying for power in republican Spain during the Spanish civil war as recounted in *Homage to Catalonia*. But such exposition is ancillary to the larger narra-descriptive intent composed of scene-by-scene construction. As Orwell notes at the outset of the chapter, "If you are not interested in the horrors of party politics, please skip." He adds, "No event in [the Spanish civil war] . . . is intelligible unless one has some grasp of the inter-party struggle that was going on behind the Government lines."[16] He acknowledges, then, that he engages in digressive exposition but only in order to inform the subsequent narra-descriptive story. And indeed he does, because after the expository chapter he returns to his extended narra-descriptive intent.

We see this again in *The Storm of Steel* by Ernst Jünger. Early in his account of life on the Western Front from the perspective of a German soldier during World War I, he writes with a hint of apology, "Although I had made up my mind to omit all comments [meaning commentary] from this book, I should like all the same to say a word or two about this first glimpse of horrors" on the battlefield.[17] After a one-page digression, expository in nature, he returns to his ambition, to describe what life was like in the trenches as a kind of miniaturist of the absurd (which I discuss more fully in the next chapter). If, then, the primary purpose of the descriptive scene in more conventional feature writing is to serve and inform the abstract point or points of the exposition, the primary purpose of exposition in a narrative literary journalism is to serve and inform the larger and dominant narra-descriptive modalities that frame and firmly anchor the story as a narrative in the traditional sense of a sequence of events. In the end, it is a matter of emphasis or degree, and, as I have noted elsewhere, there is no reason why journalism cannot do both, the writer E. B. White serving as one example frustrating the efforts of scholars attempting to engage in a too discrete classification scheme.[18] This is why such works are perhaps better examined according to the emphasis or degree of their modalities. Thus, the kind of narrative literary journalism under consideration here is more in the way of a "narra-descriptive journalism" or a "narra-descriptive documentary" when it is characterized by the dominating modalities.

By such means we can distinguish approximately between hard news, the conventional feature story, and a narrative literary journalism (or narra-descriptive journalism). But I would emphasize that these are only general distinctions with degrees or shades of difference, each merging toward the other. In practice, the result is either a movement by degree or emphasis toward conventional feature writing and ultimately into hard news, or the movement, again by degree or emphasis, into the most personal of memoirs.[19]

Bearing such distinctions in mind, we can begin to account for what makes narrative literary journalism—aka narra-descriptive journalism—such a compelling reading experience. It is because part of its influence derives from how readers imaginatively process traditional narrative. They do so in a way that the traditional feature story and hard news or breaking story cannot. As the literary historian Cathy N. Davidson has noted in her translation of critic Mikhail Bakhtin: "The complex intellectual and emotional activity of reading . . . empowers the hitherto powerless individual, at least imaginatively, by authorizing necessarily private responses to texts."[20] The responses are private because they arise amid the silence of one's reading, and because they are shaped by the infinitely different experiences individuals have in life. While she refers to the conventionally fictional novel, it is not a difficult step to make to the kind of narra-descriptive journalism discussed here, a kind of journalism that, yes, "reads like a novel or short story" except that it really happened in our phenomenal world.

This, of course, is also the basic premise behind reader-response theory (strongly influenced by Bakhtin). While it is true that all texts authorize private responses, not all such authorizations are necessarily equal. A narrative literary journalism more actively engages the imagination in the creation of meaning than either the summary lead, inverted pyramid model of journalism or the traditional feature story. As the Austrian critic Karl Krauss observed (and as recalled by Walter Benjamin), the conventional journalistic styles of the early twentieth century had a tendency to "paralyze" the imagination of the reader.[21] Of course, "paralysis" serves as a useful metaphor—and perhaps as a kind of rhetorical hyperbole, since readers' minds are not truly "paralyzed," and there is always some room for an imaginative response in negotiating meaning. But again we are looking at a matter of degree or emphasis; that is, there are some texts that prompt greater cognitive engagement of the imagination. In this case it is the emphasis on description and what it conjures imaginatively. Of the objectivist intent of the modern newspaper in the twentieth century, Benjamin notes, its purpose was "to isolate what happens from the realm in which it could affect the experience of the reader."[22] Because of such isolation or alienation, such a model is much more inclined to failure in engaging the subjectivity of the reader in a dialogue of which imagination is part and parcel. The purpose, then, of a narra-descriptive journalism is to recover more concretely the illusion of experience.

Benjamin and Krauss anticipate (as did Bakhtin) the reader-response position that novelistic narrative constitutes an engagement with what Wolfgang Iser calls a performative "reality," or "the process by which the reader 'realizes' an overall situation." In the "realizing," an imaginative reality is established. As Iser further observes, "Reading, then, is experienced as something which is happening—and happening is the hallmark of reality."[23] This is in contrast to what has been characterized as a "constative" reality, meaning "that the action denoted has taken place."[24] A "constative utterance" is a foregone matter beyond dispute. It is simply "reported," much as we see in the hard news report.

The "performative" text engages the reader with questions, according to Iser: "As far as the reader is concerned, he finds himself obliged to work out why certain conventions should have been selected for his interpretation.

This process of discovery is in the nature of a performative action, for it brings out the motivation governing the selection."[25] This process can be detected in Wolfe's "scene-by-scene" construction, and, again, in what the preposition "by" suggests about location, affinity, and relationship in the construction: Why are such scenes placed adjacent to others? What is their affinity and relationship to previous scenes as well as to those that follow? The performative action or process becomes a "performance" for the reader to engage in imaginatively.

To illustrate the distinction between a narra-descriptive journalism and hard news, I cite a hard news lead I wrote many years ago as a reporter, which read something like this: "A county police officer shot and killed an armed holdup man during a convenience store robbery in Severna Park on Tuesday." As a hard news lead it sums up the conclusion to the end of the original narrative experience—in other words, what happened in time and space. The focus of the beginning of the story is on the concluding moments of the event. (Again, in isolation, the sentence is narrative; but the article results in an anachronic digression as the discourse fades away, the information declining in importance down the page according to the selection of the reporter and editor.) The details follow, if readers care to read on, but they do not have much incentive if they know the main points—meaning the final result—of the report. We have in this conventional news lead a "constative" action that has taken place as a foregone matter beyond dispute, and one, therefore, that limits, not encourages, a reader's imaginative response.

But here is something to consider: What if the holdup man's name was Jean Valjean? What if he was stealing a loaf of bread at a convenience store so he could feed his starving sister and nephews? Now we begin to detect the outline of a story in the traditional narrative model, as Victor Hugo well understood in *Les Misérables* (except that Hugo's protagonist Valjean is not killed in the robbery, fortunately for the subsequent course of the novel and future musical). Such a narrative example—one fundamentally performative—might read something like this: "Jean Valjean lingered in the night's dark shadows behind the convenience store, just beyond the reach of the edge of yellow light cast by the streetlamp. The warm rain trickled down his face and he felt the hunger tighten in his stomach. He recalled the large, vacant eyes of his hungry sister and nephews. He put his hand in his coat pocket and felt the cold handle of the snub-nosed .38 police revolver. He stepped out into the street light, and walked slowly to the convenience store's glass door."

So we have a complication. A traditional narrative approach will engage readers imaginatively in the search for understanding, meaning, and insight. It begins the moment a narrative mystery or complication is posed. Again, to return to Jon Franklin's opening, there is Dr. Ducker's refusal to drink coffee.

Why? It culminates in some kind of resolution, though not a terribly satisfy-ing one: despite the surgeon's restraint in not drinking coffee, which could make him nervous and cause his hands to shake during delicate brain sur-gery, his patient dies on the operating table. Most important, it makes of the reader a participant in the performance because the narrative version leaves the reader with a problem or complication to resolve, which is at the heart of reader-response theory. We see how a beginning can arouse expectations for a middle and an end.

Less so, by degree, the summary hard news lead, which dispels the mystery from the outset. The result is that the summary lead has more of a tendency to discourage engagement of the reader's imagination. Here I would borrow from Jauss, since what he says of the intellectual exercises and abstracting natures of philological study and literary history can also be said of the inverted pyramid, that its content has been "reduced to a knowledge of facts,"[26] because they are "constative." The emphasis is on disengaging the subjectivity of the reader from the experience in the report, as Benjamin well understood. In short, the emphasis is on objectification—the making of the world a distant object unrelated to the reader—which is at the heart of the concept of "objective" journalism.

When Wolfe called for "scene-by-scene" construction, he was invok-ing an age-old rhetorical strategy that engages the imagination more than the abstract exposition of the inverted pyramid or the conventional feature story. (It should be noted, however, that when Sugg utilizes description in her Pulitzer-winning feature stories, she too is attempting to engage read-ers in a "performative reality." The difference, of course, is that hers is not sustained with "scene-by-scene" construction as it is in a narrative literary journalism. Rather, such description is designed only to illustrate the larger abstract points to follow. Even the concluding descriptive scene is in thrall to the same purpose.) Scene-by-scene construction is also important because of an epistemological problem—a problem of knowledge, or of what we believe we can know about our phenomenal world—that Wolfe implicitly addressed in his prescription. I have characterized it as the common sense-appeal of the shared common senses.[27] While we may differ on how to define abstract notions such as love and hate, what most of us tend to have in common are our shared sensate experiences—the aesthetics of experience—which find a meeting ground in imaginative description. It is not that all of us see the same identical image in the mind's eye, but rather that we have a shared if approximate evocation. For example, the smell of frying bacon is pleasant to my imagination, conjuring up the memory of breakfast around the campfire while camping with my family in the Blue Ridge Mountains as a child. But I had a friend who was raised a vegetarian, and the sweet, fragrant smell of frying bacon—and all pork for that matter—made her sick to her stomach. (Interestingly, I was told by a state police medevac pilot years later when I was a police reporter that burnt human flesh smells something like burnt pork; it was the kind of trauma he found the most unpleasant because the smell lingered in the helicopter cabin for days; thus my vegetarian friend's olfactory DNA may have known something mine did not because mine was overwhelmed by the fondness of a memory.) What is important is that we had in common a shared evocation, though not necessarily an identical response.

This is what Joaquín Martínez Pizarro calls the "rhetoric of the scene," of which writers have long intuited the value.[28] For example, the *History of the Franks* by Gregory of Tours relates how, in the early sixth century, King Chilperic I of Neustria (today's northwestern France) discovers the infidelity of his wife, Queen Fredegund. The king had planned to go hunting, "but since he loved his wife very much he returned from the stables to her chamber in the palace. She was in the room, washing her hair with water. The king, coming from behind, struck her on the buttocks with a stick. She, thinking that it was Landeric [her lover], said: 'What are you doing Landeric?' Looking back, she saw that it was the king, and became very frightened." Pizarro observes of such scenes, "I am talking fundamentally about the decision on the part of the narrator to . . . create the illusion that we are witnessing the events he describes."[29] By "witnessing the events he describes," he means engaging in an imaginative return to the contemporary moment located more than 1,400 years ago. Moreover, the account of the king swatting his queen's buttocks is not necessary to understand that the king discovered that she was being unfaithful when she mistook him for her lover Landeric. But it does appeal to the common sense-appeal of our shared common senses, even if it evokes different interpretations: Is this an affectionate and gentle swat by a loving husband? Is this a kind of ritualistic foreplay? Is this abuse of a wife? Here we begin to detect different possibilities of meaning. (Whatever the interpretations, Gregory claims that the scheming Fredegund had King Chilperic murdered.)

On the one hand, we interpret the description of materiality communally. But on the other, we always do so individually. Again, as Jauss notes, such a text "is not an object that stands by itself and that offers the same view to each reader in each period," for the "context of experience of aesthetic perception" will be applied differently by each.[30] (Thus to some the smell of burning pork may elicit a fond memory that for others comes closer to the fragrant sweet smell of death.)

Such an understanding of "story" as narrative, that it empowers the reader imaginatively, is supported increasingly by scientific research into how the brain investigates the world: the evidence is mounting that we do so by telling stories. This is because the brain, as E. O. Wilson has observed, "develops stories to filter and make sense of the flood of information that we are exposed to every day."[31]

Brian Boyd, in an extensive elaboration on narrative as an evolutionary response, notes that storytelling developed as part of our survival skills because it is the human way of passing on social knowledge that includes knowledge about potential threats and self-protection. Not all of us can experience those dangers, but "with narrative we could, for the first time, share experience with others who could then pass on to still others what they had found most helpful for their own reasoning about future actions. We still have to act within our own time, but with narrative we can be partially freed from the limits of the present and the self." To that can be added his observation: "We are not *taught* narrative. Rather, narrative reflects our mode of understanding events, which appears largely . . . to be a generally mammalian mode of understanding."[32]

To return to cognitive psychology, researchers have found in studies that readers of narrative are more engaged by traditional storytelling as opposed to discursive exposition. An expository model that has analytically migrated or evolved away from narrative, such as the inverted pyramid model, confronts a significant problem: "The results of these studies are compatible with the claim that narrative text is recalled approximately twice as well as expository text and is read approximately twice as fast."[33] Moreover, narrative is perceived of as more "real." This is because one experiences what is characterized in cognitive psychology as an increased sense of psychological "transportation" into the more traditional story world.[34] "Transportation" is "defined as an integrative melding of attention, imagery, and feelings, focused on story events."[35] Furthermore, as neuroscience research has revealed, the more realistic stories are, the more actively the brain responds to them.[36] In other words, the more "real" a mediation appears, the more the brain reacts to the aesthetic appeal and engages in the "psychological transport."[37] Our brains, then, are designed for telling stories, and a narra-descriptive discourse captures the imagination in a way that more abstract and objectified models of discourse cannot: "We tell stories about other people and for other people. Stories help us to keep tabs on what is happening in our communities. The safe, imaginary world of a story may be a kind of training ground, where we can practice interacting with others and learn the customs and rules of society. And stories have a unique power to persuade and motivate, because they appeal to our emotions and capacity for empathy."[38]

One of the distinctive features of a narrative literary journalism is the effort, if not to engage in an exchange of subjectivities, then at least to narrow the distance between subjectivities by means of the common sense-appeal of the shared common senses.³⁹ The result is, as noted, empathy. But it must be emphasized that empathy is not necessarily the same thing as sympathy. It may be, but does not have to be. Empathy is "the ability to identify oneself mentally with a person or thing and so understand his feelings or its meaning."⁴⁰ There is a difference between understanding, on the one hand, and approving and accepting another's actions and emotional stance (and ultimately values), on the other, as we find in sympathy. For most it would be difficult if not impossible to accept and approve of why Perry Smith slit Herb Clutter's throat, as recounted in *In Cold Blood*. But one can understand and perhaps even identify with the profound existential dilemma Smith exhibits—driven by the fear that he is an existential nobody, as I examined in my *History*—a frustration that drives him to engage in the same kind of act that prompted Rodion Raskolnikov to murder a pawnbroker in *Crime and Punishment*.⁴¹ That empathy is not the same as sympathy is important when we consider not only such heinous acts but parody and satire as well in a narrative literary journalism, an issue I explore later.

It is for these reasons that even the beleaguered American newspaper industry has increasingly recognized the value of a more narrative and descriptive style.⁴² At least they did until the recession of 2008–2009, after which the industry went into an economic free fall from which it has not recovered. But the pre-recession recognition was driven in part by studies demonstrating what reader response has long claimed. The Readership Institute of Northwestern University's Media Management Center confirmed in 2000 that an approach that is more narrative is in turn more reader-friendly. In a survey of 37,000 newspaper readers across the United States, such writing was identified as more accessible: "Papers that incorporate a narrative writing style in their coverage of a wide variety of topics—not just traditional features content—are seen as easier to read."⁴³ This is because such writing recovers how people naturally inquire into their world, by means of narrative and description. A similar 1998 report by the American Society of Newspaper Editors called for improved approaches in reporting that better "engage" or "connect" with the reader: "It includes such things as having media spark your emotions, reflect your beliefs and values, or be surprising."⁴⁴ Sparking emotions, of course, points to the inherent nature of a narra-descriptive journalism, namely, that it is a more subjective form that elicits empathy. As Ronald Weber, one of the pioneers of narrative literary journalism scholarship, has observed of the form, "In the obvious . . . novelistic artistry of scene and characterization the writer makes his presence and his shaping consciousness known."⁴⁵ The presence of the shaping consciousness invests such writing with a clearly more subjective stance or voice that is freer to engage in an aesthetic appeal, prompting the emotional response.

This has significant consequences for our traditional concepts of journalism because of the basis on which the idea of an "objective" journalism was constructed, particularly its rhetorical embodiment in the summary lead and inverted pyramid. The objectivist model is in no small part a consequence of the positivist paradigm that came to cast a long shadow over journalism practice in the late nineteenth century, something Michael Schudson ably explored.[46] The upshot has been a rhetoric—the "objective" news style—whose claim was founded on the belief that it was serving the cause of modern science. Associating itself with science effectively legitimized the "objective" model as the professionally correct model. But given what science is telling us, one must conclude that the "objective" model was not "scientific" despite the claims, because it is not how the mind naturally inquires into the world. As it turns out, the critical hegemony of "objective" journalism was constructed on a false premise, one that has a tendency to result in more of an epistemological disconnect for readers in terms of what we can know or think we can know about the material world. In violating how we naturally inquire, it delivers the consequences of the phenomenal world to us as a cognitive fait accompli. This is the problem that is particularly inherent in the "inverted pyramid" model. It leaves us disengaged because we have not participated imaginatively in the journey or process of the story.

It is also apt to note, if it is not obvious, that the scientific method is a variation on what storytellers have been saying all along: we inquire into the world around us by telling stories that "filter and make sense of the flood of information that we are exposed to every day," as Wilson concisely explained. And we do so by starting with a complication or question and taking it through the various stages of testing—the developmental stages inherent in narrative—in what we call the scientific method.

The inverted pyramid in particular is an unnatural form of inquiry precisely because it starts with the resolution and builds one digression upon the other. To be sure, such a model provides for quick access to important results. And I emphasize that mine is not an advocacy for dispensing with the model. After all, it does have its utility, something I keenly appreciate as a former reporter. But it is too easy to overlook its shortcomings. Specifically, the initial emphasis on the end results denies the often challenging journey in which a reader can imaginatively participate in the performance by "realizing" what is happening.

This recalls, in a variation, what the French sociologist of science Bruno Latour observed back in the 1980s, before the recent groundswell of scholarship in the study of narrative literary journalism, namely that the genre is indispensable for exposing the impenetrability of science to the understanding of the lay reader. When we follow by means of the aesthetics of experience the "journey" that scientists take, we imaginatively participate with them in their discoveries, their triumphs, and their failures.[47] For example, imagine this scenario: It is 1904 and Albert Einstein sneezes, interrupting himself as he pours a glass of port for his mother, Pauline, in the dining car of the train from Berlin to Zurich. Opening his eyes, post-sneeze, he catches sight from the corner of his peripheral vision of a raven in flight. On observing the raven recede across the sky, he detects at the same moment the swollen Rhine River, which he knows is moving at flood stage in the opposite direction to the train. The train is southbound while the river flows north, except that because of his movement on the train, it does not seem that the river is moving at all. All of which—northbound flood, south-bound train, raven flying in an indeterminate direction—is spatially dis-orienting. Dimly he recalls his earlier departure from the seeming solidity and centrality of the Potsdamer Platz, where it was said at the time that the crossroads of Europe converged, and now how it is a distant world slipping farther away. The world is in constant motion, Einstein realizes as he starts to pour the wine again while his mother says, "*Danke,* Bertie," squeezing his other hand affectionately as if he were still a little boy. So what emerges as he responds absentmindedly, "*Bitte,* Mama," with his thoughts elsewhere, is the first intimation of his Special Theory of Relativity (that even as we move through space, the world around us in its variety moves independently of our own motion, because there is no fixed, unmoving Potsdamer Platz of the universe) as well as the seeds of his General Theory, which would account for changes in movement. Now we can begin to prize open the black box of science, making us imaginative participants in Einstein's moment of recog-nition. (Disclaimer: Insofar as I know, none of this happened. I simply use it as a hypothetical example.)

This brings us to a paradox in that laypersons can engage science in a meaningful way subject to the writer's subjectivity selecting from the aesthet-ics of experience—the sneeze, pouring the glass of port, perhaps the silhou-ette of Burg Maus on its promontory slipping silently past us as Burg Katz looms up, as if ready to pounce. In other words, in the attempt to convey the "absolutes" of science we are, paradoxically, reduced to doing so subjectively by means of traditional narrative.

Admittedly, if the purpose of journalism is to provide information in a timely manner, putting the result off until the end of a traditional narrative story would seem an indictment of the form. But that is if timeliness is always the overriding consideration for what constitutes journalism. This brings us back to a simple observation: we engage in stories in order to make sense of our complex world, and for that reason, I would suggest, narrative engages us in a degree of psychological transport that the inverted pyramid and conventional feature stories cannot equal.

The observation also has implications for the call in recent years for a more public journalism. In other words, news organs need to better engage their communities. As Jay Rosen has identified the issue (or at least part of the issue, because it too is a complex one), journalism should "address people as citizens, potential participants in public affairs, rather than victims or spectators."[48] To get the public to participate is to better engage their subjectivities and elicit an empathic response, which is central to what a narra-descriptive journalism attempts to do. Telling traditional stories imaginatively engages the reader's consciousness in sorting through the complexities of community problems. John J. Pauly has long subscribed to the position that the New Journalism of the 1960s and 1970s uniquely engaged readers in such a manner.[49] More recently, he has noted that a literary journalism could better engage citizens in civic life by "portraying the life of groups and organizations with as much subtlety as it does individual characters and interpersonal relations. Perhaps all forms of journalism necessarily sacrifice some analysis for the sake of drama; that may be the price of creating a widely shared narrative of our common life."[50]

It is for these reasons, then, that there is a kind of refreshing critical integrity to a narra-descriptive journalism which the "objective" lacks: narra-descriptive journalism acknowledges personal valuations initially in the personal voice of the author making selections of description from the phenomenal world. To these, readers then bring their own interpretations. In a sense, this invests a narra-descriptive journalism with a truer kind of "objectivity" because it is a discourse that inherently acknowledges its limitations and denies the spurious kind of omniscience that so-called objective journalism seems to imply and that makes of readers passive spectators. This, clearly, is an incentive for telling the news "naturally," and helps contribute to our understanding of the genre's location among other genres.

2

Telling the Leaves
from the Forest

In 1927 Ernest Hemingway wrote a passage describing a motoring tour he took in Italy, this as part of an article that was to appear in the *New Republic* later in the year:

> A big car passed us, going fast, and a sheet of muddy water rose up and over our windshield and radiator. The automatic windshield cleaner moved back and forth, spreading the film over the glass. We stopped and ate lunch at Sestri. There was no heat in the restaurant and we kept our hats and coats on. We could see the car outside, through the window. It was covered with mud and was stopped beside some boats that had been pulled up beyond the waves. In the restaurant you could see your breath.
>
> The pasta asciutta was good; the wine tasted of alum, and we poured water in it. Afterwards the waiter brought beef steak and fried potatoes. A man and a woman sat at the far end of the restaurant. He was middle-aged and she was young and wore black. All during the meal she would blow out her breath in the cold damp air. The man would look at it and shake his head. They ate without talking and the man held her hand under the table.[1]

Some might say vintage Hemingway, the prose lean and uncluttered. But there is more to be detected in the passage's plain and indeed almost utilitarian nature in what Mary McCarthy has described as the "trite symbolism of ordinary life."[2] Because within that modest passage lies a complication that bears directly on the aesthetics of experience reflected in a narrative literary journalism: we often hear that one of the reasons why such a journalism is so compelling is that what is being reported is "real" (which, so often, is conflated with "truth," as in truth is reality and reality is truth). The claim recalls Tom Wolfe's loud boast that the attraction of the New Journalism of the 1960s was the "rather elementary and joyous ambition to show the reader real life—

24

'Come here! Look! This is the way people live these days! These are the things they do!'"[3] Of course, part of understanding such a reality is that we trust to "the testimony of the senses," as characterized by Stephen Greenblatt.[4] In doing so, such a testimony is forever tethered by perception to a distinctive time and space. But in addition, we also know that at whatever level of consciousness, something has been left out of those perceptions. In other words, there is always an absence attending to what we have perceived. The result is that the "real life" with which Wolfe is so enthusiastically comfortable (given the exclamation marks) turns out not to be so plain and simple despite the seemingly irrefutable testimony of our senses. "Real life," "reality," "actuality," or whatever we call it, is in fact not so "elementary" as he suggests.

This is what I explore in this chapter, and in doing so I hope to further contribute to distinguishing the genre from conventional fictions, as well as more traditional mainstream journalisms.

Wolfe's claim about "real life" is undoubtedly comforting (hence the enthusiasm) because the testimony of our senses (or what those senses testify to) provides a compelling measure for making our way in a phenomenal world; the testimony is central to understanding our existential condition, given any number of circumstances and vicissitudes that can have a bearing on that condition. How can one dispute the referentiality of so seemingly un-complex and simple a scene as when Hemingway describes "a sheet of muddy water [rising] up and over our windshield and radiator," the windshield wiper "spreading the film" of muddy water across the windscreen glass, the advancing waves in the bay at the town of Sestri on the Mediterranean coast providing a backdrop to the fishing boats pulled up on the shore, or the wine tasting of alum and being diluted with water?[5]

This is why I have chosen the passage. It is relatively free of an extended and elaborate literary symbolic that we find, for example, in Shakespeare when Prince Escalus chastises the Montagues and Capulets after one of their public brawls: "Rebellious subjects, enemies to peace, / Profaners of this neighbor-stained steel. . . . / Throw your mistempered weapons to the ground, / And hear the sentence of your movèd prince" (1.1.81–82, 87–88). The steel swords of these warring families are hardly filled with "neighborly" intentions, and the bloodstains on the swords, in the play on "mistemper," suggest a steel that has been improperly finished in the metallurgical process of tempering or hardening, as if that would account for its profane anger.

This is not to suggest that an extended and elaborate literary symbolic does not exist in a narrative literary journalism. But for now I do not want to cloud unnecessarily an emphasis that focuses on the more "prosaic" nature of such prose in order to better understand the relationship between the phenomenal particular and attempts at as simple, plain, and direct a referentiality as we (or at least authors) believe possible.

Bearing this in mind, we see that Wolfe's "elementary" observations are indeed seemingly "joyous" because they hint at what most readers would likely wish to believe of themselves and as members of their community. This is that we can trust the testimony of our senses and thus have some control over our existential condition, and, moreover, that we can have an approximate consensus as a community about imagined images, no matter how differing the "context of experience of aesthetic perception," to borrow again from Hans Robert Jauss, as I did in the last chapter.[6] After all, muddy water smeared across a windshield is something many have likely experienced at one time and can, as a result, referentially imagine in the imagined reexperience. It is our response to the rhetorical "common sense-appeal of the shared common senses," as I have also noted. But in privileging the testimony of the senses, we can easily overlook that we place ourselves as individuals at the center of the perception. And that is where the world of the phenomenal starts to be not so simple—and "elementary"—and where the "joyous ambition" is only that, an ambition with which, in a sense, we permit ourselves to be seduced because it is comforting in the illusion of its seeming simplicity. There are, in other words, implications far beyond a seemingly simple and uncomplex referentiality. There would be anyway, of course, given the exchanges between our personal and cultural influences and values, or the "context of experience of aesthetic perception." And there would be anyway, given the inherent limitations of language. But there are also phenomenal implications that cannot be dismissed as merely and solely fictions, and that ultimately provide in their evidence the misty origins for all of our contexts of experience.

Here I return to Friedrich Nietzsche's intriguing and seminal essay "Truth and Falsity in Their Ultramoral Sense."[7] The 1873 essay proved, of course, powerfully influential among the mid-twentieth-century philosophers of language.[8] But in their rush to identify the frailties and failures of language, there was a tendency, reflected in the claim that all text is fiction, to sideline as more of an afterthought what provided Nietzsche his point of departure: the phenomenal particular as reflected in what he calls the "concrete metaphor."[9] Thus, Nietzsche never entirely lost sight of what we conventionally call the evidence of the external "real" outside of consciousness, again the phenomenal, albeit, as we will see, one not so simple. This is not to deny that it is understood via consciousness and language but rather to focus on what prompts perception.

Briefly, a short summary for those not familiar with the essay. Nietzsche takes note of the tendency in consciousness to essentialize distinctive phe-

nomenal experiences into comprehensive abstract generalities by the exclu-
sion of differences between the individual phenomenal experiences. He
observes that every abstract idea "originates through *equating the unequal.*
As certainly as no one leaf is exactly similar to any other, so certain is it
that the idea 'leaf' has been formed through an arbitrary omission of these
individual differences, through a forgetting of the differentiating qualities."
Such an elimination of what distinguishes or particularizes evolves into what
Nietzsche calls a *qualitas occulta,* according to which a consciousness derives
its "universal" laws—in effect, our essentializations or totalizations. As a
consequence of forgetting or erasing or eliding from consciousness the differentiating qualities of individual phenomena, a person, Nietzsche suggests,
begins to submit "his actions to the sway of abstractions; he no longer suffers himself to be carried away by sudden impressions, by sensations; he first
generalises all these impressions into paler cooler ideas, in order to attach to
them the ship of his life and actions. Everything which makes man stand out
in bold relief against the animal depends on this faculty of volatilising the
concrete metaphors into a schema, and therefore resolving a perception into
an idea."[10] Hence, of course, we detect the fallacy that results from reification.
Here Nietzsche assaults the premise behind the Aristotelian commonplace
and the intervening centuries of Neo-platonisms, and this has generally been
the lesson that recent philosophers of language have taken from it.

But it is also revealing what Nietzsche does not say in his essay: he does not
say that the evidence of the phenomenal does not exist. As he notes, we perceive "sudden impressions, by sensations." But those sensations are inevitably
derivative of responses to phenomena—the aesthetics of experience—which
we recall referentially. Like it or not, we cannot dismiss the evidence of the
phenomenon we respond to—especially if it should pose a threat to us existentially. Ma'sud Zavarzadeh reminds us, "The subjectivity involved in all acts
of human perception of the external world does not deny the phenomenalis-
tic status of the experiences transcribed."[11]

I return to McCarthy's observation about the "trite symbolism of ordinary
life." The challenge to Nietzsche's paler and cooler ideas can be detected in
McCarthy's reflexive examination of an earlier example of narra-descriptive
journalism she published in the March 1953 issue of *Harper's.*[12] The "story,"
"Artists in Uniform," provided a true account of a conversation she had with
an American army colonel on a train journey in which the latter expressed
his anti-Semitism. Her follow-up article was published nearly a year later
in the February 1954 issue of *Harper's.* In it she reacted to letters she had
received from readers in response to the initial article. What troubled her was
the desire of some readers to see an elaborate literary symbolic in the first, in
effect to seek levels of extended and complex allegory. One English professor

wrote to McCarthy and asked her how to symbolically interpret her wearing two shades of green with pink accents, the appearance of nuns, and the fact that the colonel ordered hash for lunch and the author ordered a sandwich. Clearly this was interpretation of literary symbolism run amok—that one was expected to find examples of the elaborate or extended literary symbolic. McCarthy noted in her response that these—the concrete metaphors—were simply what they were. As she flatly stated, "There were no symbols in this story; there was no deeper level."[13] She drew a distinction between "centripetal" and "centrifugal" symbols. On the one hand, the centripetal, according to her interpretation, finds words drawn back to a more direct referentiality to the phenomenal evidence: hash is hash (chopped and fried corned beef, potatoes, and onions), and a sandwich is a sandwich (perhaps bacon, lettuce, and tomato with a dollop of mayonnaise between two slices of toasted white bread), in what she characterized, to note again, as the "trite symbolism of ordinary life." On the other hand, an extended and elaborate literary symbolism "is centrifugal and flees the object, the event, into the incorporeal distance, where concepts are taken for substance and floating ideas and archetypes assume a hieratic authority."[14] McCarthy is talking Nietzsche. A narrative literary journalism attempts to resist such "volatilization," that metaphor for conversion from a liquid to an abstract gaseous state. The abstract schema to which we attempt to attach the "ship of our lives" is then a kind of metaphorical gas.

What is easy to overlook amid the abstract constructions of consciousness, constructions that also make a claim to our existential condition—peace, love, war, death—is just how much the originating phenomenal status of an experience, however imperfectly understood and articulated, is located at the intersection of a unique, distinctive, and one-of-a kind time and space that cannot be replicated. This recalls Mikhail Bakhtin's concept of the chronotope. In the chronotope, time (chronos) and place (topos) are inseparable. While the concept has provided much inspiration to literary scholars, Bakhtin's essay on the chronotope is exploratory in nature, and he acknowledges: "We do not pretend to completeness or precision in our theoretical formulations and definitions. . . . Here and abroad, serious work on the study of space and time in art and literature has only just begun."[15] The result is that the chronotope has been interpreted differently by subsequent scholars.[16] What is clear is that the concept has been privileged as literary gesture.[17] But it is not privileged exclusively, because like Nietzsche, Bakhtin identifies what provides him with the point of departure for the chronotope: the evidence of phenomenal experience. "Out of the actual chronotopes of our world (which serve as the source of representation) emerge the reflected and *created* chronotopes of the world represented in the work (in the text)."[18]

The kind of chronotope I am suggesting is at work in a narra-descriptive journalism takes its cue from this observation by Bakhtin. It is one that is both phenomenal *and* linguistic, or that openly acknowledges and is indeed initially defined by the evidence of the phenomenal as it is negotiated by the linguistic, a claim that cannot be made by the strictly fictional, in which there is either no such relationship or at best an indirect relationship, resulting in what is fundamentally allegory, which I examine shortly. As Wolfgang Iser observed of fiction, "There is no outside object with which to relate the image."[19] What we see in such an approach to a narrative literary journalism is a dynamic process, not a static intellectual concept, as acknowledged by Bakhtin. While emphatically cautioning against confusing the evidence of phenomenal experience with linguistic expression, he adds, "They are nevertheless indissolubly tied up with each other and find themselves in continual mutual interaction; uninterrupted exchange goes on between them."[20]

To be sure, chronotopes can be detected in the more mainstream and objectifying models of journalism—the hard news story and the conventional feature story. But their treatment, compared to a narra-descriptive journalism, is different, as I noted in the previous chapter. Again, the rhetorical ambition of the hard news model, the inverted pyramid, abstracts from the outset both narrative and descriptive modalities in emphasizing digression and discontinuity in which the specificity and distinctiveness of the chronotopes (composed of concrete metaphors) located uniquely in one time and place decline in order of importance, so that such details have a decreasing claim to cognitive value. With regard to more conventional feature writing, the chronotopes of descriptive scene construction usually serve, again, the purpose of illustrating an expository—and thus abstract—claim. In other words, in both forms of journalism the chronotopes are in thrall to the abstracting rhetorical ambition—the larger schema of a rhetorical *qualitas occulta*. This contrasts with a narra-descriptive journalism in which the concrete metaphors of such chronotopes resist the abstracting inclination by insisting on and foregrounding the differences between the individual leaves (and as reflected in the passage from Hemingway).[21]

Paula Bock, a reporter for the *Seattle Times*, detected and highlighted this distinction in a 2002 account about AIDS in sub-Saharan Africa when she posed an epistemological challenge at the beginning of her article by noting: "Listen to Ruth's mother cry, and you'll never think of the number 2.3 million in the same distant way." Three sentences later she reiterates: "Two million three hundred thousand. A number too big to get your arms around, a number easier to calculate than to comprehend." And again, after an explanatory paragraph describing the AIDS epidemic, she writes: "If you've ever wondered whether 2.3 million deaths make any single death less

painful, listen. Imagine wind moaning, tires screeching, goats being stran-
gled."[22] Thus she invites the reader to participate in the world of the narrative
in her examination of one dying life in Harare, Zimbabwe. In the one dying
life lies Nietzsche's differentiating qualities of the concrete metaphor. Significantly, Bock takes aim, in the mantra-like refrain of "2.3 million," at conventional reportorial models according to which the story of the AIDS epidemic
in Africa generally has been reported in the news, models that might read
something like this: "Some 2.3 million Africans have died of AIDS, according
to the World Health Organization." And clearly Bock and her editors sensed
the limitations implicit in the objectivist paradigm so long dominant in journalism practice, namely, that it interprets the world in only "a distant way,"
as she defined the issue, or as a constative report, as reader response would.
Bock's account seeks escape from the cooler, paler ideas.

Such a claim for the chronotopic documentary is one, I would suggest,
that solely traditional fictional accounts cannot make in the same way. This
is because traditional fictions, in the sense of wholly invented or made-up
stories, as suggested earlier, are fundamentally allegorical. Few would dispute the power of *Les Misérables* as fictional novel. Its power stems, at least
in part, in its remove from the distinctive chronotopes located in time and
space outside the covers of books.[23] This is because the remove provides for a
powerful cognitive freedom in imaginative interpretation, but one, it must be
emphasized, that can only be conjectural or speculative. But liberated from
the chronotopes located in one phenomenal time and space outside the covers of books, it has only one ambition in which consciousness can proceed:
in the centrifugal direction of allegory, the *qualitas occulta.* When literature
is discussed as transcendent, it is allegorized, from which arise, in an illustration of Nietzsche's abstracting volatilization, claims to the bromide of Great
Literature to which the fustian litterateur attaches the allegory of the ship of
his or her life.

Clearly the inseparability of evidence from a distinctive time and place is
detected in the passage from Hemingway. For example, the "sheet of muddy
water [rising] up and over our windshield and radiator" and the windshield
wiper "spreading the film over the glass" derive from a singular time and
place outside the cover of books. This is not a claim that conventional fictions
can make, for they lack such a phenomenal referent. In a narra-descriptive
journalism, humans may choose to ignore the differentiating qualities of the
evidence reflected in those perceptions or the testimony of the senses, as the
college English professor did in seeking a higher-order and extended level of
symbolism, but the ignorance is theirs as part of what Nietzsche concludes is
part of our natural inclination—for better or ill.

One presumes that we do need to acknowledge our ontological or phenomenal world in an epistemological act, given that the epistemological act is the only recourse available for conveying to others the experience of our existential condition: we cannot ignore existential consequences. Herein lies an important distinction from conventional fictions. Journalism (and more broadly documentary) deals, in its end result, with the evidence of phenomenal consequences. Traditional fiction, however, deals with imagined prospects or conjecture, and so is fundamentally a form of allegory. The solely allegorical can certainly be subtle and nuanced, as the extended literary symbolic suggests. But we should bear in mind that phenomenal consequences may also be nuanced and subtle, as we will see.

In a narrative literary journalism, fundamentally narra-descriptive in the inseparable supra-modality of the chronotope, we are caught in a compromise of course, since the testimony of the evidence of the senses must ultimately be reflected in language—in its many varieties or media. But even if we concede that all discourse is a kind of "fiction," not all fictions, I emphasize, are equal. Rather, there are qualitative differences, because there are those mediated forms that attempt, however difficult and challenging the effort, to reflect or reference the evidence of phenomenal consequences, prompted as they are by those differentiated qualities selected by the author and located at the intersection of a unique time and space. Conventional fictions in the sense of made-up stories deriving from imagination alone are *only* symbolic, or allegorical, or exist at a greater remove, and indeed are severed from the differences inherent in the time and space of phenomena. Again, as Wolfgang Iser observed of fiction, "There is no outside object with which to relate the image." In a sense, fictions as allegorical constructions are another variation on Nietzsche's paler, cooler ideas, because they deny the phenomenal status of the attempt at experiences described, to rephrase Zavarzadeh.

One must acknowledge the messy boundaries between traditional narrative fictions and a narrative literary journalism. There are, after all, examples where, despite claims of veracity, the author nonetheless fictionalizes, as Truman Capote is accused of having done with *In Cold Blood*.[24] More egregiously (though there was a different historic sensibility at the time), Daniel Defoe did the same in *Robinson Crusoe* when he said the story was true.[25]

Then there are examples in which it is later discovered that traditional fictions drew from phenomenal chronotopes. To cite one, there is the best-selling 1898 American novel *David Harum: A Story of American Life*, in its time something of a minor literary classic.[26] Based on the real-life David Hannum of Homer, New York, the volume is about a small-town banker, moneylender, and horse trader named David Harum. A cracker-barrel philosopher, the protagonist is prone to homespun aphorisms that have entered into the American vernacular, such as "Do unto the other feller the way he'd like to do unto you—an' do it fust."[27] That the fictional Harum was drawn from the phenomenal Hannum was reflected in the 1902 publication of *The Real David Harum*, which provides a biography (and something of a hagiography, given the popularity of the fictional novel) of Hannum.[28] But even though it is based on "real life," *David Harum* is still a conventional fiction. One can detect this in a comparison of the home where the real-life David Hannum lived and the fictional home of David Harum.[29] Author Edward Noyes Westcott accompanied his father as a young man on visits to Hannum in the Upstate village of Homer. The elder Westcott, at one time the mayor of Syracuse, New York, and one of the founders of modern dentistry, was an investor with Hannum in various projects, including the Cardiff Giant Hoax of 1869 (which, curiously, is not included in the fictional *David Harum;* Hannum played a role in perpetuating the hoax). The young man listened attentively to Hannum's tall tales and countrified aphorisms. But locations in Hannum's house are different in the novel. For example, the wing of the house that contains the sitting room where "Aunt Polly" and "David Harum" relax and talk is located on the opposite side of the fictional house (on the south side) from its place in the real house owned by Hannum that exists uniquely in time and space. Nor does the original have a mansard roof.[30] Moreover, the bones of the real-life David Hannum are now buried in Glenwood Cemetery on the hill in back of the village (which in the fiction is named "Homeville"). The remains of David Hannum are referential, then, to what exists and existed outside the cover of books. But the bones of the fictional David Harum are not buried anywhere, because they do not exist. They are only an allegorical invention, for they are lacking in referential correspondence to evidence of phenomenal chronotopes.

The conflation of David Hannum with "David Harum" rises to the level of the absurd, however. As noted, the book *David Harum* proved a popular success. It was made into a stage play, a silent movie in 1915, and a talkie in 1934 with Will Rogers playing the role of the fictional Harum. In 1936 it debuted as a soap opera on the NBC radio network, and later the CBS radio network, lasting until 1951. Another reflection of how much it captured the popular imagination (and an early marketing synergy) is the numerous commercial products named for Harum, including a waltz, cigars, fishing line, denim overalls (the company's logo was "David Harum Uwarum Kanttarum"), animal feed, canned vegetables, a child's piggy bank, and even a variety of peony (crimson in color). The absurdity emerges in what happened to the real-life Hannum house and David Hannum's photographic image. The original home was, during the heyday of the popularity of the book and the character David Harum, the frequent subject of postcards identifying it as the "David Harum House" or the "Home of David Harum," and again later when the Will Rogers movie version appeared. One variant of the postcard includes the house with a photo of the real-life David Hannum identified as the fictional David Harum, certainly evidence of the cultural apotheosis of phenomenal consequence elevated to an allegorical prospect or conjecture in defiance of the laws of physics. This is only one example.[31] Such is the difference between phenomenal consequences and the allegorical illusion of the conjectural or speculative.

Given the nature of a narra-descriptive journalism, we find ourselves disinclined to deny the evidence of the phenomenal status "of the experiences transcribed" because there can be existential consequences that derive from the "differentiating qualities" of the phenomenal chronotopes. Herein lies part of the unique influence over the imagination of such documentary accounts. There are, after all, the bones of French and German soldiers lying in the Verdun ossuary as a result of that 1916 battle. Because accounts of these are referential—mediated—we are forced, on the one hand, to acknowledge that the victims are neither you nor I. But on the other, we are also forced to acknowledge that we could in a phenomenal world face similar evidence of existential consequences. (To some extent, one detects this, too, in the proverb "There but for the grace of God go I.") Here we observe a difference between conventional fictions derived solely from the imagination (or claiming so) and those mediations claiming to be referential to the phenomenal evidence. In acknowledging that the existential consequences could apply to us in our phenomenal world, as opposed to the allegorical reflected in the purely fictional, we cannot afford, in an act of denial, to turn our backs— physical, emotional, psychic, spiritual, or whatever combination—on the differentiating qualities inherent in the phenomenal. This is because we cannot assume that similar experiences will not rise up and devour us. With the unambiguously fictional (meaning allegorical), we can always deny it—or as I would say as a child (watching grade-B horror movies in the late 1950s and 1960s, holding my father's hand for reassurance), "Oh, this isn't real." This is not a claim one can so comfortably and smugly make with accounts referential to the evidence of phenomena.

Clearly such differentiating qualities in phenomena can pose profound challenges to our paler, cooler ideas—those ideas we have constructed both individually and culturally. This is because the abstracted ideas in which we take our comfort—propagating further as they play off, moderate, and inflate one another—are always confronted with a dilemma. As they evolve into the larger schema, they must either eliminate or incorporate newly perceived differentiating qualities of the unfamiliar phenomenal particular, or else the paler, cooler ideas must be reshaped, whether to a larger or smaller degree, to the challenge posed by what is "novel" that cannot be eliminated or incorporated. When we are exposed to stories generally, including conventional fictions, as the cognitive psychologists Roger C. Schank and Tamara R. Berman have noted, "we seek to *match* what is being told to us to ideas we have already stored in our memories. We are essentially attempting to confirm the beliefs we constructed earlier. If we have difficulty doing so, we may learn something new, or we may revise a belief."[32] The last sentence is revealing, because when the novelty of the concrete metaphor that is reflective of the chronotopic evidence cannot confirm beliefs constructed earlier, we are forced to revise those beliefs. This is, for example, what documentary accounts accomplished during the European period of exploration and discovery, when explorers brought back tales of strange species of plants and animals from newly discovered worlds, whether it was tomatoes or kangaroos.[33] The novel phenomena discovered on those voyages of approximately the fifteenth through the eighteenth centuries contributed to challenging the medieval worldview with what the latter could not incorporate into its spiritual allegory of what constituted "reality." Simply put, the authors and keepers of the Christian Bible, the definitive documentary text of the medieval European mind, knew nothing about such strangenesses as tomatoes and kangaroos.

Victor Shklovsky's concept that literature makes the familiar unfamiliar helps us understand how influential the distinctive concrete metaphor—in which the differences have not been elided—can be in reshaping the way we interpret our personally and culturally constructed world. As Shklovsky notes:

> Art exists that one may recover the sensation of life; it exists to make one feel things, to make the stone stony. The purpose of art is to impart the sensation of things as they are perceived and not as they are known. The technique of art is to make objects "unfamiliar," to make forms difficult, to increase the difficulty and length of perception because the process of perception is an aesthetic end in itself and must be prolonged. *Art is a way of experiencing the artfulness of an object: the object is not important.*[34]

To "recover the sensation of life . . . to make one feel things, to make the stone stony . . . to impart the sensation of things as they are perceived and not as they are known" is, of course, an early iteration on the "aesthetics of the everyday," even if the term was not used at the time Shklovsky articulated his concept of the unfamiliar (which was in 1917).[35] I would only dispute, in the case of a narra-descriptive journalism, that "the object is not important."

In fact, its perceived "differences" make all the difference in converting the familiar of what we believe we know into the estranged or unfamiliar.

To recover "the artfulness of an object" arises because our relationship to the world suffers from "habitualization," Shklovsky suggests, noting elsewhere that "all of our habits retreat into the area of the unconsciously automatic."[36] Thus, when the world reflected in literature becomes too familiar so that we take it for granted—or to rephrase a colloquial expression in the spirit of Nietzsche, we cannot see the individual leaves for the forest—we require a new literature that helps us see the world anew, one that provides new insights. This requires violating our cultural and/or individual assumptions. In the case of a narrative literary journalism, this is possible because of the insights gleaned from the distinctiveness of differentiating qualities in the phenomenal chronotopes that need not necessarily obey the constraining expectations of our assumptions. The result is always the possibility of a cognitive disruption or estrangement to be found in the unfamiliarity of the individual leaves of the individual trees, not the familiarity of the generalized forest as one vast global expanse of green reflected in the cooler, paler ideas. The blinders of our idealizations or totalizations have been removed—or at least diminished—and we detect the phenomenal world anew as well as our place in it. (Nor is there any reason why this cannot be true even in those instances where we do find an extended or elaborate literary symbolic in works of narra-descriptive journalism.) Thus we have been placed in a new relationship with both the evidence of the phenomenal and our personal and cultural values and assumptions, and we see the world and ourselves reflected and refracted in a new or different light, no matter how nuanced. In a sense, such a new relationship is a liberation from the old habitual relationships.

Chronotopic accounts of war especially lend themselves to understanding the familiar that becomes unfamiliar because what we so often detect is dramatic contrast—or dialogue—between the violence of war and our everyday, taken-for-granted and insignificant banalities which establish how we see the world. Simply, we detect irony. Ernst Jünger, for example, repeatedly reveals an uncanny aesthetic ability for detecting this quality in *The Storm of Steel*, his account from the German side of life in the trenches on the Western Front. In one scene we find him in a French house that has been partially blown away. Amid a bombardment, as the French bomb the Germans (the familiar, or what we would expect—there was, after all, the loss of Alsace and Lorraine to avenge) but also their own homes (more unfamiliar, or what we would be less inclined to expect, because the French are bombing French houses), Jünger the alien German sits down in a comfortable French chair and picks up and starts reading an old book, observing that this is "where a lover of beautiful old things must have lived." Then, amid the bombardment in the half-blown-away house, reflecting its aura of banal domesticity or the comforts of home, he says: "I felt a violent blow on my left calf. . . . There was a ragged hole in my puttees, from which blood ran on to the ground. On the other side there was the round swelling of a shrapnel bullet under the skin"—juxtaposed against a home where a lover of beautiful things once lived.[37] So we have the familiar made unfamiliar in such a juxtaposition of domesticity and the violence of war. Bruce Chatwin, a narrative literary journalist in his own right, would note, regarding Jünger's aesthetic sensibility in identifying such contrasts, "No one but a man of Jünger's composure could describe the appearance of a bullet hole through his chest as if he were describing his nipple."[38]

Jünger, in his later journals from World War II, when he was stationed in Paris as a cultural liaison officer with the German army, described an Allied air raid viewed through a glass of burgundy in which strawberries floated.[39] Again we detect the familiar made unfamiliar. After all, a glass of burgundy with strawberries floating in it could all but represent the banal gesture of a sybarite of culturally refined and elegant tastes. And the Allied air raid with bombs dropping from the sky has become all but a visual cliché we have inherited from grainy black-and-white documentary film of the period. It is, however, the juxtaposition of the two—Jünger watching through a raised glass of red wine in which strawberries float as bombs drop from the sky— that introduces us to a new unfamiliar. Of course, it will not represent a new unfamiliar for those who routinely watch air raids through a glass of wine in which strawberries float, but I suspect they are among the exceptions.

Clearly, such images are estranged from our habits of seeing or knowing. Jünger takes note of this critical phenomenon near the beginning of *The Storm of Steel* when, as mentioned in the last chapter, he says he will refrain from engaging in discursive commentary. But the passage bears repeating in its entirety because of his critical perception of the aesthetics of experience, this from someone who survived as a storm trooper on the Western Front:

> Although I had made up my mind to omit all comments [commentary] from this book, I should like all the same to say a word or two about this first glimpse of horrors. It is a moment so important in the experience of war. The horrible was undoubtedly a part of that irresistible attraction that drew us into the war. . . . Among other questions that occupied us was this: what does it look like where there are dead lying about? And we never for a moment dreamt that in this war the dead would be left month after month to the mercy of wind and weather, as once the bodies on the gallows were.
>
> And now at our first glance of horror we had a feeling that is difficult to describe. *Seeing and recognizing are matters, really, of habit. In the case*

of something quite unknown the eye alone can make nothing of it. So it was that we had to stare again and again at these things that we had never seen before, without being able to give them any meaning. . . . But finally we were so accustomed to the horrible that if we came on a dead body anywhere on a fire-step or in a ditch we gave it no more than a passing thought and recognized it as we would a stone or a tree.[40]

In other words (note the added emphasis), how we perceive derives, at least in part, from our habits of seeing, meaning our volatilized schema to which we have attached the ships of our lives and actions, "ships" that are larger metaphors for those totalizations to which we subscribe. And it is the unfamiliar of phenomena that disrupts the familiar schema—strawberries in red wine in a glass raised skyward in a toast, almost as if to receive those grainy black-and-white bombs descending from the Flying Fortresses.

Perhaps it is not so remarkable that Jünger and Shklovsky, who both served in World War I, arrived at similar critical positions: that our habits of seeing or our habitualizations need to be disrupted in order to "see" the world, phenomenal and literary, anew. By the same token, we can detect the opposite, the familiar confirmed by habits of seeing, in the "routinizing" of conventional news that presents the unexpected to the reader as the conventional.[41]

When we discuss the perception of the seemingly deracinated particular, complete in all its differences (in the "trite symbolism of ordinary life," centripetal in orientation back to an original), what we discuss is how the particular exists to some extent beyond the ritualistic confirmations of our experience. Again, "*Seeing and recognizing are matters, really, of habit. In the case of something quite unknown the eye alone can make nothing of it.*" Hence the cognitive disruption of what is perceived as unfamiliar, and the power of the phenomenal concrete metaphor uniquely located beyond the covers of books to challenge our personal and cultural assumptions. In a sense I am discussing an anti-aesthetics that challenges conventional and ritualistic aesthetics whose interpretations are dictated by the schema. We see that Jünger is a kind of "an-aesthete" in such a writing that overrides convention with an "an-aesthetics" of experience. Of course, eventually the unfamiliar can very much evolve into the familiar, and the cognitive disruption can be overcome, as Jünger acknowledged when soldiers became so accustomed to the horrific of the trenches. But not before it has introduced to us a new way of seeing.

War lends itself uniquely to making the familiar unfamiliar because the nature of the horrific reminds us of this most convincingly. But making the familiar unfamiliar can also be detected in more pacific accounts (relatively speaking). Consider James Agee's *Let Us Now Praise Famous Men*.[42] In my

earlier history, I adopted William Stott's characterization of a narrative literary journalism from the 1930s as being either "instrumental" and designed to
prompt social change or "descriptive" and designed to let the reader draw his
or her own conclusions. I initially placed Agee in the instrumental category.[43]
But I am less disposed to do so today, and see his work as in the descriptive
category also (if not more so). This is because in recent years I have been
researching the work of the early twentieth-century German-Czech journalist Egon Erwin Kisch, a staunch communist who was undoubtedly the
most widely known promoter in the world proletarian writers' movement of
a "literary reportage" during the 1920s and 1930s.[44] Such work, needless to
say, was often tendentious. Kisch's example reveals just how different Agee's
intent was from the usual "instrumental" intent of the proletarian writers' movement. In a statement that reflected the value Kisch saw in such a
reportage, and in what is clearly a rebuke to the bourgeois tradition of James
Joyce and others who explored interior consciousness in fictional novels, he
declared: "Psychological novels? No! Reportages! The future belongs to the
really true and courageous far-seeing reportage."[45] Kisch was writing in support of Marxist ideology. The material evidence was the revelation.

Agee was different. He wrote in support of examining one's personal
relationship with those who had been consigned to the social and economic
"Other" (much as both communists and capitalists tended to do). Not that
Agee did not reflect instrumental qualities. His was less a material instrumentality, however, and more a psychological and philosophical instrumentality
aimed at trying to help readers (and himself) understand the subjectivities
of poor white southern tenant farmers by means of the concrete metaphors
reflecting distinctive intersections in time and space. (In a sense, he was
attempting in his own way a kind of cultural documentary reflected and
refracted through interior consciousness.) What he discovered was that the
tenant farmers possessed their own existential dignity *despite* their material
hardships and poverty. But such a dignity clearly flies in the face of Marxist
political correctness: here were not necessarily the downtrodden masses so
neatly pigeonholed and in need of deliverance by Marxism-Leninism. Ultimately, Agee's subject was the existential condition, and he wrote on a cosmic
stage, as Paul Ashdown has observed.[46]

From whence arises this resistance to the political screed? It can be
detected in Shklovsky's concept of the familiar made unfamiliar. It is revealed,
for example, in Agee's almost microscopic examination of farmers' blue jean
or denim overalls, an examination that goes on for more than a page:

Try . . . to imagine and to know, as against other garments, the difference
of their feeling against the body; drawn-on, and bibbed on the whole belly

and chest, naked from the kidneys up from behind, save for broad crossed straps, and slung by these straps from the shoulder; the slanted pockets on each thigh, the deep square pockets on each buttock; the complex and slanted structures, on the chest, of the pockets shaped for pencils, rulers, and watches; the coldness of sweat when they are young, and their stiffness; their sweetness to the skin and pleasure of sweating when they are old, the thin metal buttons of the fly.[47]

So Agee proceeds in close detail in a description 387 words long. Moreover, it is a description he resumes a few pages later. It is true that at the end of that initial passage he describes the overalls as a "blueprint: and they are a map of a working man."[48] Given the political tenor of the 1930s, this last would seem to consign the description once again to an instrumental purpose, namely, to show the working class through its labors; in effect, to reveal the *qualitas occulta* of the political screed. This cannot be entirely denied, and it helps us realize that the issue is in part how well an author negotiates between the concrete metaphors and the paler, cooler ideas, and whether he or she emphasizes one more than the other.

At the same time, there is at least as much reason to believe that Agee is being ironic, or that he is celebrating the man who works as an individual, not necessarily the mythic proletarian "working man" representative or symbolic of the "working class." This is because he cites Marx's call for revolution—"Workers of the world, unite and fight"—at the beginning of the book and then in a footnote observes: "These words are quoted here to mislead those who will be mislead by them." He aims at those who will respond with a knee-jerk reaction to the catchphrase of communism. Again, that can include communists and capitalists. As part of what he characterizes as his "theme," he refers the reader to a passage from *King Lear,* printed on the opposite page, in which the king says, "Expose thyself to feel what wretches feel. . . . And show the heavens more just." But Agee is not attempting to place the "wretches" like puppets on a politically ideological stage, because he observes in the conclusion to the footnote "that neither these words nor the authors are the property of any political party, faith, or faction."[49] Hence his focus on the individual as individual.

This intent is expressed elsewhere. For example, when he stops on a back country road in Alabama to ask for directions from two men and a woman sitting on the front porch of their ramshackle farmhouse, he observes, "Since . . . they existed quite irrelevant to myth, it will be necessary to tell a little of them."[50] So he attempts to break through conventional habits or "myths" of seeing that consign or objectify the individuals as poor Alabama dirt farmers. As with the denim overalls, he engages in minute description. Among them, the young woman's "body also was brass or bitter gold, strong to stridency beneath the unbleached clayed cotton dress, and her arms and bare legs were sharp with metal down." The color gold takes on the taste of bitterness thus disrupting one sense—color—with that of another—taste. Moreover, the woman wears the cheapest of cotton, unbleached and suggestive of the quality of clay. What Agee describes is muslin calico, which is a cotton fabric not fully processed; in its less processed form it may even contain fragments of the cotton plant's husk. (In this instance calico should not be mistaken for colorfully printed calico; calico originally meant the nature of the fabric, its processing and weave.) Natural muslin calico is the color of a very light tannish gray. While this may be the color Agee is suggesting when he references the quality of clay, it could equally mean a color derived from the pigments of clay dyeing, a primitive and cheap method of dyeing which can come in the various shades of clay. Whichever, we detect his pushing the boundaries of the common sense-appeal of our shared common senses in the effort to capture the distinction of what he sees. Similarly, regarding the arms and legs "sharp with metal down," this suggests an abrasive quality from hair that could only contrast with the sophisticated cosmopolitan world of women's waxed or shaved legs. So Agee approaches the tenant farmers as autonomous individuals by attempting to recover the distinctive differences in the leaves that Nietzsche discussed. In the differences lies the unfamiliarity from habits of seeing.

Agee's volume raises the issue of visual journalism, given that it is not only Agee's but Walker Evans's volume as well, because included are the latter's black-and-white photographs of the sharecroppers who are introduced at the beginning of the book without comment or identification. (It should be noted, too, that the names of the sharecroppers were changed by Agee in the printed text.) As Agee observes, the photographs "and the text, are coequal, mutually independent, and fully collaborative."[51] My emphasis for the moment is on the printed text independent of the photographs. But a critical perspective on the two media juxtaposed or in collaboration offers promising inquiry, especially in our contemporary moment, when we see a "convergence" of media in cyberspace. I will save that assessment for the concluding chapter.

In any event, what we have in such examples in the printed text is the attempt to make the familiar unfamiliar in order to arrive ultimately at a new but estranged relationship, or an estrangement from the symbolic assumptions, cultural and individual, that we may take for granted. After all, how often have we taken blue denim or jeans for granted, even turning them into a kind of high fashion—well scrubbed with holes in the knees for contemporary teenagers to make a fashion statement? In still another sense, Agee recovers what denim was originally intended for. Tough and durable, it was meant for utilitarian purposes.

To return to Hemingway's account of his motoring tour of Italy in 1927, how does making the familiar unfamiliar apply in such a prosaic scene as I opened with? After all, one could view the spray of mud on the windshield as a larger confirmation of an existing perception or habit of seeing with regard to the primitive state of Italian transportation infrastructure in the 1920s, the kind of concern that someone could write an engineering dissertation on. But can we always count on such differentiating qualities being eliminated from or incorporated into the larger idea? One might say, hypothetically: "'Italian roads are bad. They are always bad,' he muttered, and shrugged his shoulders with indifference." Instead, as with the Renaissance voyages of exploration and discovery, the potential is always there to prompt a reconsideration and revision. Hypothetically, some Fascist functionary, embarrassed by the article in the New Republic, could consider for the first time a highway-building program in Italy—a multi-laned autostrada. In other words, the differentiating qualities of the intersection where time and place meet always have the potential to provide a new perception, not necessarily the confirmation of an existing paler, cooler one. Thus we might see a challenge to business as usual regarding the state of Italian roads in the 1920s.

Nor can we predict or anticipate what other challenges might be posed by the differentiating qualities to the established *qualitas occulta*. Those ideas consonant with an ideology may attempt to absorb the differentiating qualities of the phenomenal through erasure, or through equating the unequal of the differentiating qualities in a kind of willed ignorance of what makes them different. But the mud sprayed on the windscreen derives its irreducible singularity from that one time and place which resists wholesale absorption into allegory. To put it differently, the concrete metaphor may strain toward totalization resulting in the abstract—to which we would attach the ship of our lives—but there can never be an absolute absorption into an idealization, because the intellectual process always remains tethered to one unique and discrete time and place and the contents therein, which as phenomena cannot entirely be volatilized, to use Nietzsche's description of the critical process. Simply put, we can never disallow that there will always be differentiating qualities posing their challenge no matter how much we engage in forgetfulness or erasure.

The resistance to generalization of the unfamiliar concrete metaphor located in time and space is reflected in Hemingway's emerging prose style in the 1920s. His history as a journalist is well documented, how he learned the journalism craft at the *Kansas City Star*, and later wrote for the *Toronto Star* in Europe.[52] What benefits from closer examination is his transition from a mainstream objectifying journalist to a narrative literary journalist emphasizing the descriptive phenomenal particular. Such a transition is illustrative of the process of reversed Nietzschean "volatilisation," or of essentialized ideas descending or reducing to a profane particular—a precipitation, in other words.

The shift can be detected in a piece Hemingway did for the *Toronto Star* in 1922, when he covered the evacuation of the Greek populace from eastern Thrace. In the article Hemingway still engages in a generalizing inclination, when, for example, he notes that the refugees' "brilliant peasant costumes are soaked and draggled."[53] In the plurality of the costumes, he presents a generalizing summarization. Hemingway is indulging what Nietzsche sees as the irrepressible human disposition—humankind, after all, "depends on this faculty"—to engage in generalization or "volatilisation."

But in the same paragraph Hemingway's writing reflects a different direction, that of a writer with his gaze focused on the evidence of the ontological particular: "An old man marches bent under a young pig, a scythe and a gun, with a chicken tied to his scythe." The old man is one of a kind, not a generalized plurality, who is further distinguished by carrying a one-of-a-kind young pig (long since consumed, one presumes), a one-of-a-kind gun, and a one-of-a-kind scythe with a one-of-a-kind chicken tied to it, all located at the intersection of that singular and irreducible time and place. As such, the old man may become suggestively representative of a people in flight, but only suggestively, because in the aesthetics of experience he is still one of a kind, in which the differentiating qualities can never be entirely elided. Hemingway has reversed the abstracting tendency of mainstream journalistic style. And this is prompted by what lies beyond the covers of books. In another example in the same paragraph Hemingway writes: "A husband spreads a blanket over a woman in labor in one of the carts to keep off the driving rain. She is the only person making a sound. Her little daughter looks at her in horror and begins to cry."[54] Hemingway would use this material again as part of a vignette in a collection of short stories.[55] In other words, he recognized the literary possibilities of the aesthetics of experience in the journalistic claim to being referential. Yet this is a referentiality that resists complete assimilation into the cooler, paler ideas.

Thus we detect part of the importance of the concrete metaphor which insists on not eliminating the differences between the leaves. But as I noted at the outset, there is another quality to the concrete metaphor that asks for scrutiny precisely because of the nature of the evidence we perceive. For on closer inspection we detect that the concrete metaphor of "leaf" is a lot less solid and stable, and more ambiguous in its phenomenal status, than we may initially think or wish to think when we are first introduced to it. This is, of course, in part because it is a linguistic construction influenced by the personal and cultural and the exchange between. Certainly they apply. But they are not the only reasons, since their origins in turn derived from concrete metaphors.

The problem arises because the evidence is never complete. On closer examination, the tangible we characterize as "real life," which we take so much for granted, serves as a veil for the phenomenal evidence beyond our knowing. Or, better yet, "real life" is a kind of euphemism that deceives. The danger of Tom Wolfe's confidence in "real life" is that it reflects a belief that one can trust the testimony of one's senses. But of course one cannot, even if we are forced to as an existential defense. Nor is this only because we can be mistaken in the initial perceptions and frailties of memory. There is that, too. But additionally (and this helps to account at least in part for mistaken initial perceptions subject to the frailties of memory), the reality of the evidence of the "real" of the phenomenal world is that the seemingly plain, simple concrete metaphor is ultimately not so plain and simple, because it speaks not only to what is recognized ontologically but also to what is not included in the recognition. The result is that there is always a potential for still newer phenomenal unfamiliars to emerge, associated with the concrete metaphor, that challenge our familiar assumptions.

Few would dispute that there is much beyond our knowing, and indeed that there is much more beyond our knowing than we can ever know. The reason we can so easily overlook this circumstance has to do with the allure of turning "real life" into a comforting habit of seeing, or in effect a platitude. Like all platitudes, it lulls us as a kind of Nietzschean *qualitas occulta* to which we attach the ship of our lives, one holding the promise of existential command, which we are only too eager to embrace. It is not difficult to understand why Wolfe's "real life" appears to result from a simple "elementary ambition," much in the way we view Mendeleyev's periodic table or chart as "elementary" for defining chemical properties. Except that maybe what is "elementary" is not necessarily so.

To illustrate, I return to Hemingway's description of mud sprayed on a windscreen. Can we be confident that at whatever level of consciousness—linguistic or otherwise—the universe of differentiating qualities intersecting in time and space have been entirely assimilated into the linguistic metaphor? Of course not. Hemingway might, for example, have examined the mud on the windscreen as a geologist would for the kind of soil it derived from—cambisols, which are generally alluvial soils of varying layers of brown, as well as red and gray, in the Sestri Levante commune in Italy, where the story takes place. From still another perspective, the town's castles are not mentioned. Had Hemingway selected these details for his article, they would in their own way have contributed to how we interpret. But for whatever reasons, conscious or otherwise, Hemingway did not indicate their presence by means of his perceiving aesthetics of experience.

To examine other parts of the passage: "The pasta asciutta was good; the wine tasted of alum, and we poured water in it. Afterwards the waiter brought beef steak and fried potatoes. A man and a woman sat at the far end of the restaurant. He was middle-aged and she was young and wore black. All during the meal she would blow out her breath in the cold damp air. The man would look at it and shake his head. They ate without talking and the man held her hand under the table." What remains undescribed here (literally) is what has gone missing. For example, why the alum taste in the wine? There could be any number of possibilities. To suggest a hypothetical example from the vantage point of an oenophile: "You could tell that they used bad clay to clarify the wine. I hate it when they use bad clay. It ruins the wine. I hate it."[56] Clay used for "fining" or clarifying wine can contain alum. Nor is the middle-aged man further described. Did he have a big nose with a heart-shaped wart five millimeters wide on the right nostril sprouting two gray hairs? Or a sebaceous cyst oozing oil? What was the young woman wearing that was black? Of what fabric was her dress made? Black worsted wool and she is still cold? Were the man and woman lovers? Or father and daughter? Or uncle and niece? Or uncle and niece and lovers? Of course, such are just some of the infinite possibilities, and it is not difficult to project through reductionism, or a critical atomization, that the details and their context would multiply to beyond comprehension of the aesthetics of experience.

When Democritus formulated his idea of the atom, he contributed to modern physics a problem yet to be fully deciphered, if ever it can be given that the atom can be further divided, and we now have the Higgs boson particle, which has only further complicated the matter. The atom and the Higgs boson are abstract, or paler, cooler ideas, located at a critical remove from the testimony of the senses, so much so that they can only be perceived abstractly through the extension of sophisticated technology, such as the super–atom smasher known as the Large Hadron Collider in Switzerland. But there can be no direct testimony of the senses, no direct aesthetics of experience that appeals to the common sense-appeal of the shared common senses that we can expect most readers to have in common, even if they interpret experience differently.

Of course, what we detect in the Hemingway passage is his shaping consciousness in his selections. For the moment I am less interested in the shaping consciousness (and the personal and cultural contexts that attend any shaping) than in what the act of making selections about the phenomenal implies. For it ultimately results in incompleteness, since something is excluded, either intentionally as part of the selection process, or because it is unobserved. There are, then, those phenomenal differentiating qualities that are beyond the momentary appreciation of the author's aesthetics of experience. They are the unassimilated. Thus those who are courageous enough to acknowledge as much are reminded that there is always something we cannot know—at least for the moment—while those who are unquestioning will tend to accept at face value the platitude or euphemism of "real life" as elementary and fundamental to their habits of seeing. To the latter, the concept of the unassimilated may appear counterintuitive.

As Mary Poovey notes, the idea of the unassimilable is not new: "Ciceronian skepticism was essentially epistemological, for [Cicero] held that the frailty of the human senses renders certainty about the natural impossible."[57] We are, in a manner of speaking, talking about the phenomenal excess beyond our knowing.[58] As Poovey further observes, in a discussion of the emergence of the concept of the modern fact during the late Renaissance as a result of the Baconian scientific method, "If one had to resist premature generalization, after all, and if one could produce systematic knowledge only by reasoning from the phenomena one observed [Baconian induction], then it was imperative to know how one moved from the particulars one saw to knowledge that was sufficiently general *to explain things one had not seen*."[59] Of course, "things one had not seen" are the hidden flaw in the Baconian formulation of the scientific method, she notes. It is the unassimilated or excess of what we do not know. It was ironic that Bacon's intent was to try to address the peculiar, the anomalous, the abnormal that did not fit so comfortably into his era's Aristotelian commonplaces as the norm, whether it was a secular or theological norm—or habit of seeing—in the hope that eventually the result would be general deductive laws. Thus the concept of the modern fact was born, Poovey suggests, but was inherently flawed and contradictory from the outset. While the scientific method has worked reasonably well in the hard sciences, it has been a more difficult matter for the social sciences, such as communication studies, in which journalism has generally (though not entirely) been housed as a discipline. "Communication science seeks to understand the production, processing and effects of symbol and signal systems by developing *testable* theories, containing *lawful generalizations*, that explain phenomena associated with production, processing and effects."[60] The emphasis is again added because the testable lawful generalizations reinscribe communication phenomena in Aristotelian deduction resulting in abstract commonplaces—Nietzsche's *qualitas occulta*. Bacon never squared induction with deduction, or the "imperative to know how one moved from the particulars one saw to knowledge that was sufficiently general *to explain things one had not seen.*" On this, Poovey notes, he was vague.

This circumstance also helps to account for why a narrative literary journalism born of the evidence of the aesthetics of experience that focuses on the concrete metaphor of the phenomenal particular fell largely outside of the communication academy: it was outside the paradigm of the deductive testable and "lawful" generalizations about journalism.[61]

Can we conclude that the excess or the unassimilated can never be assimilated? No. Nor can we conclude that all differentiating qualities in the excess can be assimilated. This is true not only of assimilation into the paler, cooler ideas but also, and significantly, with the "trite" concrete metaphors. What we detect, then, is a recognition of our limitations tied not just to the concrete metaphor but to what about the evidence of the concrete metaphor has not been assimilated, or what we do not know.

Recent studies on modern narrative have also detected to varying degrees the concept of the unassimilated. Iser, citing Arnold Bennett's observation that "you can't put the whole of a character into a book," adds, "He was thinking of the discrepancy between a person's life and the unavoidably limited form in which that life may be represented."[62] Thus we detect that something has been excluded. As David Herman succinctly notes of human limitations, "Persons are constituted by but not wholly reducible to (collections of) material particles."[63] A similar observation has been made of history. Jauss observes, in interpreting and then quoting the German historian Johann Gustav Droysen, that what we believe in "is the illusion of the complete process. Although every historian knows that our knowledge of history must always remain incomplete, the prevailing form of the narrative creates 'the illusion and wants to create it, that we are faced with a complete process of historical things, a finished chain of events, motives and purposes.'"[64]

The result is that the vague notion of the unassimilated or the excess hangs suspended (to use a metaphor for an absence) and out of reach of consciousness, as opposed to the selected description or concrete metaphors of the text. To assimilate all differentiating qualities into the concrete metaphor is, of course, impossible, given the nature of cognitive reductionism that must end increasingly in an abstract realm, and ultimately in the abstraction of subatomic particles well beyond the common sense-appeal of the shared common senses, or the personal aesthetics of experience. Our knowledge of the phenomenal is indeterminate because of, inevitably, the limitations of the testimony of the senses to perceive every aspect of phenomena. This, of course, is why Mendeleyev created his periodic chart, because of the limitations of the testimony of the senses. And it provides only one small attempt at an extension of the testimony that moves us cognitively into the realm of the paler, cooler ideas of abstraction, the periodic table as *qualitas occulta,* although admittedly one with utility in a phenomenal world the way modern mainstream journalism has a more abstract utility. (But, as discussed, "abstract utility" reveals its own inherent contradictions that also problematizes such cognitive attempts.)

It is, of course, difficult to grasp the concept of the unassimilated since it is beyond our knowing. For a genre making a referential claim to the seeming solidity of the phenomenal—to "real life"—this is epistemologically unsettling, and indeed it seems counterintuitive, because it means that what we say is and perceive of as "real life" is not entirely tangible. The referent, after all, is always reflective of some degree of incompleteness, not simply because of language but also because of our sensory limitations, which cannot perceive all of "real life."

To better understand the unassimilable, we can detect an insightful parallel from the study of quantum physics. As Lee Smolin, a leading contemporary theoretical physicist, has observed: "Quantum mechanics does not give a complete picture of reality. . . . This means that there are things that are true about the world that quantum mechanics cannot represent."[65] He refers, then, to what has not been assimilated into human cognition. But that does not mean that quantum mechanics is necessarily wrong, he adds. Instead, it means that the entirety of a hypothetical physical universe is incapable of being perceived. In his interpretation of the Nobel award-winning physicist Niels Bohr—one of the formulators of quantum mechanics in addition to Werner Heisenberg—Smolin writes, "Properties are defined only relationally, and . . . physics is an aspect of our relations with the world." In other words, we cannot know what exists beyond our relations with the universe because our knowledge is determined by the confining capabilities our limitations impose, or the questions we ask. "For him [Bohr], physics was an extension of common language, which people use to tell each other the results of their observations of nature," Smolin says.[66] What they can arrive at, then, is only approximate understanding and meaning, not essential understanding and meaning, because the testimony of the senses has inevitably proved inadequate.

Nor is the connection between quantum mechanics and a narrative of the evidence of the phenomenal merely a borrowing of a useful metaphor from the world of physics. It reminds us of how Samuel Johnson and James Boswell anticipated the discoveries of Bohr and Heisenberg in their own versions of an early narrative literary journalism, their two separate accounts of a joint walking tour they took of Scotland and the Hebrides in 1773. The significance lies in their attempts to reflect the same phenomenal world. What they discovered is that they reported differently on the same observations. For example, on the Isle of Iona, Johnson made note of the "black stones" where "the old Highland chiefs, when they made contracts and alliances, used to take the oath, which was considered as more sacred than any other obligation." Boswell, in a footnote to Johnson's observation, "swore an oath there [and] claimed it was one stone."[67] The incident reflects the different responses Johnson and Boswell brought to the enterprise of observation on the same experience. Johnson acknowledges this when on the Isle of Mull, he, Boswell, and their party investigate MacKinnon's Cave on the western coast of the middle peninsula. Of it Johnson remarks in his account, "He who has not made the experiment, or who is not accustomed to require rigorous accuracy from himself, will scarcely believe how much a few hours take from certainty of knowledge, and the distinctness of imagery; how the succession of objects will be broken, how separate parts will be confused, and how many particular features and discriminations will be compressed and conglobated."[68] The issue reflects the fundamental instability of observation refracted from the testimony of the senses through consciousness and language. In the case of Johnson and Boswell it comes as no surprise, since each brings to bear his own "context of experience of aesthetic perception," according to Jauss.[69] In the "loss of particular features," as Johnson expresses it, we detect the loss of differentiated qualities from the intersection of one time and place. In the cognitive compression or "conglobation" we detect the natural cognitive movement toward paler and cooler ideas.

As Bohr observed, *how* each of us sees contributes to shaping *what* is seen in "Quantumland," as Smolin likes to characterize the quantum universe. The physicist is speaking the language of reader response. And the emphasis on the *how* reveals just how much we detect the rhetorical ambition. This of course speaks to the central role of a shaping subjectivity in a narrative literary journalism, as any number of critics have noted.[70]

It is here that aesthetics and physics make uncanny common cause, which has implications for any discourse characterized as "literary" and yet at the same time makes a claim to reflecting phenomenal experience, or in other words, the world of physics. Indeed, it is no longer clear whether we are in the world of poetics or physics. But given our subject, a narrative literary journalism that draws from the aesthetics of experience, this should come as no surprise. Again, as the literary critic Mark Edmundson has noted, literature ultimately escapes critical closure because, as he says, it "resists being explained away,"[71] just as Heisenberg and Bohr recognized that not all empirical information can be accounted for and explained. Or, as John Keats said, poetic experience (in the form of a Grecian urn) forever "teases us out of thought."[72] Heisenberg and Bohr, too, detected a relationship between the languages of physics and poetics.[73]

It is no wonder then that a narrative "literary journalism" is by no means the only terminology by which such a shifting form or genre can be identified, or that it is any more privileged than "New Journalism," "narrative journalism," or "narra-descriptive journalism," or, for that matter, a "chronotopic journalism," to add still another possible contender. Each reflects the particular questioning brought to bear on such phenomenal accounts. Ronald Weber is closer to the truth than he may have fully anticipated when he noted, "Here I shall be using a simple descriptive term: literary nonfiction."[74] His announced reflexivity ("I") reveals the particular perspective he has at the moment on a discourse.

What is the basis, then, for how we choose the concrete metaphors we select? What are our motivations? And it is here that the full complexity of cultural and individual influences comes into play. But what cannot be discounted—elided—is that because each phenomenon is different, it always poses in the differentiating qualities the potential for eliciting new ways of envisioning, of disrupting and revisioning taken-for-granted assumptions if the differences are outside the reader's habits of seeing, and, moreover, if more differences—the initially unassimilated—are later detected. For that reason, human beings are not exclusively cultural automatons, their strings orchestrated by culture in a cultural symphony. Undoubtedly a cultural symphony is there. But in the perception that there can be a seemingly deracinated particular lie opportunities for a cognitive dissonance to the symphony—and liberation from those habits of seeing. For example, in John Hersey's *Hiroshima* we discover an empathetic if not sympathetic portrait of Japanese, as reflected in the differentiating qualities of individuals, who survived the atomic bombing of the city. The result is that we (I am speaking of Americans like myself) are empathetic if not sympathetic with those who had been our enemy.[75] Something similar could be said of the southern white tenant farmers in Agee's *Let Us Now Praise Famous Men*, to whom many Americans, understandably, would have difficulty relating. Thus differences always run the risk of introducing exceptions to the assumptions of the paler, cooler ideas. For example, in 1946 the Japanese could all too easily be demonized because of Pearl Harbor and the Bataan Death March. Or, in the 1930s poor southern white sharecroppers could be viewed as uneducated racist rednecks. Such are assumptions or habits of seeing. But all it takes are differentiating qualities, such as those described by Hersey and Agee, to infiltrate and counter dominating assumptions, which then have to be either renegotiated and possibly reaffirmed, or discarded in favor of new envisionings and interpretations.

Moreover, it is the gratuitous random and distinctive details lacking in obvious centrifugal symbolism (outward directed) that in some ways are the most resonant, precisely because, in a sense, they yearn futilely for unfulfilled larger symbolic meaning, the *qualitas occulta*, that we as humans desire. The reason is clear: lack of context—or the personal and communal values (and platitudes) we might normally supply. It is a case of unrequited love. The more denied, the more the desire; we seek to be in command of what eludes our understanding. In the Hemingway examples of the old man as refugee and the refugee family, they are potentially suggestive, as noted, of a larger condition, that of refugees, even as the old man and the family are—resolutely—one of a kind.

Hemingway was aware of this consequence posed by the rendering of differentiating qualities, as have been many literary critics. For Hemingway, it was reflected in his aesthetic theory of omission, which he outlined in *Death in the Afternoon*: "If a writer of prose knows enough about what he is writing about he may omit things that he knows and the reader, if the writer is writing truly enough, will have a feeling of those things as strongly as though the writer had stated them. The dignity of movement of an iceberg is due to only one-eighth of it being above water."[76] Hence, too, the seeming randomness of the chronotopes selected by Hemingway in the passage this chapter began with.

Bearing Hemingway's theory of omission in mind, I would suggest that this is what the English professor was confronted with in asking Mary McCarthy what the symbols meant in her account of anti-Semitism. But she draws, perhaps unintentionally, too airtight a distinction between a narrative literary journalism that is centripetally oriented back toward the distinguishing qualities of the phenomenal and ultimately the unassimilable, on the one hand, and on the other, a discourse centrifugally oriented outward in an extended literary symbolic. Centripetal and centrifugal referentialities are, of course, metaphors, and at the risk of mixing them in an oxymoron at odds when contradictory forces in nature collide, I would only suggest that you can have both at work at the same time. Indeed, that dynamic tension may contribute to what makes such a discourse compelling. McCarthy was clear in her mind that her wearing two shades of green and eating a sandwich had no more symbolism or ulteriority of meaning than that of a simple and unambiguous (and "trite") phenomenal description. But we cannot conclude that such a circumstance must always be the case, and that the description of materiality may not have centrifugal ulteriority at the same time, including one that arises beyond the intent of the author. Similarly, we cannot conclude that a narra-descriptive journalism loses its differentiating qualities, seen and unseen, at a unique location in time and space.

.   .   .

Nietzsche was right, of course, regarding our human nature, because we have seen confirmation in recent years of what he induced as a philosopher in 1873, that it is in our human nature to try to erase the differences between the leaves in order to create a generality. Again, as Schank and Berman note, when we are exposed to stories, "we seek to match what is being told to us to ideas we have already stored in our memories. We are essentially attempting to confirm the beliefs we constructed earlier." They add, "We group together similar experiences to make generalizations of our conceptions."[77] As Brian Boyd similarly observes: "Individual memory first evolved because sufficient regularities exist in the world for roughly similar situations to recur frequently. But since situations never repeat exactly, minds need to match similarities loosely. Through something like massively parallel distributed computer programming, advanced brains became able to pattern-match memories and present predicaments, to allow them to bring to bear on present choices even distantly remembered events and the emotional weightings attached to them."[78] In effect, we detect the disregarding of dissimilarities or the "differences" that Nietzsche identified, or the evidence that they "never repeat exactly."

This is one reason why it is easy to erase the differences between fictional and documentary (or nonfictional) stories. For example, it would be easy to do so when one considers Iser's note that "contingencies and complexities are reduced to a meaningful structure" when we write stories.[79] I would suggest that the "meaningful structure" is less true of a narra-descriptive journalism, or at least different, because such contingencies and complexities in the latter are only in temporary abeyance until a new unassimilated previously unrecognized from the phenomenal world emerges to challenge what was all along a temporary narrative structure. I do not suggest that the meaningful structure is entirely absent but rather that it contains loose ends—contingencies—as yet unexplained and perhaps never to be explained. For example, consider Joan Didion's "Some Dreamers of the Golden Dream," which has been described as iconic, and which I explore more thoroughly in the next chapter.[80] In Didion's tale of adultery and murder, Lucille Miller, who is charged with killing her husband, is convicted and goes to prison. She is also pregnant. While the legal defense in the court case suggested that the pregnancy was a result of Miller's wanting to mend her marriage with her husband, one cannot help have doubts, given the adultery and that Miller faked her husband's death as an accident.[81] Didion leaves this ambiguity from real life unanswered for the reader. It is one of those contingencies that remain unassimilated. As Jonathan Harr has noted, after completing his monumental *A Civil Action*, "the facts of a real event sometimes don't occur in a way that lends itself to narrative elegance."[82] In narrative elegance lies the desire for a perfect narrative symmetry balanced at the least with a beginning, a middle, and an end; part of fulfilling that structure is tying up the loose details. One detects this in Anton Chekhov's admonition: if you introduce a gun (or rifle) onstage, you should fire it.[83] In other words, foreshadowing should not be gratuitous. Instead, the expectations aroused in the audience should be fulfilled. The result is the conventional portrait of reality deriving from causal verisimilitude: we can believe it when the gun is fired because it was there all along. In "Some Dreamers of the Golden Dream," the consequences of life with the ghost of the contingent unassimilated clearly defy the literary axiom for a perfect (and elegant) narrative account.[84]

This also helps to explain why Capote invented material for *In Cold Blood*. The conclusion serves as one example. Detective Alvin Dewey, four years after the murder of the Clutter family, visits their gravesite, where he runs into Nancy Kidwell, who had been victim Nancy Clutter's best friend.[85] They talk about life moving on—Nancy Kidwell is now in college. That life can move on in a conclusion to a book about murder makes for a convenient narrative elegance. Except that the scene did not happen in the real-life world outside the covers of books. What one detects here is the human ambition— Capote's specifically—to force-fit the account into a narrative elegance it does not have.

Instead of viewing the ambiguity of such loose narrative ends outside the cover of books as shortcomings, I would suggest that there is instead a kind of cognitive integrity to such incompleteness because, in a sense, it more honestly reminds us of our existential condition: we will always have to confront the phenomenal unknown or contingent. This is, after all, why "reality" can appear stranger than the verisimilitude of assumption-constructed fictions. One could view the unassimilated as a vague form of foreshadowing, one that arouses a vestigial survival instinct. Experience alone will intimate such a circumstance. We know that there is much more out there than we can ever accommodate in our understanding. After all, how many times have we later discovered of experience what seemed all so obvious—after the "fact," or after our confrontation with a fact or facts with which we were not familiar earlier?

Of course, this challenges a common viewpoint on the relationship between fiction and documentary. It is that traditional fictions are somehow privileged and superior.[86] I suspect the claim is a hangover from the belletristic elitism of the past. Perhaps we see it most egregiously in Keith Oatley's "Why Fiction May Be Twice as True as Fact: Fiction as Cognitive and Emotional Simulation," in which, of course, he claims that fiction is twice as true as factual accounts.[87] Oatley is a noted cognitive psychologist who retired to write fictional novels. Elsewhere Brian Boyd claims, "Stories, whether true or false, appeal to our interest in others, but fiction can especially appeal by inventing events with an intensity and surprise that fact rarely permits."[88] Of factual or documentary accounts he says, "The 'appetite for the true' model 'spectacularly fails to predict large components of the human appetite for information.'"[89] Here he quotes John Tooby and Leda Cosmides, who elsewhere make the sweeping claim that "when given a choice, most individuals prefer to read novels over textbooks, and prefer films depicting fictional events over documentaries. That is, they remain intensely interested in communications that are explicitly marked as false."[90] What Oatley, Boyd, Cosmides, and Tooby seem to be unaware of is the existence of a journalism that is indeed narrative, and they appear to conflate narrative and fiction as one and the same. What is missing is the inability to distinguish between the conjecture of fiction as allegory, and the narrative accounts of consequences outside the cover of books. Undoubtedly, with regard to traditional fictional novels such as *Les Misérables*, there is greater room for unhindered imaginative "play," as Boyd (among others) characterizes it.[91] Again, as Iser notes of traditionally fictional efforts, "There is no empirical outside object with which to relate the image."[92] Hence the greater cognitive freedom of the purely fictional, because it is unconstrained and unhindered, and draws on our existing accumulated knowledge—cultural and personal—to "see" the wholly invented fiction. Undoubtedly a narra-descriptive journalism lacks this kind of freedom because to some extent it is constrained by the demands of maintaining some veracity to referentially based concrete metaphors.

But I would also suggest that an advantage (and superiority) of a narra-descriptive journalism is precisely its restricting referential claims to the phenomenal, given the findings, as noted in the previous chapter, that began emerging in the late 1980s "suggesting that higher degrees of [cognitive] incorporation are achieved when subjects believe they are learning real information."[93] Again, the more real the perception, the greater its cognitive acceptance. And still again, the result is what has been described in cognitive psychology as "psychological transport."[94] While psychological transport is experienced in both conventional narrative fiction and a narra-descriptive journalism, it is perceived as more "real" in the latter, given the more active response of the structure of the brain.[95]

Moreover, the creative freedom of fiction can, paradoxically, constitute not only a strength but also a weakness. Again, as Schank and Berman note, "when we hear stories we seek to confirm our existing beliefs by comparing the new input to familiar/similar indexes in our memories."[96] Thus a fictional story or narrative is double-edged. It can introduce new critical horizons and the implications they have for changing our beliefs, or it can confirm our existing beliefs. It is the latter that can reveal a weakness in conventional fictions.

While the absence of the outside referential object results in a greater cognitive freedom, one that more courageous readers will welcome in challenging their "habits of seeing," it is also one in which the more timorous of nature may find it more comfortable to retreat into the safety of their personal and cultural assumptions—otherwise described as the "indexes in our memories," or the "context of experience," or "existing world knowledge." It was also to such a habit of "narrative seeing" that Capote fell victim in his grasping for a narrative elegance, one in which he could erase the shadows of contingencies for which he could not account.[97] In a sense, he displayed aesthetic cowardice in avoiding the inconveniences of the aesthetics of experience. That is one of the dangers in the temptations of conventional fictions. The virtue of the evidence derived from phenomenal consequences—the referent outside of the mediated image—is that the differences in the concrete metaphors can pose a challenge to those assumptions or preconditions because it is more difficult to dismiss the phenomenal referent as not existing. If we do so, we are accused of being out of touch with "reality." At the least this is a social constraint. But it could also be a matter of existential survival.

It has been suggested that fiction is not subject to judgments of truth and falsity the way nonfiction is.[98] That position, moreover, has also been challenged, namely, that fiction can have its own kind of truth, although I do not mean here belletristic transcendentalism.[99] But both fiction and nonfiction have their merits, because I do not see them as necessarily in opposition. Rather, they speak to the differences inherent in the discourses and how the reader distinguishes between them. As Herman observes, "Readers orient differently to stories that make a claim to fact, or evoke what is taken to be a (falsifiable) version of our more or less shared, public world, than they do to fictional narratives."[100] He adds, "Strategies for interpreting situations and events will be affected, in part, by the referential status that accrues to storyworlds via assigned genre categories—such as fiction versus memoir."[101] Granted, each discourse or genre has the capacity for varying degrees of psychological transport. But a narra-descriptive journalism is more subject to judgments of truth or falsity in phenomenal reality where time and space uniquely intersect and what that implies about the heightened brain response to what is perceived as more "real." As Richard J. Gerrig rightly notes, this does not mean that psychological transport does not occur in fiction—a transport that has the potential to affect real-world judgments.[102] It can. But still the perception of what is believed to be more real is more cognitively stimulating.

Given the phenomenal unassimilated, there is a consequence that further reveals what about a narra-descriptive journalism is distinctive. Implicit is that, because of the unassimilable or excess or absence, a narra-descriptive journalism can continue to change and grow in the phenomenal world in a way that conventional fictions cannot. This is because conventional fiction exists in a "sovereign world," as it has been described, independent of phenomena.[103] In that sovereignty we detect a narrative closure. Similarly, Oatley notes in his own translation of Aristotle, "a poetic mimesis, then, ought to be . . . unified and complete."[104] We detect this sovereignty, too, in medieval allegory and the religious need at the time to provide a spiritual ideology; conventional fiction, to some extent, evolved out of that experience, resulting in literary transcendentalism.

Documentary or nonfiction can never be "sovereign" in the same way as a conventional fiction. Consider their conclusions. They are only temporary. For example, Hersey added a significant sequel to *Hiroshima* by picking up where he left off with the first version. In the first version, published in 1946, he ended with the immediate aftermath of how six individuals survived the bombing. But forty years later Hersey added a new chapter after returning to Japan to find out what happened to the survivors. The revised paperback edition with the additional chapter adds sixty-two pages to the original account of ninety, extending the book by more than two-thirds. Nor is *Hiroshima* the only work of narra-descriptive journalism that has prompted sequels, given that there can never be an ultimate conclusion. We see this in *Let Us Now Praise Famous Men*. In 1989 Dale Maharidge and Michael Williamson published a sequel, *And Their Children After Them*, an account of what happened to the tenant farmers' families in the forty years since.[105] It won the Pulitzer Prize for general nonfiction in 1990. While conventional fiction, too, can have sequels, as demonstrated by the *Harry Potter* series, they only require imagination and have no referential obligation to what may emerge from the previously unassimilated in the phenomenal world.

Of course, there is a corollary to this. If there is no final conclusion in a narra-descriptive journalism, or it is only a temporary conclusion, the same can be said of beginnings: that there is no true beginning, or at best just temporary beginnings. When Hersey begins his volume, he describes where his six protagonists were and what they were doing in the minutes before the atom bomb detonated. For example, Dr. Fujii was sitting on his back porch in his underwear reading a newspaper.[106] But of course there were beginnings well before this as part of the endlessness of time as it is accessible to us by means of the aesthetics of experience (or until the universe collapses on itself). It could have started twenty years earlier, when (hypothetically) Dr. Fujii made the mistake of opening his medical practice in Hiroshima instead of Osaka, as his wife (who was from Osaka) might have urged. "I don't have a good feeling about Hiroshima," she could have said (hypothetically). Fictional allegory, because it is sovereign and self-contained, lacks dictinctive referents to such unfolding locations in phenomenal time and space. Some may say that makes fiction superior. But consider: Is self-containment how life's stories really play out? Or is narrative unity itself a fiction with which we can deceive ourselves by believing we have, in our hubris, a global view? I emphasize again that the more courageous will embrace the inconclusive, while the more timorous will be inclined to turn to all-encompassing and predictable comforts as found in the allegories of fiction. When you finish reading a work of narra-descriptive journalism, you know at some level of consciousness or subconsciousness that of course the story does not end. People's lives go on, and that disrupts "the illusion of the complete process," as Jauss said of history.[107]

If Boyd is correct, that storytelling is part of an evolved strategy for the tribe on how to survive by means of stories about the dangers that lurk in dark shadows (what otherwise has been characterized as literary Darwinism), one question is: Which is more advanced along the evolutionary path, conventional narra-descriptive fiction or narra-descriptive journalism? Fiction would seem a logical choice, given the critical freedom it permits consciousness. But consider again: narra-descriptive journalism referential to phenomena in concrete metaphors establishes and imposes constraints that require closer collaboration with the phenomenal, and, most important, the demand for dealing with and accounting for unavoidable consequences, no matter how disagreeable. Is that further along on the evolutionary path? After all, in the solely fictional transport, without real-life constraints subject to judgments of truth and falsity, one can always conveniently fall back again on one's comforting assumptions, the schema, the *qualitas occulta*. In a sense, fiction offers the path of least resistance. Undoubtedly, that was very helpful as we evolved. But just as it can teach us to survive, it can also teach us to flee unnecessarily from what causes discomfort. After all, today we can watch the Cartoon Network twenty-four hours a day.

Perhaps at this point the best we can say is that both narrative fiction and a narra-descriptive journalism are different in terms of how they influence readers. If, indeed, storytelling or narrative is part of an evolutionary survival strategy, each has evolved for a reason. Fiction provides greater or wider cognitive negotiation in terms of speculative or conjectural outcomes. Documentary ties us to the evidence of outcomes or consequences, which we are disinclined to ignore for "real-life" existential reasons, complex and paradoxical.

In *A History of American Literary Journalism*, I posited that a narrative literary journalism was a form of the novel or narrative of the inconclusive present, as articulated by Mikhail Bakhtin.[108] What I have said in this chapter will,

I hope, provide additional evidence for that claim. Such a narrative of the inconclusive present results from the observation of the fluidity (often with an ironic humor at our expense) of the aesthetics of experience inherent in our discovery of what had hitherto been cognitively unassimilated, or what Bakhtin characterizes as the "carnivalesque."[109] As at a carnival, we are bombarded by the moving collage of sights, sounds, smells, and other sensations to which we cannot resist responding. (And then we tell stories to filter and make sense of the flood of experience.) Such reactions resist the straitjacket imposed by the deductive method of the Aristotelian commonplace seeking to establish "generalizable laws." In other words, it makes an irony of the vanity of human ambition ensconced among its paler, cooler ideas. Such a narrative is in opposition to what became the formulaic fictional novel, because the former "took shape precisely . . . when the object of artistic representation was being degraded to the level of a contemporary reality that was inconclusive and fluid. From the very beginning the novel was structured not in the distanced image of the absolute past but in the zone of direct contact with inconclusive present-day reality."[110] In effect, the evidence of the inconclusive present is observed and selected by the writer attuned to the aesthetics of phenomenal experience who emphasizes the differentiating qualities and resists "forgetting" those differences under pressure of the irrepressible cognitive inclination to volatilize or abstract. So new interpretations are prompted. The opposite is the "novel" or narrative of "the distanced image of the absolute past." These are today the predictable potboilers and bodice rippers, and there is no reason why there cannot be the equivalent in a narra-descriptive journalism. The inevitable happy ending for the superhero we find in Hollywood movies is still another example. And in their own hackneyed way they are a variation on paler, cooler ideas in the distanced image of an absolute past constructed to reinforce our assumptions, our habits of seeing, personal and cultural, especially when they seduce us with the promise of a happy ending.

The interpretive possibilities suggested by those differentiated qualities, as well as the potential for the unassimilated to emerge later, helps to provide a dynamic that accounts, at least in part, for the appeal of so much narrative literary journalism. Such a journalism resists the pull of the distanced image of the absolute past—the tendentious platitudes and bromides of the paler, cooler ideas—by attempting to keep the reader cognitively in imaginative participation with phenomena that exist or existed as evidence outside the covers of books located at the intersection of a distinctive time and place. It is the suggestive performance we re-create that helps us realize a new reality, as Iser put it.[111] Such suggestiveness reflects the power of the specific furnishings of space, the concrete metaphor reflecting evidence, in other words.

One must add a caveat, however, to such an interpretation of a narrative

literary journalism as a variation on the narrative of the "inconclusive present." It is that such a narrative aspires to such a state. Because it is not always
so easy to distinguish between a narrative of the inconclusive present and a
narrative located in the distanced image of an absolute critical past. It would
be too easy to view Bakhtin's position as one of either/or. From a more pragmatic perspective, there are undoubtedly those accounts that reflect both.
After all, recall that Agee described farmers' overalls as a "blueprint: and they
are a map of a working man."[112] In the metaphor of the "blueprint" lies the
allegory of the distanced image of the absolute past. It is perhaps more apt
to ask whether a narrative literary journalism tends more toward one or the
other even as it may often contain varying degrees of both. Much the same
could be said of Nietzsche, that the claim of differentiating qualities exists
alongside the flabby essentializations of paler, cooler ideas. What draws scrutiny is the relationship between the two, as well as which dominates.

I hope that what is clear in this discussion is the paradox in the relationship
between documentary accounts and the conventionally fictional novel. We
tend to think of the material or phenomenal as stable because it is demonstrable outside the covers of books. And we tend to think of the fictional or
allegorical as less stable precisely for not having such a referentiality. But consider: the material or phenomenal has its own inherent instability, given the
endless carnival perceived by means of the aesthetics of experience. And the
ether of the fictional or allegorical, existing in its abstract sovereignty, has in
a sense an abstract stability precisely because it is not demonstrable and thus
is not as subject to the challenges of truth and falsity regarding phenomenal
experiences—the "inconclusive present." Nor is this to dispute the virtue of
fiction, given its greater latitude for interpretation. Yet the strength of our
endless interpretation of the phenomenal lies in both its challenge to the fictions of assumptions and the courage required to engage in that challenge.

I hope, too, it is clear that the result of resisting volatilization into cooler,
paler ideas is an inherent opposition to critical closure because of the attempt
to embrace the differentiating qualities of materiality, known and unknown.[113]

This is what we detect in Hemingway's motoring tour of Italy, even in the
most prosaic of scenes, which is why I selected them. The emphasis is on differentiating qualities in the interest of a dialogic open to interpretation. We
see this in the conclusion to the sketch because it is indeed left open to interpretation. Thus it serves to mock a rhetorical ambition that seeks to provide a
global message. In the last line of "Italy 1927" Hemingway writes, "Naturally,
in such a short trip, we had no opportunity to see how things were with the
country or the people."[114] But his denial as to how things were in Fascist Italy
is ironic understatement, for he has provided a carnival of evidence in concrete metaphors reflecting the inconclusive present in scenes and conversa-

tions committed to differentiating qualities. Among others, he is solicited by prostitutes in a restaurant. Also, he is shaken down by a petty Fascist official for having a dirty license plate. And the passage I began this chapter with reflects a seeming randomness of the evidence of experience. To say that Hemingway could not see how things were is ironic because, of course, what he has committed himself to and provided his readers with is a carnivalesque tapestry of contemporary life in Fascist Italy. Nor can we conclude that the differentiating qualities—including the unassimilated—have been forever eliminated. In the end, it is all in the details and their infinite promise. Again, as Peter Dear has noted, "The singular experience could not be evident" or fully constituted in the mediation, "but it could provide *evidence*" of what contributed to constituting the mediation.[115]

3

The Death of the Dream
of Paradise

To WHAT END, then, a narrative literary journalism, narra-descriptive in its modalities? In the last chapter James Agee provided an intimation when he focused on what existed outside the boundaries of "myth." Similarly, consider the following: in the opening chapter of Tom Wolfe's *The Right Stuff*, an account of the origins of America's space program, there is a scene in which a pilot bails out of his malfunctioning jet and his parachute fails to open. As onlookers watch from the ground, the world rises up to "smash him."

"When they lifted his body up off the concrete, it was like a sack of fertilizer."[1]

So life is vulgarly reduced, as is in a sense the cultural mythology and history of the much-vaunted American space program. There would be little argument that the accomplishments of the space program taken cumulatively represented an important national achievement for the United States during the post–World War II era. And yet, as the Wolfe example demonstrates, that interpretation is problematic: the space program in this instance is metaphorically reduced to fertilizer. Nor, clearly, is this the kind of account that one would find in mainstream journalism, which might read something like this: "A Navy test pilot died yesterday when his parachute failed to open after he bailed out of his malfunctioning jet."

The example serves as an illustration of an ambition in narrative literary journalism that has as its goal an assault on false mythologies, much as Agee suggested. Moreover, it is an assault on our popular histories as a form of mythmaking. After all, reducing America's space program to metaphorical fertilizer is clearly iconoclastic, and narrative literary journalism, or a narra-descriptive journalism, particularly if it is from the era of the New Journalism, has often proved iconoclastic, as reflected in the critical rebuke and outrage it elicited during the 1960s and 1970s.[2] This is at the heart of the kind of personally inflected cultural revelation so much narra-descriptive journalism attempts, and is what I examine in this chapter. I focus on the New Journalists because cumulatively what we can see is that they so often challenged nothing less than the shibboleth of the "American Dream," that mythic ambition—and concoction—that promises a happy ending. But I do so also because they achieved a degree of ironic insight into our cultural mythologies that in my view has not often been equaled. They still have much to offer us a half century later. In order to better understand that anti-mythic—and subversive—nature, I examine texts of narrative literary journalism by Wolfe, Sara Davidson, Truman Capote, Joan Didion, Hunter Thompson, and Michael Herr.

I would emphasize that cultural mythology and essentialized or totalized history are inextricably associated. As Mircea Eliade, the distinguished scholar of mythology, has observed, "The novelty of the modern world consists in its revaluation, at the secular level, of the ancient sacred values."[3] The secular level can include totalized history; as Eliade also notes, "The myth is regarded as a 'true history.'" Perhaps among the most obvious that he cites are the myths dealing with the historic reality—hence history—of human mortality.[4] And as Michel de Certeau intimates, history is inevitably about the otherness of our mortality that we do not know and our attempts to make peace with its psychic specters.[5] The difference between myth on the one hand and cultural myth and totalized history on the other is, as Eliade suggests, that the first is sacralized and the second desacralized.[6] What they have in common is that both are venerated as providing a communal context against which human activity is enacted. Thus the ambition of some of our most compelling narrative literary journalism lies in the challenge to false gods.

I draw on the following in my discussion of cultural myth. First, by myth I clearly do not mean the ethereal lands of lurking pagan gods but rather the kinds of story tropes that, as Eliade notes, "suppl[y] models for human behavior and, by that very fact, gives meaning and value to life."[7] Or, I would add, we believe they give meaning and value to life, but, as I will demonstrate, it can be a meaning often to our detriment. Second, Roland Barthes defines myth as a semiological problem, or as a problem inherent in a system of signs. As a journalistic example, he cites a photograph of a black French African soldier on the cover of *Paris Match* from the 1950s. In an accumulation of signs derived from an associated series of signifiers, volatilized, in other words, from concrete metaphors, the myth emerges as one about a French empire inclusive of all races, and the realization of the French republican ideals of *liberté, égalité, fraternité*. "Myth wants to see in only a sum of signs, a global sign, the final term of a first semiological chain," to cite Barthes.[8] As he further notes, such myths (or the ideals of *liberté, égalité, fraternité*) are an all-encompassing or "global" mask for the ideology of French imperialism (republican imperialism, no less) and the moral imperative for France to maintain its colonies; Barthes was writing at the time of the Algerian insurrection against French rule. Moreover, France, after a bloody conflict, had only recently been forced to withdraw from Vietnam. The *Paris Match* photo, then, is an attempt to bolster a tattered imperialism with a mythic appeal.

Finally, A. Bartlett Giamatti, the late commissioner of baseball, provides a vernacular simile for myth that helps us to understand the mythic nature inherent in narrative. If, however, Giamatti is the late commissioner of baseball, he was also the former president of Yale University and a distinguished scholar of English and Italian Renaissance literature. Thus he was adept at negotiating between the abstract world of scholarship and the dust and sweat of the baseball diamond. Baseball is the acting out of a narrative myth, according to Giamatti. He characterizes the game as a "communal poem about separation, loss, and the hope for reunion . . . the Romance Epic of homecoming America sings to itself." It is how the game of baseball is played that provides the basic operation for myth as narrative: "In baseball, the journey begins at home, negotiates the twists and turns at first [base], and often founders far out at the edges of the ordered world at rocky second—the farthest point from home. . . . There are no dragons in baseball, only shortstops, but they can emerge from nowhere to cut one down." Third base is, of course, followed by the return journey home. The result, according to Giamatti, is that we watch baseball in order "to imitate the gods, to become godlike in our worship of each other and . . . to know for an instant what the gods know." This is because baseball "aspires to the condition of paradise," which he characterizes as a "dream of ourselves as better than we are, back to what we were."[9] Or, one might add, back to what we believe we were.

On the one hand, Giamatti's observation demonstrates a point made by Eliade that myth and basic narrative are "consubstantial with the human condition and hence irreducible" from each other. Eliade also notes: "What we consider important is the fact that in modern societies the prose narrative . . . has taken the place of the recitation of myths in traditional and popular societies. . . . [T]he modern passion for the [fictional] novel expresses the desire to hear the greatest possible number of 'mythological stories' desacralized or simply camouflaged under 'profane' forms. . . . [P]eople feel the need to read 'histories' and narratives that could be called paradigmatic, since they proceed in accordance with a traditional model." Moreover, myth for Eliade is about origins, or, in effect, the attempt to conjure up or reclaim an Edenic and paradisiacal past, the time of what he calls the "beginnings."[10] Baseball, then, provides a reenactment of narrative as myth. Clearly, journalism as narrative is implicated, too.

On the other hand, the narrative structure of baseball draws its support from the accumulation and orchestration of Barthesian signs. But in this semiological construction, the results are mythic illusion, a point echoed by Giamatti, who characterizes the mythic narrative of baseball as "a trick, an illusion . . . a pleasurable self-delusion."[11] It is, as Giamatti notes, a "dream." Like the front cover of *Paris Match*.

The observation that mainstream journalism is embedded with mythic elements is not new. Among notable examinations is *Media, Myths, and Narratives: Television and the Press*.[12] Still another is *Daily News, Eternal Stories: The Mythological Role of Journalism*.[13] It is not difficult to see how mythic elements inhere in mainstream journalism. One can readily detect this in *New York Times* coverage of the September 11, 2001, World Trade Center disaster in New York:

> The horror arrived in episodic bursts of chilling disbelief, signified first by trembling floors, sharp eruptions, cracked windows. There was the actual unfathomable realization of a gaping, flaming hole in the first of the tall towers, and then the same thing all over again in its twin. There was the merciless sight of bodies helplessly tumbling out, some of them in flames. Finally, the mighty towers themselves were reduced to nothing. Dense plumes of smoke raced through the downtown avenues, coursing between the buildings, shaped like tornadoes on their sides.[14]

In his account, the *New York Times* reporter has invoked by means of such generalities and clichés (Barthes's "global" signs) as "horror," "chilling disbelief," "unfathomable realization," "merciless sight," "mighty towers," and "reduced to nothing" no less than the eschaton, or the mega-myth of the destruction of the world and the primordial existential fear not just of individual annihilation but of mass human annihilation. It would be an understatement to note that vast, incomprehensible destruction is a staple of mythic lore. After all, besides Babel, there is the Apocalypse. In a more contemporary world longing after myth, there is the finale to *Götterdämmerung*, in which the gods self-immolate, performed by the Berlin Philharmonic as the city fell to the Red Army in 1945.[15] So we detect mythic longing.

Elsewhere in that issue of the *New York Times* the day after the attack, Serge Schmemann characterized the destruction as a "hellish storm," doing so without even the intervention of the structure of a simile.[16] Instead, in his eyes, hell on earth—the destruction of the world, the goal of all eschatologies—had metamorphosed into phenomenal reality. All that was required was for the righteous heroes to rise up against the mythic powers of darkness, and we have seen that in subsequent reportage on the "war on terrorism," battling that which terrifies as we seek to reclaim the Edenic or paradisiacal past.

Nor are mythic characterizations and archetypes reserved solely for events of such magnitude. One can detect them embedded in the structure of the simple—and ritualized—police beat story. I return to the following: "A county police officer shot and killed an armed holdup man during a convenience store robbery in Severna Park on Tuesday." What is enacted here is as old as myth, the forces of good—and authority—triumphing over those of evil. As part of a cultural and ritualized myth, one might ask, how often do we read news stories about convenience stores getting robbed? How often are they robbed by gunmen? How often are gunmen shot and killed by police officers? Unfortunately all too often in an incantation that becomes ritual. It is the "shoot and kill" ritual of journalism. In the treatment we detect a professional ritualization that draws unconsciously on mythic archetypes. As Stanley Cohen and Jock Young have observed of such news, it "is a main source of information about the normative contours of a society. It informs us about right and wrong, about the parameters beyond which one should not venture, and about the shapes that the devil can assume. A gallery of folk types—heroes and saints, as well as fools, villains and devils—is publicized not just in oral tradition and face-to-face contact, but to much larger audiences and with much greater dramatic resources,"[17] meaning, of course, it can be found in the news media. The police beat example is perpetuating, then, the mythic exemplars.

S. Elizabeth Bird and Robert W. Dardenne attribute the mythic nature of conventional news at least in part to the fact that "Journalists have to make . . . 'assignments' or 'news judgments' quickly, and inevitably resort to existing frameworks. 'Normality' is good, difference bad or deviant (or amusing)." The result is that the "assignments reflect the interests of the status quo . . . [and] the prevailing maps of meaning have come to be perceived as 'natural' and 'common sense,' blinding us to the fact that even 'common sense' is culturally derived."[18] Here they borrow from the anthropologist Clifford Geertz on the nature of what we take to be "common sense."[19] Or again, as Ernst Jünger put it, such reports derive from our "habits" of seeing.[20]

Bird and Dardenne add insightfully, "News stories, like myths, do not 'tell it like it is,' but rather, 'tell it like it means.' "[21] For that matter, the same could be said of totalized or essentialized histories against which human events must take place—the "march of time" with the "Grim Reaper" reminding us of our mortality, the ultimate existential dilemma.

But there is a consequence. As Barthes notes, cultural myths are fundamentally "parasitical" because they feed off an accumulation of signs, "impoverishing" them by directing the reader how to see the meaning.[22] The result is that such myths rob signs of the epistemological vitality of the original concrete metaphors derived from the testimony of the senses responding to the aesthetics of experience. This provides one reason for the seeming repetitiveness, or, in the end, ritualization, of mainstream journalism. In hard or spot news, such ritualization is reflected once again in the professional mantra of writing according to the structure of the "inverted pyramid." The emphasis reflects a deprioritization of *initial signs* in the descent through the story, what Barthes characterizes as "first-order signs," while the emphasis in the prioritizing *ascent* to the capsule lead of the story is clearly toward abstraction—and mythification in the form of an accumulation of multi-order systems, of "telling it like it means." (And while unusual aspects—meaning particulars—of the story may be included in the lead to help make it distinctive, the discursive gravitational pull in the lead is still toward abstraction, which is only a pale, anemic reflection of the original first-order signs, one that relies on cultural mythification and ritual for interpretation.) As James W. Carey observed in his 1975 call for an examination of communication as ritual, such an account "operates to provide not information but confirmation, not to alter attitudes or change minds but to represent the underlying order of things."[23] One might add that it is the *perceived* underlying order of things.

Nor, I must emphasize, is narrative literary journalism necessarily free of mythification. Rather, both myth and anti-myth can very much exist side by side and in an ongoing tension, and indeed struggle. Tom Wolfe, in *The New Journalism*, astutely observed this dimension of mythification in narrative literary journalism in what he called "status" or "symbolic details" as fundamental to the form.[24] Thus we see Pete Conrad, the aspiring future astronaut, and his wife, Jane, the protagonists in the first chapter of *The Right Stuff*, living in a white house with black shutters shining in the sunshine with green pines as a backdrop, which is idealized as a "dream" house.[25] The characterization fulfills one of the promises of the American Dream, that mythic ambition—and concoction—in which our suburbs attempt to reflect the desire to return to "primordial perfection," as Eliade says,[26] or the condition of paradise, as Giamatti terms it. So Wolfe detected a mythic nature in his variety of New Journalism.

Similarly, Norman Sims observed in 1984 that narrative literary journalism reflects "symbolic *realities*."[27] He coins the term in an interview with the literary journalist and Pulitzer Prize winner Richard Rhodes, who seeks in his writing to reflect the "transcendentalist business of the universe showing forth, the sense that there are deep structures behind information."[28] What "symbolic realities" encompass, however, poses a problem, not an answer. Are we discussing here myth as transcendental and metaphysical? Or in the "deep structures behind information" are we discussing the transparency—the lifting of veils or masks—provided by irony and paradox that reveals the ideologies which lie behind so many of our cultural myths, an unmasking that permits us to realize a personally inflected cultural revelation? There is, after all, something transcendental in revelation because one unveils what heretofore could not be seen.

Or, as I would suggest, do "symbolic realities" potentially reflect both, given that there can be an ongoing mythic and anti-mythic struggle in such work? So we detect mythic appeal, for example, in Tracy Kidder's 1985 *House*, an appeal that reflects the ambition to re-create primordial paradise when the Judith and Jonathan Souweine family hire contractors to build their custom-designed home in western Massachusetts. What follows is the mythic quest for the ideal home, a quest with trials and tribulations. Finally, it is built, the new owners are happy, and the American Dream has been realized. In the epilogue, the architect receives an award for the house's design, and for the owners "the house kept improving, as it became a lived-in thing."[29] But unlike the examples I will be examining for anti-myth, *House* in the end is a celebration not only of the completion of the home but also of the unambiguous and symbolic realization of mythic ambition, in this case of what Eliade calls "the obscurely felt need for an entirely new beginning, of an *incipit vita nova*—that is, of a complete regeneration."[30] So one symbolically reclaims paradise.

The unambiguous and symbolic realization of mythic ambition—the desire to return to paradise—is also clearly at work in John Hersey's *Hiroshima*. Here the mythic ambition is the Orphean return trip from hell—or, as noted earlier, surviving the atomic explosion in Hiroshima in 1945, and how six Japanese individuals did so and in the end achieved a degree of heroic triumph by recovering some sense of normality in their lives (but only some). They seek to return to the safety of home on the baseball diamond of life. Again, such symbolic realizations are unambiguous and in the end fundamentally lacking in the kind of irony and paradox embedded in the types of narrative literary journalism I explore next, those whose "symbolic realities" result in the unveiling of (or in the revelation of personally inflected cultural) anti-myth. (Though *Hiroshima* also contains an anti-mythic element, in that it shows the Japanese, who had been demonized in the United States during World War II just as Americans had been in Japan, as human beings, evidence again of the point that such works can contain both myth and anti-myth.)

Wolfe takes caustic aim at affirming mythological tropes when he notes the kind of extended symbolism long associated with the fictional novel by the belletrist, namely, that it attempts "to illumine a higher reality . . . the cosmic dimension . . . eternal values."[31] It is the mythic, in other words. Thus it is his purpose to subvert myth with anti-myth. When that unfortunate pilot in *The Right Stuff* falls back to earth, he is only one of several experimental test pilots and astronauts-in-waiting who come to similar ends in the first chapter of the book. In the rendering of their deaths can be detected a key to Wolfe's anti-mythic—and antihistorical—subversion. This is because Wolfe the journalist declines to idealize his characterizations of death. Here he embraces Barthes, who suggested, "Since myth robs language of something, why not rob myth?"[32] To do that he calls for the creation of a counter "artificial" myth, which Wolfe does. To put it more colloquially—and bluntly—America's space age heroes are being set up for a fall, literally and figuratively. We detect it in the mythic title of the chapter: "The Angels."[33] Indeed they will prove to be "fallen" angels.

To understand this, we must appreciate better the myth inherent in the story before we see what the anti-myth is challenging. I have noted already the symbolic realization by Pete and Jane Conrad of the myth of the American Dream as reflected in their home. In addition, Jane is described as looking "a little like the actress Jean Simmons." Thus she is associated with the Hollywood mythos. Pete is described as the "Hickory Kid sort," the primitive country boy, the all-American Huckleberry Finn prototype. Nonetheless he was "on the deb circuit," because that is where he met Jane.[34] In other words, they met at that institution where America's social royalty are anointed: the debutantes' ball. At such moments a country of rather lowbrow origins could live the mythic illusion that they were indeed royalty. Meanwhile, she attended Bryn Mawr and he Princeton, both of which have taken their own mythic places among American colleges and universities as finishing schools for America's future elite—and heroes. It is only the mythic quest that they must now embark on, with the promise of paradise at the end.

It is here, however, that the quest grimly turns into something other than heroic, because Wolfe takes the signification of "death" and disconcertingly reduces it to the banality of something edible. Indeed, throughout the opening chapter the motif of food is invoked as a simile and metaphor for death. For example, "burned beyond recognition" was an "artful euphemism to describe a human body that now looked like an enormous fowl that has burned up in a stove, burned a blackish brown all over, greasy and blistered, fried, in a word."[35] The passage is noteworthy for several reasons. First, Wolfe the literary journalist understands at some level the true nature of euphemism. It is in itself a kind of myth, with the ideological design of avoiding what his protagonists do not wish to confront: death. Or, as the Nobel Prize–winning poet Joseph Brodsky has observed in a similar context, "Euphemism, generally, is inertia of terror."[36] Second, Wolfe pointedly avoids inflating death into an abstract idealization. He could, for example, have characterized death in an idiom generally accessible within an ideological framework for a broad American reading public, in other words, "told it like it means," as Bird and Dardenne noted. Thus death could have been described as "heroic," "tragic," or "sacrificial," or in other words the sacred (and historical) ground against which it is determined that human activity is defined and enacted, and must be defined and enacted.

Third, by utilizing simile (and elsewhere metaphor), Wolfe is further fulfilling Barthes's prescription for demythifying myth by developing an anti-myth. Even as simile suggests a resemblance by means of likeness, an ineluctable part of its tropological nature derives by virtue of difference. The description "like an enormous fowl that has burned up in a stove, burned a blackish brown all over, greasy and blistered, fried" acknowledges only a passing similarity at best. The result is an unappetizing incongruity of associating death with what we eat.

Wolfe continues to draw on the food motif for his act of demythification, describing, for example, the wives of aviators "sizzling" as they await the news of their husbands' deaths, and of receiving the news "like a fish" "on ice" from a clergyman or officer. Elsewhere, a dead pilot's brains are likened to "yellowish curds," and the pilot's head is described as having been "knocked" "to pieces like a melon."[37] Thus the abstractions of life and death are vulgarly reduced, in these instances to what we find in our neighborhood supermarkets. The banal motif of the edible acting as simile and metaphor may be in "bad taste," but it is nonetheless effective because it makes a visceral appeal to what readers can perceive in a phenomenal or de-sacralized world, not a mythic one. The familiar has been made unfamiliar. So the narrative engages in a kind of insurgency because a country's heroes are reduced to metaphors of food. The result is a dark parody of how our contemporary heroes are conventionally represented, and in a material sense this is the only true kind of reverse volatilization that can occur, as the abstract, "life," is converted into the material. As if to reinforce by way of irony that his is anti-myth, Wolfe's narrative in the last death in the chapter, of the pilot whose parachute fails to open as the earth rises up to "smash" him, results in the evolution of the motif of death as edible into what food inevitably must be reduced to: fertilizer.

Wolfe has the literary good taste to leave out the evolutionary stage between food and fertilizer.

Of course, the obvious mythic parallel to Wolfe's account is the Greek myth of Daedalus and his son Icarus. They escape from imprisonment by King Minos, using wings Daedalus constructs of feathers and wax. Icarus, however, not heeding his father's warnings, flies too close to the sun. The heat melts the wax, his wings disintegrate, and Icarus falls into the sea and drowns.[38] But the difference between the original myth and Wolfe's version is that there is still something heroically tragic about the Daedalus version, the dramatic crash into the realm of King Neptune because of a young man's hubris and ambition for flying high. In contrast, it is difficult to see death reduced to the edible, which is ultimately reduced to fertilizer, as tragically heroic.

We can detect similar characteristics in further examinations of work by Wolfe, and as I indicated in the work of others. And what we find is nothing less than an assault on the myth of the American Dream that evolved into a kind of cultural triumphalism in which the United States basked following the end of the Second World War. By the beginning of the 1960s, when the New Journalism emerged, no other country was as materially powerful and rich. Astronauts landed on the moon in 1969, which was a triumph for American ingenuity, know-how, and a can-do philosophy. Yet few would dispute that the sixties were an era of social and political crisis in the United States: witness the civil rights movement, assassinations, and the drug culture. Vietnam proved not only a quagmire but also a challenge to the idea that American ingenuity, know-how, and a can-do philosophy, all idealized constructs, could overcome all obstacles. The period challenged what many Americans believed about their time, that it was the "American Century," another idealized construct. What was happening, then, in the 1960s is that Americans were discovering the limits of an empire of ideas, including that overarching palliative the American Dream, with its promise, its entitlement, that all would have a happy ending. The New Journalism would uncover a growing psychic dread underlying the triumphalism. Its rise can be traced in the following examples.

Wolfe's "Kandy-Kolored Tangerine-Flake Streamline Baby" provides a revealing cultural foreshadowing of the social distress and transformation to come. In some ways, it might be more appropriate to explore Wolfe's *Electric Kool-Aid Acid Test* as representative of the iconoclasm of the New Journalism. Indeed, it shocked the establishment when it appeared in 1968, because Wolfe described Ken Kesey, author of the critically acclaimed 1962 fictional novel *One Flew Over the Cuckoo's Nest*, and his companions known as the "Merry Pranksters," traveling across the United States in an antiquated school bus painted in psychedelic colors. During the journey they ingested copious amounts of illicit drugs, such as LSD, the "acid" in the title, which was added to, among other beverages, Kool-Aid, the sugary American drink with little nutritional value for children, which took on its own status as a pop cultural icon in the 1950s and 1960s.[39] Wolfe's account revealed how far the country had come by 1968 in challenging the sober righteousness of the postwar triumphalism, and in doing so was not very subtle, and indeed unambiguously iconoclastic.

But "The Kandy-Kolored Tangerine-Flake Streamline Baby" is culturally revealing because it is an earlier work in which the vulnerabilities of the American Dream are intuited. It is probably more widely known as the work that made Wolfe's initial reputation. The account of the custom car subculture, which appeared in *Esquire* magazine in the fall of 1963, proved difficult to write. Wolfe says he turned his notes over to his editor, incapable of finishing the project, and the editor published the notes much as Wolfe had written them.[40] The article is divided into two parts. The first is about affluent American teenagers "consumed" by a consumer culture, and thus is representative of the kind of cultural probing the New Journalism engaged in during the early 1960s. The second discusses the builders of custom cars. I will focus on the first, because it reveals young people immersed in the hubris of the cultural innocence of the American Dream.

The account examines a custom car show in Burbank, California, a suburb in the greater Los Angeles area, which was sponsored by the Ford Motor Company to try to attract youthful drivers to the Ford brand at a time when Chevy was the dominant automobile marque for America's hot rod set. What emerges is a social portrait of callow young people seduced by the success of an American consumerism that hijacks the original intent of the American Dream, articulated at the beginning of the Great Depression as a more altruistic ambition.[41] Instead, the ambition gets commodified by consumerism. In a swimming pool a Chris-Craft cabin cruiser filled with teenagers goes around in circles. Chris-Craft has a long history in the United States as a manufacturer of power pleasure boats appealing to the middle and upper classes for recreational purposes. Clearly, too, a swimming pool is a symbol of middle- and upper-class success. Elsewhere, two hundred teenagers dance to a rock band on a raised platform, doing the "hully-gully, the bird and the shampoo." Wolfe observes that the young people dress alike. The teenage women-girls who are barely adults (Wolfe calls them "nymphets") have bouffant hairdos. The teenage men-boys have their hair combed back, and "none of them had a part," meaning that the hairstyles were likely greased back *à la* the early style of Elvis Presley. (The mop-topped Beatles, and their hairstyle, would not begin to become popular in the United States until their music was introduced nationwide in December 1963.) Wolfe characterizes the event as "Plato's Republic for teen-agers. Because if you watched anything at this fair very long, you kept noticing the same thing. These kids are absolutely maniacal about form. They are practically religious about it. For example, the dancers: None of them ever smiled. They stared at each other's legs and feet, concentrating. . . . They were all wonderful slaves to form."[42] They were, in effect, finding comfort in conformance to an idea as they innocently danced out their youthful American Dream.

Initially, it is not immediately clear how there is an exchange of subjectivities, or at least a narrowing of the distance between subjectivities, which is one ambition of a narrative literary journalism, as opposed to an objectifying journalism that makes experience emotionally remote and inaccessible.[43] Instead, Wolfe's account appears as more of a sensational treatment, seeking to emphasize the differences between the innocent, fatuous teenagers and, presumably, the mature, sophisticated readers of *Esquire*. But one must examine closely the nature of postmodern parody to understand what Wolfe is doing. While the account does not result in the kind of sympathy suggested by an "exchange of subjectivities," a term coined by Alan Trachtenberg that has been applied to a narra-descriptive journalism,[44] there is nonetheless a narrowing of the distance between subjectivities, resulting in a kind of empathy, but one not necessarily sympathetic. As I noted in the first chapter, an empathic response is to see oneself as possibly in the other person's shoes. But that does not mean you share the person's values, emotional or otherwise, as we find in sympathy. At the heart of the matter is the way in which the chronotopes (the phenomenon as representation) are arranged that defy the secular myths. A result of parody (as a form of satire) is self-realization in the form of "There but for the grace of God go I." Therein lies parody's peculiar if rather cold-hearted empathy, in seeing what the subjects of the representation do not see about themselves. In parody the reader discovers how she or he is implicated. While not as empathic as non-parody—say, Hersey's *Hiroshima*—parody nonetheless serves as self-instruction for the reader, and therein lies its appeal, which of course is small comfort for those parodied. To cite Linda Hutcheon's articulation of postmodern parody, we thus detect how parody provides insight: it targets the representations of our assumptions and conventions, and then challenges and calls them into question: "It is the complicity of postmodern parody—its inscribing as well as undermining what it parodies—that is central to its ability to be understood," Hutcheon notes.[45] This is detected in the representation of fatuous teenagers described as "slaves to form" while dancing the "hully-gully, the bird and the shampoo"

in their innocent celebration of Ford hot rods and Chris-Craft cabin cruis-
ers. Madison Avenue could only respond with glee. Such is the real nature of
the American Dream. The initial innocence of the teenagers and the dream
is replaced by conformity to consumer convention. The result is, Hutcheon
adds, "the intrinsically political character of parody and its challenges to the
conventional and the authoritative."[46]

Perhaps it goes without saying that we can also detect a more subjective
examination on the part of the shaping consciousness of the author, one
that engages, through description, in more of an exchange of subjectivities
than one would find in the traditional abstracting hard news story. Such an
objectifying story might read something like this: "Some 500 Los Angeles–
area teenagers turned out at the Ford Custom Car Caravan in Burbank on
Saturday to admire the art of the custom hot rod." The issue is one of degree
between the two kinds of voice, Wolfe's being more subjective in the selection
of descriptive detail, while the objectified version would be neutered of such
revealing details as the way the teenagers danced in the same manner, as if
orchestrated by some Platonic puppeteer. Wolfe's representation of the details
prompts again the very strange empathy of postmodern parody as a survival
strategy, and we detect one discursive representation subject to that parody:
the conventional news report.

Wolfe's account serves, then, as an important cultural statement looking
back toward social innocence but also forward in anticipating a cultural crisis
of confidence that was slowly overwhelming the 1960s. In effect, innocence
was on trial, and Wolfe was probing the fragility of the American Dream. We
know the result: the innocence of youth would soon find itself drafted for
service in war, as has so often been the case.

Perhaps more than any other work from this period, *In Cold Blood* is
about the symbolic death of the mythic American Dream. Like a *diabolus
ex machina*, two murderers appear out of nowhere and kill the exemplary
American family, the Clutters. Regarding the exemplariness, on the day
before the night of the murders, exemplary sixteen-year-old Nancy Clutter
bakes a cherry pie, the wholesomeness of which is another American mythic
trope, and volunteers to tutor a younger student, this on the family farm in
Kansas.[47] She is the ideal teenager, and like that staple persona of American myth, Dorothy from *The Wizard of Oz*, Nancy Clutter could almost be
expected to launch into "Somewhere Over the Rainbow"—coincidentally
also in Dorothy's Kansas. We have, in effect, the innocence of paradise, the
realized American Dream.

But in the aftermath of the murders there can be no return to paradise.
This is because the effort to know who the Clutters are recedes as Capote's

intention becomes clear: to explore the psychologies of the murderers, their lives, how the murders came about, and how the murderers were caught, tried, and executed. The Clutters—the good guys—are consigned to being dramatic foils to the murderers: the heroes of the American Dream are merely supporting characters. Thus Capote takes his place alongside Dostoevsky, who focused on the murderer in *Crime and Punishment,* except as a fiction. And the result is like Dostoevsky's. What we find are antiheroes (and anti-myth). They fail to fit into the exemplary—and mythic—norms of society. Instead, the murderers' aspirations for paradise in Capote's volume end on the gallows. But unlike in the Russian *Crime and Punishment,* where there is redemption in the end, there is none in the American version. That is Capote's terrible indictment of the American Dream, achieving his literary—and philosophical—depth precisely because he challenges a culturally derived mythic archetype. His is the story of the dread lurking beneath the American mythic—and psychic—landscape, that all may not turn out well in the end. So Capote reveals cultural mythmaking for what it is: the consequence, to borrow from Paul de Man, of "an idolatry, a fascination with a false image that mimics the presumed attributes of authenticity when it is in fact just the hollow mask with which a frustrated, defeated consciousness tries to cover up its own negativity."[48] There is a reason, then, why Capote calls his a "true account" in the book's subtitle: he is engaging in anti-myth to unmask the fiction of the myth, and for our purposes that may be the book's most important contribution.

But as we know, *In Cold Blood* was not without its flaws in the claim to being a "true account," flaws that traditional mainstream journalists often pointed to in dismissing the New Journalism.[49] As I discussed in the previous chapter, Capote was accused of inventing scenes since shortly after *In Cold Blood* appeared. The charges remain troubling, given that he insisted in his acknowledgments that the book was true to life.[50] In the fictional invention, we detect Capote's inability to resist his own mythmaking (or allegory), and here, in the effort to destroy a secular myth, it is done at the cost of building another false myth to create a narrative unity.

In considering *In Cold Blood* as emblematic of the death of the American Dream, we find that there is also a larger cultural dimension for understanding it. The murders of what appear to be the near-ideal American family, a progressive farm family in Kansas—the American "Heartland," which is the breadbasket from which a country feeds itself, and which is still another mythic trope if not a cultural cliché—take place in November 1959, or at the end of the relatively culturally stable 1950s. By the time the book is published in 1965, communism is well established in Cuba, the Bay of Pigs fiasco has occurred, as has the Cuban Missile Crisis, which brings the world closer to the edge of nuclear war than at any other time during the Cold War. Civil rights protests and related race murders have taken place across the South and then some. A president who seemed to represent the ideals of what American democracy could offer has been assassinated. There are increasing doubts, and eventually antiwar demonstrations, as the United States slips deeper into the Vietnam War, propelled by the fear of a communist victory.

Lost, clearly, was the innocence of the dream—and myth. The murder of the Clutters provided a kind of prologue.

In an article originally published in the old *Saturday Evening Post*, "Some Dreamers of the Golden Dream," Joan Didion similarly challenges the myth of the "California Dream," that alter ego to the American Dream. In epic fashion Didion begins, "This is a story about love and death in the golden land."[51] It could be the beginning of a story recited by an ancient bard, appealing to those mythological tropes: love, death, the desperate quest to return to the golden land. But not only will Didion assault the myth, she will also assault what she perceives as its maker: modern media. We detect, then, an example of the challenge a narrative literary journalism can pose to the mythmaking mainstream media. After a review of what attracts immigrants to Southern California, Didion observes of their desacralized mythic quest, "Here is where they are trying to find a new life style, trying to find it in the only places they know to look: the movies and the newspapers."[52] Again, as Giamatti said, they are aspiring to "the condition of paradise."

Didion proceeds: "The case of Lucille Maxwell Miller is a tabloid monument to that new life style." Thus, what Didion suggests is that tabloid media have erected a monument—a celebratory myth—to husband-murderer Miller. Lucille Maxwell Miller killed her husband by burning him alive in his Volkswagen. She did so because she was engaged in her own mythic quest, her own attempt to realize California's Golden Dream. This meant killing a husband she has tired of in order to find happiness with her lover, "a man who might have seemed to have the gift for people and money and the good life that Cork Miller [Lucille's husband] so noticeably lacked."[53] Her lover, attorney Arthwell Hayton, has a real-life name reflecting a kind of genteel British refinement that might just pass for that of a grade-B Hollywood actor like Stewart Granger or Errol Flynn in a way that "Cork Miller" never could. But Arthwell abandons Lucille. She is charged with her husband's murder and is convicted. Such is the nature and result of her quest, and it would be easy to conclude that she has simply struck out on the baseball diamond of a myth in search of paradise.

But as Didion discovers, "what was most startling about the case that the State of California was preparing against Lucille Miller was something that had nothing to do with law at all, something that never appeared in the eight-column afternoon headlines but was always there between them: the revelation that the dream was teaching the dreamers how to live."[54] Didion is echoing Barthes, seeing the source of the problem as mythification embedded in media. The result is a siren song as we watch movies and read the newspapers in order, as Giamatti noted, "to imitate the gods, to become godlike in our worship of each other and . . . to know for an instant what the gods know."[55] Thus, those in search of the Dream—including Lucile—long for a "dream of ourselves as better than we are, back to what we were,"[56] or what we believe we are entitled to.

Moreover, during the course of the trial Lucille continues to dream her dream of paradise. This can be detected in the status detail of her hairdo as something more than just a hairdo. At the opening of her trial she is described as "a meticulous woman who insisted, against her lawyer's advice, on coming to court with her hair piled high and lacquered."[57] Her vanity, then, her belief that she is better than she is (or at least than her lawyer believes she is), gets the better of her in her mythic conceit.

The trial also takes on mythic proportions. As Didion observes: "Two months dragged by, and the headlines never stopped. . . . Two months in which the Miller trial was pushed off the [Los Angeles] *Herald-Examiner*'s front page only by the Academy Award nominations and Stan Laurel's death."[58] In other words, the only events that could displace Lucille from the front page were the elevation of secular heroes by the Academy Awards to movieland Valhalla, and the death of one of movieland's long-standing (anti-)heroes, comedian Stan Laurel, a jester at the court. As Barthes recommended, Didion is challenging myth with anti-myth. In the end, what we detect in Didion's eye for irony and paradox is again a postmodern parody, in this case of media engaged in aggressive news coverage. Didion cites conventional social representations and then undermines them. From that the reader can take instruction: Approach with caution what you read or see in the media.

With her characteristic understatement, Didion concludes the article with one last salvo aimed at cultural myth. Lucille's lover, Hayton, spurned her in order to marry his children's young Norwegian governess. In a seeming narrative misdirection, Didion concludes the article with word of the new Mrs. Hayton's wedding: "The bride wore a long white *peau de soie* dress and carried a shower bouquet of sweetheart roses with stephanotis streamers. A coronet of seed pearls held her illusion veil."[59] In Didion's hands, the passage becomes a parody of wedding announcements that often appeared in the society sections of newspapers in the United States at the time (and still do to some extent, as can be routinely detected in the Sunday *New York Times*).

But that this young bride is wearing an "illusion veil" speaks to the cultural and linguistic resonance Didion marshals that reflects a use of myth against myth. While the illusion veil is a staple of weddings, one must also ask what illusions has the new Mrs. Arthwell Hayton, she twenty-seven, her groom forty-four, when they marry in 1965? Meanwhile, Lucille has gone to prison, pregnant, amid the debris of her own illusions—and myths.[60]

Sara Davidson's "Real Property," her highly subjective account—it began as a personal journal—of living in Venice, California, in the 1970s—similarly reflects a resistance to cultural myth. Hers is a secular quest, its mythic stature reflected in where the account takes place (one reflective of its own kind of mythic ambition in a secular world): "Venice." As Davidson notes, Venice, California, was built as an imitation of the original by cigarette maker Abbot Kinney in the first decade of the twentieth century. "Kinney raised the money to build canals, lagoons, bathhouses, and bridges with fake Italian design, roller coasters and cottages with docks so people could visit each other by gondola." Kinney aspired, then, to his Venetian version of paradise, a land of play and salubriousness. But by the time Davidson arrives, Venice has, with ominous foreshadowing for the collective American and California dreams, declined: "In time, the novelty wore off and the resort fell to seed. The canals turned stagnant and the unheated cottages became substandard housing for the poor."[61]

With such a backdrop of paradise-in-decay, Davidson embarks on what becomes a traditional progression from one quest trial to another, recalling the quest trials implicit in Giamatti's interpretation of baseball—and the desire to reclaim, in this case, paradise from paradise-in-decay. What emerges, however, is the rupture of the mythic quest by anti-myth.

The first trial the narrator undergoes is a search for "an unscarred man" following a failed marriage. The narrator dates Bruce until one day he tells her there is "no more cheese in the relationship." Davidson concludes, "So much for that dream," intimating the fraudulence of the myth of the unscarred man, the exemplary hero. It was, after all, just a dream. The next trial in the quest is to buy a house one could call home because of its promise of a sense of permanency and rootedness. But that too leaves her unfulfilled so that she is left to observe that the mania for buying real estate in California in the 1970s was part of a "feeding frenzy": "The only problem . . . is that you can never have enough."[62] The result is that "real estate" becomes an ironic metaphor for what is no more real—such as possessing substance, permanence, and rootedness—than any other cultural myth that claims to constitute reality. We begin, then, to detect here another literary journalist's commitment to resisting the elevation of the aesthetics of experience into myth. Davidson is seeing through the mythic illusions about being fulfilled by love, and about the rootedness of owning a home. She is removing the masks of self-deception, as the familiar becomes the unfamiliar.

Increasingly desperate in her quest, the narrator proceeds to take up listening to reggae and making trips to Israel. Reggae is infused with Rastafarian mystic and mythic belief, particularly belief in the Ethiopian emperor Haile Selassie as the "Lion of Judah," the descendant of King David's union with the Queen of Sheba, according to tradition. Similarly, when the author-protagonist travels to Jerusalem in her quest, she is enacting a mythic pilgrimage repeated by countless pilgrims of all faiths to the City of God. Yet in the end, reggae is only a kind of metaphoric shortstop, and Jerusalem a kind of third base. More ominously, they are failures because she finds that she is no happier.

Finally, still unfulfilled in her mythic quest, she takes up roller skating on the Venice boardwalk in what becomes an (existential) act of desperation. Because this appears as the final goal of the narrative in what becomes a false climax, it should represent the metaphoric home plate. And it should illuminate the accomplishment of the mythic homecoming. Clearly, however, it is hardly existentially satisfying and hardly the return to paradise. In taking up roller skating, Davidson notes, she is following the example of one of her friends, who says to her, "Now I can float along with the rest of the flakes." Characterizing the narrative's roller skaters as "flakes" belies the metaphor's use as a much more profound trope for what drifts, albeit whimsically, with indirection. Here we have an ironic form of symbolic realities with "flakes" as a metaphor for a lack of existential substance. We have realized parody or satire again among the beautiful people seeking California's golden dream on the beach. Moreover, when the narrator is incapacitated because of a bad fall, she notices others who have had similar experiences, including a surfer with a dislocated shoulder. When she asks him why he continues to skate, he responds, "What else is there to do?"[63] Thus we see the uncertainty and indirection that accompany metaphorical "flakes" drifting down the boardwalk on roller skates. The American and California dreams are transient and adrift. The result is not myth but anti-myth as the reality emerges that there is no paradise.

But roller skating turns out to be a false climax. At the end of the narrative, as a result of the discouragements that derive from Barthes's concept of resisting myths with anti-myths—demythification—the narrator intuits (by means of those pesky differentiating qualities of the inconclusive present resisting incorporation into a *qualitas occulta*) even more existential inconclusiveness in what becomes the true climax. One could say she is returning to the dugout after striking out in the baseball game of life. Returning home, the

narrator accidentally runs over a homeless drunk lying in her driveway. Inex-
plicably—Davidson is at a loss to account for this—the drunk is unhurt.
(Once again we have one of the loose ends of narra-descriptive journalism
that conventional fiction would avoid in its effort to achieve a perfect narrative unity.) The drunk in his intoxication takes on the qualities of an oracle,
except in this case he becomes a kind of anti-oracle. When Davidson-the-
narrator questions the drunk about why he was lying in her driveway, he
says, "I wanted to sit down here . . . think about shit." He adds a moment
later, in what in its ritual repetition becomes a scatological incantation, "I got
shit on my mind." The narrator takes up the incantatory refrain obliquely
with an unspoken but nonetheless telling ellipsis that also serves as a pause to
be filled in by the reader: "I'm just glad you weren't hurt. It scared the . . . life
out of me." So she pauses to avoid the scatological expletive of the cliché. Now
the drunk limps away, and the incantation fades to a faint echo resonating at
the end of her thought: "As I stood there, I realized that I was thirty-five and I
was still waiting, expecting to wake up from all of this."[64] Ultimately, what is
"all of this"? Davidson does not explain. But the drunk's incantation can only
echo suggestively in our minds.

And so "Real Property" reflects a resistance against secular myth. There is
a myth of sorts in "Real Property," one that evolves and whose chronology is
detectable in the quest theme. But instead an anti-myth is constructed that
leads to roller skates on which people "will fly out of control and there is
nothing to hold onto,"[65] literally and, perhaps more important, figuratively
in the different and indeterminate meanings that the figurative can reflect,
including existential. The result is implied in the irony of the title to the piece:
there can be no secure "Real Property."

Hunter Thompson's "gonzo" journalism occupies an anomalous position in
relation to the kind of narrative literary journalism discussed here. Yet his
work is often discussed as literary journalism, albeit described as "gonzo," or
outrageously challenging conventional social values.[66] Part of the difficulty is
that while often narrative, his works such as *Fear and Loathing in Las Vegas*
engage in satire so outrageous that they raise the question of just how true
they are. Thus we detect one reason why his work can be anomalous.

In the case of *Fear and Loathing in Las Vegas*, Thompson ostensibly goes
in search of the American Dream in the heart of America's gambling mecca.
But again, Thompson engages in satire or parody that invokes its own kind
of empathy, one that need not be sympathetic. In doing so, he holds up a cultural mirror to largely white, well-to-do Americans (not that those parodied
will see what he and we see). In the representation lies cultural revelation,

personally inflected. And such parody may well be part of the answer regarding the relationship of "gonzo" journalism to a narrative literary journalism. Thompson's gonzo journalism represents, to borrow from postcolonial criticism, the colonial "Other" writing back to the empire. In the satire, the "empire" (or the American Dream as the case may be) is forced to see a side to itself that only the "Other" can provide, in this case that of a psychedelic drug user. But if Thompson's outrageousness casts doubt on what constitutes the truth of the truth claims, what is "true" becomes part of his cultural critique. The satire not only spurns traditional American values but also challenges the very notion of what constitutes the correct state of consciousness (sobriety?) for reporting on the world. After all, another cultural myth is that of the hard-drinking American newspaper reporter.

This brings us, finally, to Michael Herr's *Dispatches*. Again, as Mircea Eliade has observed, the purpose of myth is that it "supplies models for human behavior and, by that very fact gives meaning and value to life."[67] But the models can all too easily lose that value in the face of trauma, since the rhetoric of the inherently fictive myth is not necessarily the same as the consequences that exist in the material world. This is reflected in Herr's Vietnam War account.

What repeatedly surfaces in *Dispatches* is the incongruity between the material reality and American cultural triumphalism. It is rarely noted that many of the young American soldiers in Vietnam were the children of the generation that fought in World War II, which was the generation that had earned the cultural triumphalism. But the fathers and the sons were involved in very different wars. World War II may well have been the last righteous war, assuming one is not a pacifist (for whom there is no righteous war). What we detect in *Dispatches* is a disconnect from the triumphalism. For example, there is the surgeon in a tent hospital in the jungle who drinks a can of beer while doing surgery. Or four dead marines are brought into camp from a firefight and another soldier walks by singing quietly, "When you get to San Francisco be sure and wear some flowers in your hair," a reference to one of the pop music anthems of the counterculture in the United States at the time.[68] A captured Viet Cong is brought in for interrogation, his arms tied behind his back, and it is clear that the interrogation will not be in accordance with the "civilized" rules of war.[69]

Then there is that phenomenon that became popular in the United States in the 1950s and 1960s, the Top 40 rock-and-roll radio station. Its mirror image in Vietnam is an American military radio station that also plays Top 40 rock songs, and listening, a soldier could think he was back home. But after an Otis Redding song, an announcer begins to discuss the importance of thoroughly cleaning a machine gun after using tracer bullets because the ammunition leaves deposits that can jam the barrel in later use. Thus the commercial break during the Top 40, in an instance of the familiar made unfamiliar, turns into an advertisement for how to conduct war—and kill— and not one selling automobiles or suntan lotion as commercials would do back in the United States. One soldier wants to turn the radio off, but another says to leave it on because he wants to hear the sports news from the States.[70] In that we see the desire to return to the primordial paradise, the American Dream, and the realization of mythic desire inherent in sports..

Then there is the drug abuse, and not all of it illicit. Medics dispense Dexedrine—speed—to night patrols. One American soldier takes them "by the fistful." Or, after an assault by the Viet Cong, wounded enemy are not treated but instead executed as Americans walk around shooting them. Meanwhile, soldiers smoke marijuana out in the jungle and continue to listen to the Top 40: "Have You Seen Your Mother Baby Standing in the Shadows, Best of the Animals, Strange Days, Purple Haze, Archie Bell and the Drells, 'C'mon now everybody, do the Tighten Up.'"[71] In our cultural memory rock and roll becomes a kind of postmodern parody of a Greek chorus amid the firefights.

What emerges from a flood of Herr's subjective impressions is not the triumphant values of American democracy, nor defeat, but rather a psychic disengagement from the trauma taking place around the soldiers—the kind of psychic disengagement Ernst Jünger identified in the trenches of the Western Front nearly a half century earlier: "But finally we were so accustomed to the horrible that if we came on a dead body anywhere on a fire-step or in a ditch we gave it no more than a passing thought and recognized it as we would a stone or a tree."[72]

Because it is disengagement, it resists incorporation into the euphoria of cultural—and mythic—triumphalism. These are the children of the triumphant GIs from World War II who came back from Europe and the Pacific to try to build the American Dream. The young Americans in Vietnam are the baby boomers trying to drown out a triumph that has now become empty history. Psychic disengagement becomes a survival skill.

Such evidence, then, is suggestive of how anti-mythic subversion runs throughout notable examples of narrative literary journalism from the New Journalism. To be sure, mythic archetypes can never be entirely escaped— these iterations of a *qualitas occulta*. But the subversion is no small matter when we consider the ultimate effect: the disruption of taken-for-granted ideological assumptions of how life should be prescribed—myth, in other words. It is a disruption that can only make such works all the more compelling as postmodern parody that reflects an "intrinsically political character" by challenging the conventional and the authoritative. This helps to account for why New Journalists such as Wolfe were accused of deflating cultural icons. It is in a resonance of irony and paradox, the transcending of being told what something should mean, that we achieve at least one understanding of "symbolic realities," and the "transcendentalist business of the universe showing forth, the sense that there are deep structures behind information."[73] So we aspire in a compelling narrative literary journalism to remove the veils from our myths, for better or worse.

4

The "Elasticity" of
Literary Reportage

As journalists, Svetlana Alexievich and Anna Politkovskaya have long puzzled me. Both have been described as writers of "literary reportage" and its variant "reportage literature." Yet they pose a riddle in genre studies because their journalistic work is strikingly different. Alexievich's work is one, I would suggest, in which the narrative and descriptive modalities predominate, more in keeping with the American tradition of a narrative literary journalism with which I am familiar (which is not to say that somehow she is more American, or influenced by the American form; I have no reason to believe so). Indeed, one American anthology has firmly placed Alexievich as an author of a narrative "literary journalism," and I agree with that assessment.[1] Politkovskaya's work, by contrast, is clearly one in which a discursiveness—expository and argumentative in nature—predominates. How, then, can both journalists be described as writers of literary reportage, but only one characterized as a writer of a narrative literary journalism? After all, given the similarities in terms, it would be easy to assume that as narrative "literary reportage" and "literary journalism" are one and the same, given the similarities of terms.

As I examine this puzzle, what emerges is that "literary reportage," also characterized as reportage literature and sometimes simply "reportage," is a genre of many variants, and is indeed "elastic" as my title suggests.[2] What also emerges is that much, but not all, of the literary reportage tradition, is fundamentally anti-dialogical, locked, in other words, in Mikhail Bahktin's distanced image of the absolute past, which I discussed in chapter 2.

Such an examination is necessary if we are to better understand similar narrative traditions of journalism in other countries. This is especially the case because the literary reportage tradition with European origins is little recognized and understood in the United States. And yet it is or has been extant elsewhere not only as a national expression but as a transnational one that has spread beyond European borders. I begin by comparing Alexievich's and Politkovskaya's styles to demonstrate more fully the nature of the problem. Then I examine the Russian tradition in which they write, going back to the early nineteenth century, followed by an exploration of the influence of the international proletarian writers' movement in the twentieth century, and finally that of the Soviet tradition. Alexievich and Politkovskaya provide a point of departure, but in the end they are the heirs to these many influences.

I have defined a narrative literary journalism in part as a genre that emphasizes a personally inflected cultural revelation by means of largely narrative and descriptive modalities. But when looking at how others define it, we find that the trail seems to lead inevitably back to Tom Wolfe's imprecise definition, namely, that a narrative literary journalism is "journalism that would read like a novel" or "short story."[3] Edd Applegate, in his *Literary Journalism: A Biographical Dictionary of Writers and Editors*, appears to take his cue from Wolfe in positing that "literary journalism uses the techniques of the novelist," although such materials are still factual and fundamentally journalistic.[4] Gay Talese takes the position that "the new journalism, though often reading like fiction, is not fiction. It is, or should be, as reliable as the most reliable reportage although it seeks a larger truth than is possible through the mere compilation of facts."[5] In his case, the American usage of "reportage" is synonymous with conventional mainstream "journalism." Richard Goldstein echoes Talese, noting that a narrative literary journalism combines the "mythmaking power of fiction and the credibility of reportage" (and, again, "reportage" is here synonymous with mainstream "journalism").[6] One detects the need to compare the form to fiction—the novel and short story—even though most of the tropes associated with chronotopic documentary existed well before the modern fictional novel and short story.[7]

"Literary reportage," or "reportage literature," depending on which of the terms serves as modifier, has proved less stable as a designation. Moreover, at times the noun "reportage" alone has been applied to the whole (as we will see), which raises still other issues of instability, given an American English-language dictionary definition for "reportage" as "the act or process of reporting news,"[8] which can include mainstream American models of the twentieth century—"objective" news, in short.

Definitions of reportage of the "literary" kind discussed here, whether it stands alone for the whole or serves as the modified or the modifier, can bear distinct similarities to Wolfean literary journalism. For example, the

Portuguese writer and journalist Pedro Rosa Mendes writes, "Reportage literature is an engagement with reality with a novelist's eye but with a journalist's discipline."[9] The British publication *Granta*, a mainstay of "reportage" of the literary kind, has provided this definition: "The art and craft of reportage—journalism marked by vivid description, a novelist's eye to form, and eyewitness reporting that reveals hidden truths about people and events that have shaped the world we know."[10] As one can detect, the definitions are largely in accord with Wolfe's. Some scholars have all but equated a narrative literary journalism and literary reportage as the same. Rudolph G. Wagner, the German scholar of the Chinese version, observed in his 1992 study that "literary reportage" is "now called 'new journalism.'"[11] Peter Monteath takes a similar position in his 1990 study concerning narrative reportage on the subject of the Spanish civil war.[12] And when one examines such traditions as the Norwegian, Slovenian, and Cuban, among others, this does indeed appear to be the case.[13]

But there are still other contemporary definitions and delineations of literary reportage that push at the equation of the two and hint at the difficulties of definition. The journalist Anne Nivat of France provides the following: "I think one of the first things for literary reportage should be to go into the field and to try to get the other side of the story. Reportage should give a fresh vision of a topic."[14] But what is a "fresh vision"? Why the fieldwork? Svetlana Alexievich similarly engages in a broad definition: "Documentary prose ought to transcend the strict boundaries between the formats of literature and journalism. The person of the author, his mentality, his philosophy and his sensitivity must be unified by a good writing style. Documentary work means using reality as the raw material to create a new reality."[15] But what are the formats of literature? Can they include poetry? Drama? What constitutes a "good" writing style? Is the creation of a "new reality" possibly the creation of fiction in the conventional sense? The German-language Czech journalist Egon Erwin Kisch, of whom I will say more, characterized literary reportage as a "milieu study."[16] But a milieu study can leave much to the imagination. It could be narrative literary journalism, or an expository sociological or anthropological study.

Then there is a dictionary definition for the Chinese version, which is called *baogao wenxue* and translates most directly as "reportage literature."[17] Of it, Wagner writes: "Reportage literature is a literary genre, a type of prose; also an umbrella term for sketches and the *texie*," the latter often synonymous with *baogao wenxue* and when first used in the 1930s in China meant "close up," a term borrowed from cinematography.[18] Elsewhere: "It is a fast and timely representation with adequate artistic processing, of real people and real events that are drawn directly from and regarded as typical of real life. As such it serves the current political agenda and is said to be the 'light cavalry' of literary production."[19] But the definition raises questions, among them: What is "adequate artistic processing"? And how is it the "light cavalry" of literary production? What is clear is that such a reportage has been politicized to serve a political agenda.

Moreover, the Russian term for such writing, *ocherk*, can mean simply "essay." But it is also translated as "literary sketch." In the last version of *The Great Soviet Encyclopedia*, completed in 1979, *ocherk* as "literary sketch" is defined broadly as dealing "with the problems associated with slice-of-life literature. Thus, the sketch has a greater degree of cognitive diversity than the short story or novel. It usually combines the characteristics of *belles lettres* and journalism."[20] The last sentence could be interpreted as defining the form as similar to a narrative literary journalism. But it need not be.

What accounts, then, for these differing versions—and visions—of literary reportage, to the extent that the adjective is dropped, for instance in Nivat's definition, where initially she uses it, then dispenses with it in what appears to be an act of synecdoche? It would be easy to dismiss such differences as reflecting different cultural outlooks. Yet what remains remarkable is just how consistently the translated terms "literary reportage," "reportage literature," and "reportage" have been used cross- and indeed interculturally outside the United States.

It is Isabel Hilton who has characterized the form as "elastic." A highly esteemed British journalist, she has served as a juror on the Lettre Ulysses Award committee, the now expired international award for literary reportage. As she notes, "Though reportage was widely practiced and its best examples long remembered, its boundaries seemed elastic."[21] And while she embraces the Wolfean definition, winners of the prize have not always fit that description; witness first-place winner Politkovskaya in 2003.[22] As I will show, she is fundamentally an expository polemicist, while Alexievich emphasizes narradescription.

Svetlana Alexievich (also transliterated as "Alexiyevich"),[23] recipient of the Nobel Prize for Literature, achieved recognition in the West with publication of the excerpt "Boys in Zinc" in *Granta*, taken from her book *Zinky Boys*. The excerpt and book provide an account of how loved ones coped with the deaths of Soviet soldiers in the Afghanistan war of the 1980s. More recently she authored *Voices from Chernobyl*, an account of those who did and did not survive the 1986 nuclear disaster.[24]

Anna Politkovskaya is perhaps best known for her journalism about the war in Chechnya in the 1990s collected in the volume *A Dirty War* (under the French title *Tchétchénie: le déshonneur russe*), which was awarded the first Lettre Ulysses Award in 2003 in Berlin (and for which Alexievich was a juror).[25] The award, then, confers on the work the status of literary reportage by one standard.

Alexievich is a Belorussian national who publishes in both Russian and Belorussian. "Boys in Zinc" was published in *Granta* in 1990, the same year the book-length version was published in the Soviet Union. Zinc refers to the regulation zinc coffins in which the bodies of dead soldiers were sent back to the Soviet Union. The English translation, *Zinky Boys*, appeared in 1992. Prior to the book's publication in the Soviet Union, Alexievich was more widely known in her country as the author of *War's Unwomanly Face*, an account of the memories of Soviet women from World War II.[26]

"Boys in Zinc" clearly reflects a more active narra-descriptive modality. One moving example involves Tamara, the wife of a professional army officer killed in the war, after he had told her, "You can't imagine how much I don't want to die for someone else's country."[27] When she arrives with his parents at an airport to pick up his coffin, this is what she found:

> "We've come to collect . . . "
> "Over there," he pointed over to a far corner. "See if that box is yours. If it is, you can take it."
> There was a filthy box standing outside with "Senior Lieutenant Dovnar" scrawled on it in chalk. I tore the board away from where the window should be in a coffin. His face was in one piece, but he was lying in there unshaven, and nobody had washed him. The coffin was too small and there was a bad smell. I couldn't lean down to kiss him. That's how they gave my husband back to me. I got down on my knees before what had once been the dearest thing in the world to me.[28]

"Boys in Zinc," I should emphasize, is not strictly a formal interview—in this case Alexievich interviewing Tamara Dovnar. Alexievich's style reconstructs not only the event but also the telling of the event, so that it appears that the narrator—the Soviet wife Tamara—is speaking directly to us. This is part of the Russian tradition of *skaz*, which means a tale not told in the voice of the author but by a first-person narrator created by the author.[29] But unlike in fiction, Alexievich is not creating a fictitious narrator. Rather she is giving "voice" to an identifiable speaker with a living presence. Indeed, Alexievich describes such a form as a "voice genre."[30]

Alexievich has selected details that would resonate more deeply across Soviet and Russian culture than American. In the case of Soviet culture, she selects details that assault official mythologies. For example, "And at that time people continued to talk and write about our internationalist duty, the interests of state, our southern borders."[31] In "internationalist duty" and "interests of state" we detect patriotic euphemisms that are not unlike what Barthes identified on the cover of *Paris Match* in the attempt to reinforce French imperialism, as I noted in the previous chapter. In effect, they were euphemistic totalizations elevated to mythic stature in the Soviet Union. (Even "southern borders" takes on a mythic status, because borders are designed to keep out what challenges myth as a self-contained and global totality.) They reflect again, as Joseph Brodsky said of euphemism, the inertia of terror,[32] a terror that becomes refracted through the revealing narra-description or stories Soviet citizens shared with Alexievich. It is here that she begins to undermine or break down myth, countering it with what the young soldiers and their families confronted in an open-ended or inconclusive reality, one for which the myth did not and could not account. In the example just cited, Alexievich notes: "The censors saw to it that reports of the war did not mention our fatalities. There were only rumours of notifications of death arriving at rural huts and of regulation zinc coffins arriving at prefabricated flats. I had not meant to write about war again, but I found myself in the middle of one."[33]

Among other examples, an army private recalls, "They lined us up on the square and read out the order: "You're going to the Democratic Republic of Afghanistan to do your internationalist duty." And "Before our first battle they played the Soviet National Anthem." But such totalized invocations of "internationalist duty" and the "Soviet National Anthem" sounded hollow because of what the ideological mythology could not account for in the unanticipated differentiating qualities: "After the battle we scraped our own guys off the armour plate with spoons. There weren't any identification discs for fatalities."[34] The phenomenal particular, intimated in the concrete metaphors, undoes the myths to which the Soviet government had attached the ship of the Soviet people's lives. The familiar comforts of the myths have been confronted with the unfamiliar.

A military nurse recalls: "They told us it was a just war. We were helping the Afghan people to put an end to feudalism and build a socialist society." But it is the horror of amputated limbs "just dumped" that begins to unmask the myth for what it is, a death machine. "Twice a week we had political indoctrination. They went on about our sacred duty, and how the border must be inviolable. Our superior ordered us to inform on every wounded soldier, every patient. It was called monitoring the state of morale: the army must be healthy! We weren't to feel compassion. But we did feel compassion: it was the only thing that held everything together."[35] Thus the myths of "sacred duty" (invoked in the name of an officially atheist state, no less), "inviolable borders," and building a "socialist society" are subverted by the seemingly simple but powerful response of a visceral heart-wrenching compassion, one that takes on an ultimate value for the speaker.

A regimental press officer recalls: "Out there you felt quite differently about your country. 'The Union,' we called it. It seemed there was something great and powerful behind us, something which would always stand up for us."[36] But eventually the myth of "Union," the totalitarian state as totalized signification, is inadequate in accounting for the phenomenal realities of war.

Similarly, myths are revealed (as they were in Didion's "Some Dreamers of the Golden Dream" discussed in the last chapter), as media constructions:

> I remember, though, the evening after one battle—there had been losses, men killed and men seriously injured—we plugged in the television to forget about it, to see what was going on in the Union. A mammoth new factory had been built in Siberia; the Queen of England had given a banquet in honour of some VIP; youths in Voronezh had raped two schoolgirls for the hell of it; a prince had been killed in Africa. The country was going about its business and we felt completely useless. Someone had to turn the television off, before we shot it to pieces.[37]

What, figuratively, they wanted to shoot to pieces were the euphemistic myths of a country "going about its business" propagated by the Soviet evening news, which could not begin to reflect the horror of war even if it wanted or were permitted to do so.

But as the example of Tamara Dovnar illustrates, the myths were challenged not just on the battlegrounds of Afghanistan. More important for Alexievich's account, they were being challenged and subverted at home, because, as S. Elizabeth Bird and Robert Dardenne noted "telling it like it was supposed to mean," in this instance back in the comparative safety of the "Union," was beginning to emerge as a lie.[38] This is what "the Union," that myth of what was to be an Edenic dictatorship of the proletariat, had come to, challenged by the open-ended present.

Then, as mentioned, there are the details that would resonate more deeply across Russian culture. For example, the matter of the husband's body going unwashed is more than just one of hygiene and respect for the dead. Instead, the ritual washing of the dead is a necessary and sacred rite in Russian Orthodox funerals because it helps to release the soul from the body.[39] Similarly, the kissing of the dead is another important rite in Russian funeral culture.[40] In a sense what Tamara Dovnar was doing was returning to older Russian cultural mythologies in a repudiation of the Soviet.[41] That she had at least some knowledge of religion (as did many Russians during the Soviet period) in that officially atheistic state is reflected in her recollection that before she married, she had a dream on Epiphany, which in the Russian Orthodox Church is the date of Jesus's baptism. She dreamed that she would marry a man in uniform.[42] She knew what Epiphany was, and here we see a variation on what Barthes called for: the undoing of secular Soviet myth with, in this instance, a more ancient mythos.

Moreover, Alexievich makes it clear that what she is attempting to do is indeed intended to be literary. This is because she is reflexively literary in a way that we do not often see with American authors; indeed, from an American perspective, she may appear too consciously aspiring to be literary. Because "Boys in Zinc," as it appeared in *Granta*, is composed of excerpts, what is lost from editorial elisions are the literary references. In the complete volume *Zinky Boys*, the initial chapter that much of "Boys in Zinc" is adapted from serves to frame the book as not only a journalistic undertaking but as a literary one as well. Eleven literary references are deleted from the chapter in the *Granta* version, which are references to writers, poets, and literary critics. The first is to Shakespeare's *Richard II*, with the quote "Each substance of grief hath twenty Shadows."[43] Then in succession Alexievich cites the critic Yuri Karyakin, Franz Kafka, Fyodor Dostoevsky, Alexander Pushkin, Mikhail Lermontov, Dostoevsky again, Leo Tolstoy, singer-songwriter-poet Vladimir Vissotsky, Dostoevsky still again, and poet Boris Slutsky.[44] Shakespeare, Kafka, Dostoevsky, Pushkin, Lermontov, and Tolstoy should need no introduction. Karyakin, Vissotsky, and Slutsky are less well known in the West.[45] Also notable in the English translation of the book is that except for pages one and eight, every page through the first ten contains at least one reference to a literary figure. What Alexievich is suggesting, then, in invoking such an accomplished roster is that journalism can indeed be literary. This is not to say that American authors do not make literary references. They often do as epigraphs prior to the start of the narrative. Truman Capote does so with *In Cold Blood*.[46] What is perhaps unique from an American perspective with regard to Alexievich is how unremitting such references are in the first ten pages of the text.

It is the nature of the quotes—direct and indirect—from her literary sources that reveals her intent to undermine Soviet mythologies. Shakespeare, the first, makes reference to multiplicities of meaning beyond the source of each trauma: "Each substance of grief hath twenty Shadows." As an illustration, the Soviet state informed loved ones of the deaths in cursory fashion, as if the cursoriness—like euphemism's avoidance of terror—would decrease the pain, at least for the messenger. "In fulfillment of my duty as a soldier, I have to inform you that Senior Lieutenant Valerii Gennadievich Volovich was killed today at 1045 hours," reads one telegram quoted in "Boys in Zinc."[47] What could not be stemmed in the fulfillment of one's "duty" were the haunting "shadows" of grief that hovered above the cursory bureaucratese of the telegram.

With that as an introduction, Alexievich continues to build her case that hers is to be read as a literary document, one that consistently assaults mythologies. She quotes from Karyakin: "We should not judge a man's life by his perception of himself. Such a perception may be tragically inadequate." In the inadequacy we detect what humans cannot know about themselves (and the unassimilated). Alexievich adds, "And I read something in Kafka to the effect that man was irretrievably lost within himself." Thus, among other interpretations, we see the age-old admonition against hubris—of the fall from grace through one's overweening pride. Of the mythos associated with the warrior in the form of martial splendor and heroism, Alexievich writes, "Dostoevsky described military men as 'the most unthinking people in the world.'" So she attacks, not so indirectly, the Soviet army, liberator of civilization, in one mythology, from fascism during the Great Patriotic War, as World War II was called in the Soviet Union and in Russia today. Later, "To write (or tell) the whole truth about oneself is a physical impossibility, according to Pushkin."[48] In other words, the global or totalized conception of oneself is not possible, and we detect again the unassimilable, the excess beyond knowing, this from Pushkin, widely regarded as Russia's greatest poet.[49]

Alexievich's invocation of Lermontov engages in a role reversal. The Soviet military, ostensibly a civilizing force, is reduced to engaging in barbarities. Alexievich writes:

> In Lermontov's [fictional] *A Hero of Our Times,* Maximych [the framing narrator, who makes available the "diaries" of the main and now dead protagonist Pechorin] says of the mountain-tribesman who has killed Valla's father: "Of course, according to their lights he [the killer] was completely in the right"—although [Alexievich as author is speaking again] from the Russian's point of view the deed was quite bestial. Lermontov here pinpointed the amazing ability of Russians to put themselves into other people's shoes—to think according to their "lights," in fact.[50]

To be bestial and commit atrocities, in other words. Alexievich's observation from *A Hero of Our Times* is reinforced later on the same page: "In Dostoevsky's novel Ivan Karamazov observes: 'No man can be as cruel, so exquisitely and artificially cruel, as man.'"[51] Such is the myth that an army can be "civilizing" in the name of one's "internationalist duty."

She cites Tolstoy's observation that "man is fluid," in the sense that in the interests of the State, that global conception, he is expendable. Vissotsky, again less known in the West, was a poet and songwriter. Alexievich listens to a tape cassette of "Afgantsi" songs sung by Soviet Afghan veterans which express their ironic contempt for the ideals—the myths—that sent them to Afghanistan. "Childish, unformed voices, trying to sound like Vissotsky, croaked out: 'The sun set on the *kishlak* [Afghan village] like a great big bomb'; . . . 'Amputees like big birds hopping one-legged by the sea'; . . . 'There's no hatred in his face now he's dead.'"[52]

Alexievich quotes Boris Slutsky, one of the Soviet war poets of World War II who rose to prominence during the cultural thaw after the death of Stalin in 1953: "When we returned from war / I saw we were needed no more."[53] Such is the dim view she presents of the Afghan venture and the survivors as psychic casualties.

But there is still an additional dimension to Alexievich's literary intentions, again intentions perhaps difficult to appreciate from the American pragmatic perspective but very much inherent in her invocation of Russian literature. Russian literature is strongly inflected with a philosophical and even spiritual imperative. I do not mean to make the argument that the literary modernists and New Critics tried to make, that literary meaning can be essentialized. Rather, I am discussing a perception in Russian letters. One detects it when Alexievich invokes the Christian existentialist (and deeply devout Russian Orthodox) thinker Nikolai Berdyaev, who was also a Dostoevsky scholar. Toward the end of the first chapter she quotes Berdyaev: "Russian writers have always been more interested in truth than beauty."[54] The quote is notable not only for the preference it expresses, truth over beauty, but also because it challenges what for so long in Anglophone culture served those intent on a transcendental literature, namely, the conclusion to Keats's "Ode on a Grecian Urn," which has for some belletristic aesthetes come to represent the "essence" of literary aesthetics: " 'Beauty is truth, truth beauty,'—that is all / Ye know on earth, and all ye need to know."[55] Berdyaev is rejecting the Western view that the study of aesthetics is the study of the beautiful, and suggesting that truth can be something different. If there is any beauty, it is in the revelation of whatever "truths," or insights as I would prefer, are revealed. (Nor should the conclusion to Keats's poem be mistaken for the aesthetic principle several lines earlier that makes an irony of those famous final lines, namely, that the aesthetic "teases us out of thought" with the possibilities of meaning; truth as beauty and beauty as truth are ironic because we can never know if this is the case if we are forever teased out of thought.) More to the point, in an example of how the literary and the spiritual (or metaphysical) invest Russian literature, Berdyaev said, in a volume about Dostoevsky, that the author of *Crime and Punishment, Notes from the Underground,* and *The Brothers Karamazov* "has played a decisive part in my spiritual life. . . . He stirred and lifted up my soul more than any other writer or philosopher."[56]

So Alexievich firmly plants herself in the tradition of Russian literature. Having done so, she is led to ask a fundamental question: "Who are we, and where are we going?" The question is directed at "Russian literary people." But it could only resonate broadly with all Soviet readers. Following the question, she makes clear that myth is indeed the object of her attack: "And it dawns on us that nothing, not even human life, is more precious to us than our myths about ourselves. We've come to believe the message, drummed into us for so long, that we are superlative in every way, the finest, the most just, the most honest."[57] Much as the New Journalists assaulted the American Dream, she is attacking the Soviet equivalent. And those who doubt, she adds, will be accused of "treachery."

On the next page she quotes Berdyaev again: "I have always been my own man, answerable to no-one." Thus he positions himself outside the state, which of course would not endear him to the Soviet regime, which reviled him (he lived in exile). Alexievich responds to Berdyaev's quote: "Something which can't be said of us Soviet writers. In our day truth is always at the service of someone or something." Or of the Soviet Union for that matter, or of one's "internationalist duty," or of any of the other ideological myths she assaults. Then she writes, "Dostoevsky insisted: 'The truth is more important than Russia.'" Furthermore, after Dostoevsky she invokes the Bible: "Take heed that no man deceive you. For many shall come in my name, saying I am Christ."[58] Alexievich adds, "Russia has had to suffer so many false Messiahs— too many to mention."[59] Lenin, Stalin, Rasputin, Boris Godunov, the false Dmitry, among others. And that, after all, was a major underlying theme in much of Dostoevsky's work, especially *The Possessed* (also translated as *The Devils*), and in the chapter on the Grand Inquisitor in *The Brothers Karamazov*. Moreover, it was this chapter that proved such a powerful influence on Berdyaev's own spiritual views.[60]

So we detect an array of influences on Alexievich in the opening chapter. One need not subscribe to the view of literature as spiritually or metaphysically transcendent in order to understand that literature in her view was a moral and philosophical enterprise. And that is the insight that an examination of Alexievich provides: her literary values frame her examination.

And yet, despite the frame, hers remains fundamentally and largely a chronotopic treatment. In her commitment to the open-ended present of the chronotope, she appears more aligned with the kind of narrative literary journalism one finds in the United States. But again, one need only consider the inclusion of "Boys in Zinc" in the anthology *The Art of Fact: A Historical Anthology of Literary Journalism* as conferring on her work the generic designation of "literary journalism" as defined in the American sense.[61] According to still another measure, then, that of the anthologists, Alexievich is more in the tradition of a Joan Didion, a Tom Wolfe, or a George Orwell.

Turning to Anna Politkovskaya, we find that she is fundamentally an investigative journalist engaged in digressive reflection, expository and argumentative by nature. We detect this in her unambiguous polemics, in which she makes no attempt to conceal at times her vituperative outrage, which she weaves through her text. For example: "The war itself was a disgrace. How much more disgraceful is it to halt the exhumations [of dead Russian soldiers] for commercial reasons." And "The federal ministries and departments drawn into this system have shown their incompetence and are now washing their hands of it all." And "Millions of my fellow citizens stubbornly refuse to understand what is going on today in Chechnya. It bears no relation to the propaganda in Moscow."[62] Thus she has mounted the polemical soap box, and she violates that cardinal rule of the creative writing workshop: Show with description—the chronotope—do not tell your readers what to think.

Not that Politkovskaya eschews scene construction altogether. For example:

> It was Abulkhanov, a respected figure in Novye Aldy, who walked through the village on the morning of the Day of Judgement and persuaded people to leave their basements. It was he who chivvied the doubters: "Why do we need to hide any longer? Things will only get better from now on. If we stay in the basement the soldiers will think we are guilty of something. But we've done nothing wrong." It was Abulkhanov who took the hand of the smiling soldier who entered the courtyard and said, "Thank you my boy. We were waiting for you. I'm glad to see you come at last."
>
> "Take out your [gold] teeth, old man," said the soldier, "and bring some money as well, or I'll kill you."
>
> Abulkhanov did not understand and continued to stroke the soldier's hand. . . .
>
> They shot the old man, turning his execution into target practice that took off the top of his head. Next they killed three others.[63]

Without doubt this is a powerful scene. But the reconstruction of the aesthetics of experience also illustrates why Politkovskaya is only sometimes a literary journalist. After reporting the massacre of more than one hundred Chechen villagers by Russian troops, Politkovskaya observes: "Soon a year will have passed since the atrocity in Novye Aldy, the Khatyn of modern-day Russia. There has been no investigation. During the entire eleven months since it happened, the witnesses have not once been questioned." She makes reference to the massacre of residents of the village of Khatyn by the Nazis in 1943 in what is today Belarus (and which should not be mistaken for the Katyn Forest massacre of the Polish officer corps by the Soviet Army near Smolensk in 1940). Regarding an investigation by the state prosecutor-general's office, she adds, "They offer the shameless lie that the Chechens, faithful to their customs, refuse to allow the bodies to be exhumed and therefore the investigation is prevented from going ahead."[64]

Thus Politkovskaya tells readers what to think, using Abulkhanov's death only as an example, instead of letting readers engage in their own dialogue to sort out what has happened by means of concrete metaphors. Examples like this are not constructed "scene by scene." Rather, Politkovskaya's invocation of such a scene as an anecdotal example is designed to illustrate her discursive—and polemical—claims. From the viewpoint of modalities, she then works more according to the feature-writing tradition of journalism discussed earlier, except that Politkovskaya's is highly polemicized. In such a tradition descriptive anecdotes serve to illustrate the larger expository or argumentative point.[65]

Nor is this to suggest that because Politkovskaya is an investigative journalist and Alexievich a narrative literary journalist that Alexievich cannot then be an investigative journalist. In fact, such journalisms are not mutually exclusive. This is because a narrative literary journalism is, as I have noted elsewhere, largely a modal genre.[66] Investigative journalism is by contrast a broad topical genre. In other words, the latter is defined by its topicality, in this case a subject matter concealed from public view deemed worthy of the investigation. Other topical examples are the travelogue and the true crime account. At the same time, they can be composed in the form of the modal genre of narra-descriptive journalism.

In fairness, Alexievich can at times also engage in polemics. After all, her polemic is that what she has undertaken has a literary ambition. What distinguishes "Boys in Zinc" from Politkovskaya's Chechnya account is that Alexievich's polemics are, by comparison, few and more nuanced. Her work represents by degree a literary journalism emphasizing the irreducibility of narrative and descriptive into a *qualitas occulta* that can be read like a conventional realist novel or short story consistent with Rosa Mendez's Portuguese definition. In Alexievich's example, narrative literary reportage and narrative literary journalism overlap significantly. Politkovskaya, by contrast, draws more from the different rhetorical modalities, but especially from the argumentative.

As exemplars of a more fluid and elastic literary reportage, Alexievich's and Politkovskaya's variations draw on two important sources. These are the Russian tradition and the international proletarian writers' tradition.

The Russian tradition can be traced at least as far back as the first half of the nineteenth century and was one that most likely evolved out of the ubiquitous travelogue.[67] This appears to be the case in many cultures and societies, such as in China.[68] One of the earliest examples of a proto-literary reportage in Russia was a collection of various articles by different authors in the volume *Physiology of Petersburg*, published in 1845. It was edited by the poet and critic Nikolai Nekrasov.[69] The "physiology was based on the French model and was synonymous with 'sketch.'"[70] The French "physiologies" were often satirical sketches that could be either true or fictional. In them, a stroller or *flâneur* ambles through Paris cynically describing the street life.[71] If fictional, they were designed to provide a description of a type, consistent again with the later twentieth-century Chinese definition of "real people and real events that are drawn directly from and regarded as typical of real life." Of course, in the type lies the allegory, and we detect one early epistemological ambition. But one also detects authors drawing from the differentiating qualities of the aesthetics of experience, the carnivalesque in short.[72] In *Petersburg*, we find accounts of yard keepers and organ grinders, as well as an examination of an impoverished neighborhood along Dvoryanskaya Street north of the Neva River, and an examination of a city courtyard in which many people lived and worked.[73] In the last, for example, there is much that is recognizable as a narra-descriptive journalism when the author records an exchange between a house serf and a tenant named Kir'yanych, to which will be added a drunk:

> Finally, he stamped his foot with terrible force, wheezed solemnly, and returned to the table. His face was also solemn.
>
> "Enough of your killing spiders, Kir'yanych. Better they crawl the walls. They won't let you sleep as it is. . . . Now then, let's hold off on the vodka until it's really cold!"
>
> "It wouldn't be a sin to drink it now," Kir'yanych said smugly. "May the Lord grant health to the kind man!" He then crossed himself and drank down his glass.
>
> After a second round, the house serf reached for his balalaika, struck up a trepak, and began to sing:
>
> > *On Monday*
> > *Savka mills the seed.*
> > *On Tuesday*
> > *Savka saddles the steed. . . .*
> > [The song continues until]
>
> There was a knock at the door, followed by loud grumbling.
>
> "Well now, master, you're really in luck today," the house serf exclaimed.

"Now we'll have some fun. The teacher is coming!"

The door flew open and banged against the wall with a deafening sound. Something akin to a whiskey bottle entered the room, swinging from side to side, a human head taking the place of a cork. This is how I first thought to describe a man in a light green coat that was without a collar but which draped about his shoulders. The collar, it seemed, had been used to repair the other parts of the coat and had been missing since 1819. . . . [The author engages in a disquisition on drunkenness and then a further description of the drunk who has just entered.]

The house serf, already laughing, hailed him with his usual greeting: "Hello, there, red-nosed one!"

From all indications, the green man became quite angry but checked his anger right away. He gestured toward the bottle and said in an affectionate voice, "Greeting Egorushka. Won't you pour me a little glass?"

Slyly and without raising any suspicion, the house serf poured a glass of water from a clay mug that had been standing on the table. He gave it to the green man. The green man downed it in one gulp. The house serf and Kir'yanych guffawed loudly, stamping their feet on the floor.[74]

So one detects a mean-spirited humor at the expense of an unsuspecting drunk who is given water to drink, and clearly what we have is an emphasis on narra-description, or the accumulation of chronotopes in scene-by-scene construction.

I should emphasize that not all of the Petersburg physiologies were narrative prose, because they also included the expository essay, poetry, drama, and even literary criticism.[75] The collection was, in fact, very much like the feuilleton sections of newspapers in France then becoming popular, which I discuss later as having an important influence on the generic elasticity of literary reportage.

A second and highly influential example of *ocherki* were *A Hunter's Sketches* by Ivan Turgenev, collected and published in 1852, but which he began publishing in the literary journal *Sovremennik* in 1847 and for which Nekrasov was the editor. (It should be noted that the title in Russian is *Zapiski Okhotnika,* which translates more closely as "a hunter's notes." But the standard English translation has usually been *A Hunter's Sketches* or *A Sportsman's Sketches.*) The sketches are fundamentally narrative and descriptive in their modalities and provide an empathetic portrait of the lives of Russian serfs. The empathy for what were understood to be a kind of *Untermensch* by the upper levels of Russian society at the time so angered Tsar Nicholas I that he fired the censor who permitted them to be published and ordered Turgenev arrested and exiled from Moscow.[76]

As with *Physiology of Petersburg, A Hunter's Sketches* should be treated with some caution because it is more in the nature of a prototype for a narrative literary journalism or reportage. This was a time when the divide between fiction and nonfiction was not always clear.[77] That said, there can be little doubt that some were true, such as the sketch "Khor and Kalinich," which was the first in Turgenev's collection. The real-life Khor, a Russian serf, often read the tale with delight to visitors. Such veracity is also the case with "A Living Relic," which Turgenev described as "all a true incident."[78]

Some of Russia's greatest writers of realistic fiction, besides Turgenev, wrote narrative *ocherki*. Starting in 1855 Leo Tolstoy published the first of what eventually would be collected as *The Sebastopol Sketches*, his firsthand account of the siege of that Crimean city by the British and French during the Crimean War.[79] In 1862 Fyodor Dostoevsky published *Notes from a Dead House*, an account of exile and imprisonment in Siberia in the early 1850s for revolutionary activity.[80] Again, it is a prototype, because Dostoevsky used a fictional narrator. But it was based on his four years in a prison camp in Siberia for revolutionary activity. It also helped to establish a tradition in which Alexander Solzhenitsyn would follow with his *Gulag Archipelago*. Among other notable examples, Anton Chekhov published *The Island: A Journey to Sakhalin* in 1895, which is an account of penal colonies on that remote island outpost of the Russian Empire.[81] Chekhov's is both a personal account of the experience as well as an expository examination of the medical conditions of convicts. (Chekhov was a doctor.)

The Russian revolutionary writer Maxim Gorky, starting in the 1890s, engaged in the narrative *ocherk* with accounts of vagabonds written for newspapers. He lived as a vagabond himself, wandering across European Russia. A number of the accounts would later be collected in the volume *Through Russia*.[82] After 1900 his work became more political and more colored by his revolutionary sympathies. One example is "The Ninth of January," an account of the 1905 massacre in St. Petersburg when imperial troops opened fire on a peaceful political demonstration.[83] Gorky's work would span both the pre- and postrevolutionary periods.

Vladimir Arsenyev's *Dersu Uzala* is one of a number of accounts of his travels while mapping the Russian Far East before World War I. *Dersu Uzala* describes Arsenyev's relationship with an old native tribesman who served as his guide in the Ussuri region of Siberia from 1902 to 1907. The book was published in 1923 and thus provides another bridge from the nineteenth-century Russian tradition to the Soviet. Tendentiousness is largely absent, and yet the volume was regarded highly by the Soviet literary establishment. "The story of Dersu inspires a sense of love for the backwoods, the deep rivers and the blue hills of the Ussuri Territory," reads the book jacket, to which Gorky added, "I am fascinated and swept away by its expressive impact."[84] Gleb Struve notes that *Dersu Uzala* "was often cited by the factographers as superior to much of Soviet fiction and as a proof that fiction was dying out."[85] "Factography" was the name given in the 1920s in Soviet Russia to one variation of the *ocherk*. And as we will see, the belief that fiction would decline becomes a mantra among advocates of a literary reportage not just in the Soviet Union.

All of these examples up to the beginning of the communist period provide national predecessors for a continued evolution on into the period of the Soviet Union, a tradition of which Alexievich and Politkovskaya would prove to be part. Clearly these early examples are to varying degrees narra-descriptive journalism. While Gorky's "Ninth of January" is to some extent polemical within its historical context, *A Hunter's Sketches* is accidentally so because of how it was received by the tsar's government, and *Dersu Uzala* is relatively free of political cant.

Literary reportage or reportage literature or simply reportage was also strongly influenced by the rise of the proletarian writers' movement which in turn was part of the larger international communist movement immediately after World War I. The international nature of the movement ensured the cross-fertilization and creation of a cosmopolitan genre that breached the boundaries of national cultures—including in the United States.

Here it was not only the Russian cultural orbit in which the movement arose but also the German. As Siegfried Kracauer, the German critic and sociologist (better known in the United States as a film critic after his immigration), noted in 1930, "For a number of years now, reportage has enjoyed in Germany the highest favor of representation, since it alone is said to be able to capture life unposed." It was, he said, a reaction against the abstractness of German idealism.[86] In the aftermath of defeat following World War I, the desire to understand that defeat beyond imperial illusionism is understandable.

The "reportage" Kracauer refers to is not that of conventional journalism practice as known in the United States. A key term here is that it was "unposed," suggesting a kind of natural or impromptu spontaneity, and it reminds us of the unexpected open-ended present. Kracauer's concept of reportage reflected the *neue Sachlichkeit*, or "new objectivity," that emerged in aesthetic circles in Germany after the defeat of the war. Unlike the concept of journalistic "objectivity" as it took shape in the United States, the German version emphasized first-person witness as the only kind of witness that could make a claim to epistemological validity. Such differences in the meaning of objectivity reflect, of course, different cultural experiences. But if to the victors go the spoils, to the losers went a "new objectivity" reflecting self-doubt, or the idea that all you could trust was your own personal witness. Hence the different perspectives.

Undoubtedly the foremost advocate of a reportage based on the *neue Sachlichkeit* was Egon Erwin Kisch. As Wagner observes, Kisch, "a Prague journalist of Jewish origin, writing mostly in German, pioneered the *literarische Reportage* as a new literary genre in the 1920s, and had, with the tremendous international success of his works, contributed to make this new genre acceptable, at least among the literati on the left."[87] Kisch's example—and aggressive promotion—of "literary reportage" and the like served as a catalyst for others and was drafted for purposes of showing the conditions of the struggling working classes as well as to demonstrate the construction of socialist society.

Although he became a committed communist by the end of World War I, Kisch had engaged in a literary reportage before the war that was fundamentally narrative and descriptive in its modalities, without the heavy hand of his later political ideology. Hence much of it could also overlap with a narrative literary journalism. In 1906 he went to work for *Bohemia*, one of Prague's two German-language newspapers, as a local reporter. Crime news and news about the dark underside of life, such as his sketch about a Slovenian girl's descent into prostitution, became his specialty.[88] In 1908 Kisch began writing sketches under the title "Prague Walks" for the feuilleton section of the Sunday paper. Among examples are sketches about an insane asylum and about a shelter for the homeless. In 1912 he began contributing to a series called "Prager Novellen," or "Prague Novellas," more ambitious efforts that continued to examine society's submerged dark side. "Christmas in a Court Prison" is one example. "As the title suggests," Danica Kozlová and Jiři Tomáš note of the "Prague Novellas," "Kisch attempted a story form, largely on the borderline between artistic journalism and belles lettres."[89]

The origins of Kisch's reportage, then, can be traced back at least in part to the feuilleton, a term of French origin in the nineteenth century. Derived from the French word for "leaf," meaning a page in a book, the feuilleton was an eclectic collection of articles usually for the purpose of entertainment, as opposed to providing strictly the information of breaking news.[90] The contents of the feuilleton could be highly polemical broadsides, art criticism, or meditative essays, or they could be physiologies and sketches, narrative and descriptive in modal disposition, fictional and nonfictional. There was no one dominating modality, and the result was very much a heterogeneous collection of different rhetorics and media (since the section often included prints to illustrate articles). The feuilleton served a cultural need, then, to provide a space for what did not fit comfortably into the conventional news pages—the cultural excess, in other words. While Kisch perceived reportage as fundamentally like a novel or novella—in other words, primarily narrative and descriptive in modalities—one can detect here, too, early evidence of a "reportage" that would often go beyond those modalities. It was a nature inherited at least in part from the feuilleton and helps to account for why it flourished in the international communist movement: any and all rhetorical means were drafted in the interests of the revolutionary enterprise.

During World War I, Kisch served in the Austro-Hungarian army on the Serbian front, an experience that helped to radicalize him politically. By the beginning of the 1920s, Kisch's conception of a literary reportage had reached maturity by most accounts, according to Harold B. Segel, who, like Wagner, credits Kisch with "defining reportage as a literary genre."[91] In his exuberance for the form, Kisch, among others, proclaimed that such a journalism with literary ambition would replace the novel as the dominant literary genre of the twentieth century:

> Novel? No. Reportage!
> What to think about the reportage? I think it is the literary sustenance of the future. To be sure, only the reportage of the highest quality. The novel has no future. I say there will be no novels produced; meaning no books with imagined plots. The novel is the literature of the last century. . . . Thus, there is a special kind of reportage work that has appeared; I would call it the pure reportage, the reportage itself.
> What's more, after the war [World War I] this reportage became the general, important mode. . . . Psychological novels? No! Reportages!
> The future belongs to the really true and courageous far-seeing reportage.[92]

The passage is notable for several reasons, not least that Kisch does not attach "literary" as a modifier, nor does he convert "reportage" into a modifier attached to "literature." Hence, we see that Anne Nivat's reference—and Granta's for that matter—to a "reportage" that stands alone is not simply a case of synecdoche. Moreover, this is how John Carey interprets the term—"reportage" in isolation—in his collection *The Faber Book of Reportage*, which was published in the United States as *Eyewitness to History*.[93] While French and American definitions of "reportage" do not mention first-person witness, it perhaps comes as no surprise, given Kisch's influence in Germany, that the German does: "eyewitness account, running commentary."[94] One measure of his long-term cultural influence is that when the German magazine *Stern* founded one of the most distinguished awards for journalism in West Germany in 1977, it named the prize for Kisch—no small matter given his communist credentials during this period of Cold War and a divided Germany.[95] Moreover, formally he was a citizen of Czechoslovakia after the collapse of the Austro-Hungarian Empire and was still one at his death in Prague in 1948. Nonetheless, that the award was named for him speaks to the regard in which he was held by the German-speaking world.[96]

Kisch's discussion of "reportage" is also noteworthy because as a character-ization of the genre, it is still to some degree elastic. It seems to suggest a rela-tionship between the novel and reportage, but that relationship is not clearly delineated as much as it is by American proponents of a "literary journalism," in other words, a journalism that would read like a novel or short story.

One reason the form flourished among proletarian writers is that com-munists distrusted the idea of a bourgeois "objective" journalism, whose rise during the 1920s became the professional standard for the capitalist media in the United States. From the Marxist perspective, a dispassionate "objec-tive" journalism was an ideological ruse for concealing the true depths of the miseries of the struggling proletariat.[97] To some extent, such a viewpoint is consistent with narrative literary journalism theory. I have observed elsewhere that the purpose of narrative literary journalism is to engage in an "exchange of subjectivities," or at the least to engage in a narrowing of the distance between subject and object.[98] In other words, one should come away from such material with greater empathy for others, and in the case of Kisch, for the struggles of the proletariat. One can do so only if one engages one's subjectivity with the experiences of others, which is opposite in epistemological ambition from what American "objective" journalism has attempted to do.

Eyewitness (and thus personal) accounts provided, in the communist vision, a truer picture of the world—as long as it was ideologically correct. The ends justified the means, or in this instance the genre. Except that the genre was rhetorically many-faceted. Such texts could be largely narra-descriptive in the developing tradition of American narrative literary jour-nalism, and Kisch often wrote in that vein. Or they could engage largely in discursive—and inflammatory—polemics.

Kisch's (literary) reportage was published in book form and received wide international circulation in leftist circles. Examples include, among others, *Changing Asia; Secret China; Tsars, Priests, and Bolsheviks; Paradise America;* and *Australian Landfall.*[99] As the titles suggest, he was very much a peripa-tetic world traveler, which not only gave him writing material but also pro-vided the opportunity to spread his gospel about the virtues of a "reportage" that he believed would replace the novel.

Kisch's influence internationally in the development of the cosmopolitan genre is reflected in what at first might appear to be two polar opposites geo-graphically and culturally: the United States and China. A salient example from the United States is the work of Joseph North, editor of the publication *New Masses. New Masses* was notable because while it was a communist pub-lication, it was also "the principal organ of the American cultural left from

1926 onwards,"[100] publishing many noncommunist writers ("fellow travelers") because of their (at least temporary) leftist views, such as John Dos Passos, Ernest Hemingway, Edna St. Vincent Millay, Muriel Rukeyser, Sinclair Lewis, Upton Sinclair, Theodore Dreiser, and Sherwood Anderson.[101] For our purposes it was also an important American venue for a literary reportage that reads much like literary journalism (the Muriel Rukeyser article cited is one example), but one that could be highly polemical in the service of political ideology. North was not only the editor but also a practitioner of the form and one of its major American advocates. He specifically names Kisch as his most important inspiration, along with John Reed.[102] In what became an ideal for such a reportage, North observed: "Reportage is three-dimensional reporting. The writer not only condenses reality, he helps the reader feel the fact. The finest writers of reportage are artists in the fullest sense of the term. They do their editorializing through their imagery."[103] Such a prescription could appeal to communists and noncommunists alike, and clearly can be applied to a chronotopic journalism. Again, it recalls the dictum that has echoed down through generations of American creative writing workshops: "Show, don't tell."

Similarly, Kisch's influence ranged to the opposite side of the world. As the Chinese journalist Xiao Qian recalled: "How our *texie* eventually developed I cannot say exactly. I only remember that, during the 1930s, the Czech writer Kisch came to China, and he promoted his literary form of *texie* in our country."[104] Kisch visited China in early 1932 and out of that came his volume *Secret China,* which received international distribution. It was initially published in German in 1933. Chapters were published in Chinese in 1935, and the whole in Chinese in 1938. The first English version appeared in 1935.[105]

But knowledge of Kisch's literary reportage preceded his visit to China. As Charles A. Laughlin notes in his study of the Chinese version, the League of Left-Wing Writers, a few months after its formation in 1930, issued a declaration calling for reportage on behalf of the proletarian political struggle: "From the midst of intense class struggle, from militant strikes, the smoldering village struggles, through community night schools, through factory newsletters, wall newspapers, through all kinds of inflammatory propaganda work, let us create our *reportage*! Only thus can our literature be liberated."[106] One of the earliest references to reportage literature in Chinese came from an article published in early 1930 and translated from Japanese, "A Newly Emerging Literature in Germany." Of Kisch the article notes: "From a long life of a journalist [he] created a new literary form, which is the *Lieboerdazhiai.* This literary form has expanded the realm of literature."[107] As Wagner notes, "*Lieboerdazhiai*" is a transliteration of "reportage."[108]

Perhaps the most indicative measure of Kisch's international influence is to be found in a 1935 German-language issue of the communist journal *Internationale Literatur,* which was published in Moscow by the International Union of Proletarian Writers. The issue, observing Kisch's fiftieth birthday, celebrated his contributions to the genre. It included forty-four messages to Kisch from what amounted to a who's who of the literati and artistic community in the world leftist movement. Praise for Kisch came from such notables as the French journalist and novelist Henri Barbuse, the American communist writer Michael Gold (who was also the former editor of *The Masses* and *The New Masses* before North took over), the Soviet man of letters Sergei Tretyakov, the German playwright Bertolt Brecht, the Hungarian Marxist philosopher and literary critic Georg Lukács, and the leftist Chinese poet Emi Siao.[109] Kisch, "they all maintained, had made literary reportage into a work of art, neither forfeiting its militancy nor relinquishing artistic standards."[110]

Yet among such proletarian and "militant" belletrists (if that is not an oxymoron) the form was not perceived as exclusively narra-descriptive in line with the Wolfean definition. Again, perceptions harked back to the rhetorical heterogeneity of the feuilleton. In the English-language issue of *International Literature* dedicated to Kisch's fiftieth birthday, the leftist critic Theodore Balk wrote: "Let us compare all that today is denoted as 'reportage.' Someone writes a biography of Madame Duberry [*sic*] and he calls it *grand reportage historique*. Someone makes a trip around the world and publishes his diary: 'A Reportage from all the World.' Someone collects the reports of an Arctic expedition—it is reportage. . . . Diary, biography, reports—everything is reportage."[111] The same has happened to the meaning of the term "creative nonfiction" in English departments in the United States, where it has come to refer to any number of nonfictional subgenres, even though the term was created in the 1980s as an alternative to the "New Journalism."[112]

It is evident from his work that Kisch preferred writing a narra-descriptive discourse. Yet he not infrequently digresses into other rhetorics. But his preferred approach in doing so is to contextualize such material as a part within a larger narra-descriptive frame. One detects this in his chapter "Stalinabad— A Capital in the Making" in the volume *Changing Asia,* which is an account of socialist construction in the outer Asian reaches of the Soviet Union. In part the chapter reviews the accomplishments of the communist revolution in Soviet Tajikistan, noting, for example, how many students now attend school in a land where prior to the revolution the vast majority of Tajiks were illiterate. The chapter "Cotton Statistics" is what the title suggests, a report on cotton farming. Both chapters are contained within descriptive and narrative framing devices reminiscent of conventional American feature writing. But ultimately the accounts are outright polemic.[113]

Kisch opposed explicit propaganda, at least in principle, on the grounds that descriptive facts of the conditions of the peasants and workers should speak for themselves and the inevitability of world revolution. Indeed, he was emphatic about it.[114] But in the heat of class struggle the result was that such an approach was observed more in the breach, and he was not above ideological pandering. This is evident in *Changing Asia*. We see this in the chapter "A Visit to the City of Garm" when he concludes with a moral lesson: "But to us Khassyad Mirkulan tells the story of how, out of a mere article of female 'goods,' a free woman was made: one of the thousand and one stories of the Soviet Republic of Tajikistan." The appeal to myth—and to the distanced image of the absolute past—is unambiguous in "the thousand and one stories," drawing from the Middle Eastern *Thousand and One Nights*. Kisch shows a woman, Khassyad Mirkulan, who is liberated by the Marxist means of production from living under the tsarist authority and that of the traditional Islamic patriarchate, in what becomes a communist morality play.

One sees Kisch's ideological pandering again in the chapter on cotton, when he draws a comparison between Tajik cotton farmers and American sharecroppers: "And we think of Dixie, the cotton belt of America, where there are slaves, actually, just as before the time of Lincoln. We think of that country, where we saw figures in rags, hungry, plundered figures."[115] This was after he had toured the United States in 1928 and 1929, out of which came his ironically titled volume *Paradise America*.[116] His appeal to Lincoln is instructive in that, despite the freeing of the slaves, bourgeois capitalism defeated the purpose of the Emancipation Proclamation by coming up with a new form of slavery in tenant farming. In the ideological gloating we detect once again the Marxist screed.

Such propagandizing in Kisch's writing (as well as in the Soviet experience as we will see) accounts for why the communist Joseph North's ideal for literary reportage is, on closer investigation, ambiguous in its meaning. Again, as North noted: "Reportage is three-dimensional reporting. The writer not only condenses reality, he helps the reader feel the fact. The finest writers of reportage are artists in the fullest sense of the term. They do their editorializing through their imagery."[117] The last observation about editorializing through imagery reflects the possibility of still another meaning beyond "showing" as opposed to "telling": that the imagery should unambiguously editorialize on behalf of the ideology. The ends of world revolution justified the rhetoric. The result, so often, was didacticism and predictability in the interests of the political ideology. But the ambiguous wording would serve different interpretations for communists, on the one hand, and on the other, leftist "fellow travelers" less inclined toward the Marxist model.

While Kisch may have been credited by some as the founder of the literary reportage form, he was not. It would be more accurate to suggest that he was the form's foremost international booster during this period, leading a campaign to encourage it. As he acknowledged, his influences were John Reed, Larissa Reisner,[118] and Maxim Gorky.[119] Reed needs no introduction as the author of *Ten Days That Shook the World*. Nor does Gorky as one of Russia's most esteemed early twentieth-century Russian authors. As for Reisner, who remains largely unknown outside of Soviet letters, she published reportage on the Russian civil war in her serialized "Letters from the Front" and wrote books in the 1920s about Afghanistan, socialist reconstruction, and the failed communist uprising in Hamburg.[120] She was also a Bolshevik intelligence officer.

It "is no accident that Reed and Reisner succeeded in shaping books from bare facts and unadorned events that in power, excitement, and tension leave far behind the overwhelming bulk of novelistic literature," Kisch wrote in tribute to them.[121] Of Gorky, he said, "For our entire generation, Gorki had been the decisive experience."[122] Even though Kisch had engaged in such writing on his own since at least 1908, Gorky still could have influenced Kisch in the latter's youth. But Reed and Reisner would have been much later influences contemporary with the Russian Revolution and civil war in the teens and early twenties. Given that Kisch had long engaged in a literary reportage that was narra-descriptive, the influences of Reed and Reisner are not entirely clear. Perhaps they were more in the nature of suggesting and reinforcing how to politicize the aesthetics of experience.

The cosmopolitan and transnational nature of the proletarian writers' movement to encourage literary reportage is perhaps captured most clearly in an anecdote about John Spivak, the American communist writer and editor who was a major contributor to *The New Masses*:

When [Spivak] and Kisch met in Paris in the late thirties and became good friends, he gave the Czech a book inscribed "To the Greatest Living Reporter." Kisch laughed at the inscription and said it meant the book didn't belong to him but to the Soviet writer Ilya Ehrenburg [also a writer of literary reportage who occasionally contributed to *The New Masses*]. Kisch reinscribed the book under Spivak's inscription, and the two took it around to Ehrenburg, who was in Paris on a visit. The Russian read the inscription and said, "No, this does not belong to me. It belongs to [the American communist writer] Agnes Smedley." He signed the book and sent it off to Smedley, who was recuperating in Seattle after making the Long March with Mao Tse-tung's forces. Smedley decided the book didn't belong to her either and signed it over to her friend Anna Louise Strong. Strong read all the inscriptions, said "Oh, thank you," and kept the book.[123]

Strong was another leftist American journalist identified with the proletarian reportage movement.

Kisch's work and example served, then, as an important influence, but one in which several influences converged within him.

Literary reportage "started in Germany in the wake of Kisch's successes, became integrated into the worker-correspondent movements of Germany and the Soviet Union, and, by the late 1920s, aspired to full literary status, the first truly proletarian genre available," Wagner writes.[124] Kisch traveled to the Soviet Union twice, in 1925 and 1926, and then in 1930 to a writers' conference in Kharkov. If he had not earlier, he likely would have met Sergei Tretyakov during the later visit at the conference as he continued to spread his gospel of "reportage." The connection is important because Tretyakov has been described as an "ardent advocate" for a "factual literature" that would come to be called "factography" or a "literature of fact" during the early Soviet years, as well as one of its "pillars" as a practitioner.[125] We must bear in mind, however, that factography, like the feuilleton, need not have been fundamentally narrative. We detect this in the assessment of Nikolai Chuzhak, another "pillar" of factography (along with Victor Shklovsky). In 1929 Chuzhak, one of the leading members of the LEF literary group (Left Front of Literature), edited the collection *Literature of Fact*, a volume of literary criticism in defense of factography. (Tretyakov contributed seven articles, and Shklovsky eight.) As Dmitry V. Kharitonov notes, Chuzhak's concept of factography could include a

> sketch, *a scholarly-imaginative, i.e. masterful* monograph, a newspaper, a montage of facts, a newspaper or a magazine feuilleton, a biography, a memoir, an autobiography, a human document, a travelogue, a historical excursus, a record of a meeting or rally, a court record, a letter describing comprehensively an event witnessed by the letter's author, *a rhythmically organized speech*, a pamphlet, a parody, a satire, etc. They wrote it in the past from time to time, Chuzhak continues, although randomly and in the shadow of canonical literature; now it all has to center the new epoch's *imaginativeness*. Mixed signals are obviously given here, and not only here. One doesn't even have to know his Roland Barthes or Gérard Genette to sense that something's not exactly right with this list: the limits of a literature of fact are suddenly expanded to potentially include a multitude of factual yet clearly imaginative works."[126]

Yet among the most highly regarded were those that we would consider to be conventionally narrative in nature. As Struve notes: "Chuzhak listed some achievements in this field, allocating the first place to John Reed's *The Ten Days That Shook the World*. His list also included . . . Shklovsky's *Sentimental Journey* . . . Tretyakov's books about China, and Arsenyev's *In the Jungles of the Ussuri Region*" [of which *Dersu Uzala* was part].[127] The result of their work was the "raising of the level of craftsmanship in the *ocherk*." And like Kisch, we see Chuzhak, Tretyakov, and Shklovsky speak of the "death" of the traditional fictional novel.[128]

We do not know much about the relationship between Kisch and Tretyakov other than that they knew each other, because when Tretyakov wrote his reminiscences of writers, he said he did not include Kisch because he did not know him on a more intimate and personal level.[129] But there is no doubt that he regarded Kisch highly, given that he contributed to the 1935 issue of *Internationale Literatur* honoring Kisch's accomplishments in reportage on his fiftieth birthday.

Among Tretyakov's works are *Vyzov* (1930) and *A Thousand and One Workdays* (1934), which are accounts of farm collectivization.[130] Perhaps Tretyakov's most famous example of a narrative *ocherk* is *A Chinese Testament: The Autobiography of Tan Shih-Hua as told to S. Tretyakov*, published in Russian in 1930 (and in English in 1934). It is an example of what Tretyakov described as a "Bio-Interview" because it "embraces more than twenty-six years of a man's life."[131] While lecturing on Russian literature at the National University in Beijing in 1924–1925, he interviewed one of his students, Tan Shih-Huah, every day for six months, viewing the young man (who was not a communist) as representative of young intellectuals committed to modernizing China. But Tretyakov's account is not simply memoir or biography, for the cultural tapestry he and Tan provide of early revolutionary China goes well beyond personal reflection and revelation.

Kisch may have been the form's foremost advocate in the world proletarian writers' movement, but Tretyakov also had a wide influence, one that spread back to Germany. In 1931 Tretyakov gave a presentation on factography before the Society for the Friends of the New Russia in Germany. As Devin Fore notes of the text of the presentation:

> To claim that this revolutionary export made a significant impact on his Weimar audience would be an understatement, for in the wake of Tret'iakov's talk everyone from Siegfried Kracauer to Gottfried Benn and Johannes Becher published responses that were in many cases critical, but in every case fervent and engaged. Of course, the most remarkable reply to this talk would be Walter Benjamin's address at the Paris Institute for the Study of Fascism three

years later, "The Author as Producer." A host of Benjamin's central theses are in fact borrowed directly from Tret'iakov's 1931 talk.[132]

Benjamin saw in the form as practiced by Tretyakov one possible avenue for the future of literature. "I admit, he is only one example; I hold others in reserve," Benjamin writes in "The Author as Producer." Tretyakov "distinguishes the operating from the informing writer. His mission is not to report but to struggle; not to play the spectator but to intervene actively." Benjamin adds elsewhere: "I did intentionally quote the example of Tretiakov in order to point out to you how comprehensive is the horizon within which we have to rethink our conception of literary forms or genres, in view of the technical factors affecting our present situation, if we are to identify the forms of expression that channel the literary energies of the present. There were not always novels in the past, and there will not always have to be."[133] Benjamin's call for an "operating" writer derives directly from Tretyakov's 1931 presentation.[134] Moreover, "to struggle; not to play the spectator but to intervene actively" echoes Tretyakov's position: "I call participation in the life of the material itself an operative relation," to which he adds, "Literature becomes an actual weapon in the revolutionary, operative activity of the huge masses who have been summoned to socialist construction."[135] Also, we see Benjamin challenging the future of the fictional novel as had Tretyakov and Kisch (and as Tom Wolfe would do later in the United States).[136]

Given Tretyakov's influence, one could easily dismiss Benjamin's call for an operating writer as openly ideological. But as with North, one can detect in it at least two (double-edged?) meanings. True, the operating writer could be polemical. But at the same time, Benjamin privileges the aesthetic over the ideological. In a revealing statement, he observes in the essay: "The politically correct tendency includes a literary tendency. And, I would add straightaway, this literary tendency, which is implicitly or explicitly contained in every *correct* political tendency of a work[,] includes its literary quality *because* it includes its literary *tendency*." The emphasis is his, and the statement could only have made commissars squirm if they examined it closely, because while Benjamin appears to be emphasizing the "correct political tendency," it can just as easily be interpreted that inherent in that tendency is the literary quality determined by the literary tendency, the latter privileged in that it shapes the political. He says as much when he condemns dogmatic or tendentious writing for lacking the literary quality derived of the literary tendency.[137]

Furthermore, to not be the spectator, or the tourist at a safe distance behind the safety glass of the tour bus, but to "struggle" with the material, to "intervene actively" in its interpretation, always leaves an opening for—and does not deny—participation in the kind of performative act associated with reader response. And it echoes Bakhtin's open-ended or inconclusive present, which results in the competing voices of the dialogic. That, of course, can lead to resistance against whichever party or ideology is in power. We detect in Benjamin's position critical perspectives not dissimilar to those of other critics on the possibilities inherent in a literary reportage or journalism.

As Maxim Gorky observed in 1931, postrevolutionary reportage of the kind Tretyakov wrote had become widespread in the Soviet Union: "The broad flow of sketches is a phenomenon such as has never before existed in our literature. . . . The sketchers tell the multimillioned reader about everything that his energy is creating over the whole huge expanse of the Soviet Union, at all points where the creative energy of the working class is being applied."[138] Sketchers, it should be emphasized, is synonymous with "ocherkists," according to Gorky's Russian original.[139] Although prerevolutionary Russia had a tradition of literary reportage in the form of the *ocherk*, what had not existed before was, in Gorky's view, the "broad flow."

One example of an extended or book-length *ocherk* in the Soviet Union is *Belomor*, published in 1934. *Belomor* is an account of the construction of the White Sea–Baltic Sea canal ("Belomor" is a compressed name for the project, which was known as the "Belomor kanal," which in turn derives from "Beloe more," meaning White Sea). It was the work of three editors, of whom the most notable was Gorky. He contributed the introductory chapter.[140] As one might expect, such works often descended into unambiguous propaganda, as their purpose was to promote the construction of socialism. In *Belomor,* for example, engineer Zubrik had been a "wrecker," or saboteur, of Soviet industry. He had risen from the ranks of the proletariat to that of the bourgeoisie before the revolution. The concluding paragraph of the chapter about Zubrik notes: "Engineer Zubrik honestly earned his right to return again to the bosom of the class in which he was born. Engineer Zubrik earned this right by making a second vital exertion at Belomorstroy," where he contributed to the construction of a difficult dam project, "—the most important exertion of his life. He cast aside all his former [meaning bourgeois] views, illusions, and prejudices—all that with which the bourgeoisie had once poisoned this young proletarian, sprung from the very heart of an oppressed class."[141] In such polemics, then, the story becomes another ideological morality play on behalf of socialist construction. What is not mentioned is that engineer Zubrik performs his duties under duress, for he is a slave laborer, a part of the vast system of penal labor camps known as the Gulag.

But because the early years resulted in much experimentation, works at times did not fall within convenient genre boundaries, and the result can be genre confusion. An example is Valentin Kataev's *Time, Forward!*, a 1933

book-length account depicting twenty-four hours during which construction workers set a world record for pouring concrete at the construction site
of Magnitogorsk, one of the large-scale Soviet industrialization projects.[142]
(Kataev and Shklovsky, incidentally, were also contributors to *Belomor*.)[143]
When it comes to books dedicated to socialist construction, *Time, Forward!*
is considered one of the most successful works of socialist realism, and
indeed described as a "masterpiece."[144] But it is also problematic. Many scholars describe it as a novel, and some as a fiction.[145] More formally, in Soviet
letters, it is described as a "production" novel.[146] But what remains unclear
is whether by labeling it a "novel" that means it must necessarily be a fiction.
Even those who view it as fiction admit that it is "semi-fictional," and thus
reveal their own uncertainty with Kataev's approach.[147] The question then
is whether it is viewed as fictional because it is made up, or because it uses
techniques for so long associated with fiction but which in fact, as demonstrated elsewhere, long preceded modern fiction in nonfiction or narrative
documentary accounts?[148]

Wagner characterizes the work as an *ocherk*, which is a line taken by Harriet Borland when she places it in the camp of "sketchers."[149] But the confusion should not be surprising given that in the attempts at experimentation
"the dividing line between novelist and journalist was to be swept away, the
hybrid result being the sketch-writer, or 'sketcher.'"[150] (And recall, too, the
translation of the title to Turgenev's *A Hunter's Sketches*, which was part fiction and part true.)

Wolfgang Kasack, for one, describes the work as a "chronicle *povest*,"[151]
meaning story, tale, or chronicle in Russian, which echoes Kataev's characterization of his work as a "chronicle." Moreover, Kataev says the account
is largely true. In the second-to-last chapter Kataev addresses a letter to
"Comrade A. Smolyan," a special correspondent for the Russian Telegraphic
Agency (perhaps better known in the United States as the agency responsible
for so many socialist posters that achieved the status of avant-garde art).
Kataev dedicates the chapter to "Sasha" Smolyan because of his assistance on
the project. The author adds:

> I hope that you will not chide me especially for having invented a thing or
> two here and there.
>   For example, the elephant. There really was no elephant. I made him up. . . .
>   As for the rest, I stuck to the truth as much as possible.

Thus he corrects the record with the intent of erasing his fiction.[152] The
approach is unusual of course, especially for those who take the position that
there is or should be an absolute divide between fiction and nonfiction. At

the least Kataev is playing a mind game with his readers, because the passage comes near the book's conclusion.

Moreover, in support of his claim that the events are mostly true, Kataev used pseudonyms for the characters. In a parenthetical note in the text addressed to Smolyan, he observes: "(Of course, it is not necessary to reveal the pseudonyms to you. You have guessed them long ago, and it is all the same to the readers.)" He then signs the chapter with his initials, "V.K."[153] The use of pseudonyms is hardly new to narrative literary journalism in the United States. Again, James Agee did it with his white southern sharecroppers in *Let Us Now Praise Famous Men*. And as we will see, the use of pseudonyms becomes important to the later *ocherki* and the Chinese version. At the very least *Time, Forward!* is on the order of Upton Sinclair's *The Jungle*, which has often been viewed as journalism (albeit a muckraking version), even though its characters are fictional. But there is evidence that *Time, Forward!* is much more, given its experimental nature, and that "the dividing line between novelist and journalist was to be swept away, the hybrid result being the sketch-writer, or 'sketcher.' "

What is clear from the volume, and what a number of critics agree on, is that it is weak when it comes to reflecting interior consciousness.[154] This quality has implications that further contribute to its journalistic status, because the emphasis is on fast-paced description, or what Marc Slonim characterizes as a "cinematographic style of flashbacks, rapidly shifting scenes, terse dialogue."[155] The lack of psychological realism provides indirect evidence that *Time Forward!* is more an effort at phenomenal referentiality despite Kataev's self-confessed liberties with the facts, such as the elephant. (A circus elephant escapes—in the book—and hampers efforts at pouring concrete.) As observed elsewhere, one of the shortcomings of a narra-descriptive journalism—as opposed to conventional fictions—is that it cannot express interior consciousness unless that consciousness tells the journalist what he or she was thinking at the time.[156] The exception would be for first-person narratives, and in such cases only for their first-person narrators. In *Time, Forward!* the emphasis tends to be on description, or the "cinematographic style of flashbacks, rapidly shifting scenes, terse dialogue." At the least, the emphasis on a phenomenal referentiality *sans* interior consciousness is consistent with other narrative *ocherki*.

Slonim's description of Kataev's style is remarkable for another reason when he notes that the book "is somewhat reminiscent of American expressionists, particularly the early Dos Passos (who, in the 1930's had many admirers as well as excellent translators in the Soviet Union)."[157] Indeed, Struve says that "Kataev was certainly influenced in his technique by Dos Passos."[158]

It has already been observed that Dos Passos contributed to *The New Masses*. Moreover, when Joseph North, Granville Hicks, and Michael Gold produced their anthology *Proletarian Literature in the United States* in 1933, they included one fictional and one reportage piece by Dos Passos, thus providing more evidence of a transnational and cosmopolitan aesthetic that had developed as a result of the proletarian writers' movement.[159]

It is because of the tendentious trend in the Soviet narrative *ocherk* that Victor Shklovsky's narrative *A Sentimental Journey* in those early years of the young Soviet Union stands out in sharp relief, especially when compared to the "first place" occupied by John Reed's *Ten Days That Shook the World*. The first part of *A Sentimental Journey* was initially published in Berlin in 1923 while Shklovsky was in temporary exile (although sections had been published earlier in Russia). Shklovsky is widely regarded as one of the founders of Russian Formalism, which he helped to inaugurate during the First World War and the period of relative creative freedom of the early 1920s in the Soviet Union. One result was *A Sentimental Journey*.

The volume is at first glance a curious work but one that demonstrates a commitment to Bakhtin's concept of the "open-ended present." When *A Sentimental Journey* appeared, "it was hailed . . . as a promising new trend in the Russian novel," according to Richard Sheldon. In this instance, however, the "novel" was not fictional, and reveals again how traditional generic boundaries were being violated. Shklovsky's aesthetic theorizing would evolve, so that "extending a tendency already present in *A Sentimental Journey*, he asserted that the new Russian reading public had ceased to respond to long, intricate forms and now preferred unadorned 'factography.'" In Shklovsky's case, *A Sentimental Journey* was a narrative factography. Furthermore, Sheldon continues, Shklovsky "led the exploration and refinement of such genres as the newspaper article, the feuilleton, and the sketch, forms that became prominent during the thirties. Out of these genres, he expected a new Russian literature to develop."[160]

But Shklovsky differs from Tretyakov and Kisch in one important way with regard to a journalistic narrative, at least as reflected in *A Sentimental Journey*. The book is described as having a "disjointed, polychromatic quality," and thus reveals a commitment to the multivocal, open-ended present, one that defies a global ideology, whether political or as a narrative unity. It is true that during the repressive Stalinist years, Shklovsky survived by publicly tempering his literary views to conform with the official screeds of socialist realism. Nonetheless, *A Sentimental Journey* remained, its pages presenting to every new reader for interpretation the re-creation of the "open-ended present." (That said, when the book was published in the Soviet Union in 1924 and 1929, cuts were made for political reasons; so we detect the attempt to silence the multivocality of the open-ended present the censors feared.)[161]

A Sentimental Journey was intentionally named for Laurence Sterne's similarly named volume, *A Sentimental Journey through France and Italy*. Both Shklovsky and Bakhtin were enthusiasts of Sterne's 1768 account of the 1765 travels in which "Mr. Yorick" served as Sterne's largely undisguised alter ego (much the way "Raoul Duke" served for Hunter S. Thompson in *Fear and Loathing in Las Vegas*). To understand the significance of the title, one must understand what is meant by "sentimental." The late eighteenth-century meaning in European letters meant a display of feelings, an emotional response, and was at the time a reaction against the rationalism of the Age of Enlightenment or Reason. In other words, Shklovsky (and Sterne) embraced what today we would call a highly subjective stance.

Still, Shklovsky's version of a sentimental journey is very different from Sterne's travelogue, and the choice of title is ironic, indeed absurdly ironic. He writes of his experiences in the Russian army during World War I, the Russian Revolution, and the subsequent Russian civil war. In doing so he describes them as a series of accidents and comedies of errors with deadly and tragic consequences. To him, the Bolsheviks took power only by default. "Russia invented the Bolsheviks as a motivation for desertion and plunder," he writes. He agrees that the "Bolsheviks were strong in that their goal was definite and simple." But as a political body they were weak and few in number. In the end, exhausted by war, people simply did not care. The result was that the ascendancy of the communists was largely an accident.[162] Significantly, he does not posit a deus ex machina. Rather, Shklovsky acknowledges only an indecipherable unknown that makes an absurdity of human ambition. This is reflected in the anecdotes, long and short, which he provides, and which often beg for explanation. For example:

> I remember seeing one of my students after I returned from Persia [where Shklovsky had been temporarily posted]:
> "What are you doing now?"
> "Robbing houses, sir. If you'll indicate apartments for us to rob, we'll give you ten percent."
> Strictly a business proposition.
> He was eventually shot.[163]

The calm manner with which Shklovsky describes his encounter could be the same in which one discusses everyday banalities, like the way one negotiates with the neighborhood kid, who politely addresses you as "sir," for cutting the front lawn. Strictly a business proposition, sir. And then, after cutting the grass, the kid is shot. Such is the familiar made unfamiliar.

While posted to northern Persia, which had been occupied by Russia since before World War I, he writes about the lack of underwear for Russian soldiers. Many had soaked theirs in oil to burn for warmth. They had asked for more and were told they were unavailable. Then, as they evacuated Persia, they discovered otherwise at a supply depot:

> "What's this?
> "It's the emergency reserve."
> It was an emergency reserve of inertia.
> It was now being burned.[164]

Or, just before the October Revolution in Petrograd (which he misses by only weeks because he departs for Iran), he attends a meeting as a representative to the Petrograd Soviet to hear representatives from different political factions:

> The meeting took place in our driver's school [Shklovsky was an armored car instructor], in a hall where we had fixed up an amphitheater for students. In the upper rows, with their heads on the tables, sat some soldiers from one of the units. There were six of them; of these, three were too drunk to lift their heads.
> And Chernov droned on, with trills and crescendos.[165]

These are hardly the heroics of a revolution.

To add to the absurdity, he works on a book of literary criticism throughout the revolution, whether in the trenches or in flight from the communists, called "The Connection Between Plot Devices and General Stylistic Devices" regarding the novel, a title that changes as the narrative proceeds.[166]

He is so weary of the absurdity (reminiscent of Sartre's Roquentin in *Nausea*) of the so-called revolution that he requests the transfer that will take him to Persia: "Frustration had driven me to the brink, the way the moon draws a somnambulist to the roof. I got on a train and set out for Persia." It is no wonder, then, that later he muses in his own words on the "absurdity of life" atop a haystack in the Russian countryside, looking up at the beauty of the stars in the night sky while hiding from Bolsheviks and working out his ideas for a book of literary criticism.[167]

For these reasons, Shklovsky, again not positing a deus ex machina such as "the controlling hand of fate," embraces the narrative of the open-ended or inconclusive present. In revealing the absurdities, he writes in the tradition of Sterne.

In contrast to Shklovsky, John Reed, in his account of the Russian Revolution, *Ten Days That Shook the World*, embraces the distanced image of the past. Reed, of course, presents a problem, because he is an American and not Russian. But Chuzhak ranked Reed's book first for factographic narrative.

And the Bolsheviks saw Reed as one of their own. He is, of course, buried in Red Square in Moscow with other heroes of the revolution. Reed places the events of the revolution as part of a larger inevitability of history. "There were certain definite things for which the Russian Revolution had been made," he announces on the second page of the book. And with the establishment of Bolshevik authority on the last page, he concludes what the revolution was "made" for, citing the final words of an official Bolshevik decree at a peasants' congress that announces the "victory of Socialism."[168] Thus, in a tidy polemical package, his account is inclined toward the "distanced image of the absolute past" in much the way of the mythologies of ancient epics, except that Reed's is a secular mythology. What we hear is the monologic of a history that Bakhtin would challenge in the example of Tolstoy, not the dialogic of competing voices such as in Dostoevsky's novels.[169]

But we should not be surprised. Reed's knowledge of the Russian language was slight at best.[170] As a participant-observer he had to depend on translators, who told him what they wanted him to hear, as is the case with any translation. It is little different from what tour guides do in selling the local sights to what Americans wish to believe (or other nationalities, for that matter, who believe that Disney World is the real "America"). As it turned out, Reed's translators were often Russian American communists who had returned to Russia to participate in the revolution.[171] So poor was Reed's Russian-language facility that when he met Lenin, the latter lectured him on learning Russian.[172] Moreover, Reed wrote the book in New York City after he returned from Russia, using a Russian-American dictionary to translate Russian documents, not the most promising way for translating the idiomatic nuances of a language one does not know. It is no wonder that one historian observed of Reed's account: "As with most writers, Reed heightened the drama, and this drama sometimes took over from reality. . . . Reed's book founded a legend, one which has largely triumphed over the facts."[173] It was a legend—a myth—that could not speak, it must be emphasized, the language of which it wrote.

Compared to Shklovsky, Reed was more an American tourist reporting on the revolution. What Shklovsky's example reminds us of is that a literary reportage is meant to be inherently or covertly subversive. Paradoxically, a narrative literary journalism and to some extent revolutionary literary reportage appear to have subversion in common, but for different reasons. As early proponents like Kisch understood, they were subversives in their advocacy of world revolution. But the subversion was polemical and the ideology overt. Shklovsky's was subtle and, again, covert. Similarly, the New Journalism of the 1960s and 1970s in the United States was subversive. But like Shklovsky, the subversion is more subtle. This is because such a narrative literary journalism resists overt ideological prescriptions. In other words, there can be no absolute and global critical closure in such documentary accounts focused on the differences among the concrete metaphors.

The early advocates of such narratives in the Soviet Union did recognize the importance of the phenomenal particular as individual concrete metaphor. Chuzhak, in *The Literature of Fact* (1929), observed, "We must understand any object in its specificity and approach objects 'as intimates.'" For him, Shklovsky served as the example: "Shklovsky is also enormously attentive to the object and to its specificity. For him, 'every flea is a flea,' and there are no 'uninteresting' objects." Still, Chuzhak would reinscribe such a discourse in the construction of a grand, global plan:

> Yes, we would like it if every uncorrupted young writer were really a "soldier" for the new construction, rejecting the path of least resistance paved by devices and forms organically alien to our era [meaning belletristic fiction]. This explains our categorical aversion to two equally malignant developments ("malignant" because they consistently undermine the tasks of our time): the diversion of thousands of potential proletarian writers away from direct work upon reality, and the redirecting of their attention toward literary fiction. *We are against the literature of fiction that is called belles lettres. We are for the primacy of the literature of fact.* For too long writers have "transfigured" the world by spiriting the passive, aesthetically stupefied reader away into a world of representations. When, if not now, could we reconstruct this world through the concrete changes required by the proletariat?[174]

The italicized emphasis is his, and in the grand plan the concrete metaphor lost what made it different and distinctive in the interests of communist literary values.

Such would be the case until the 1950s and the death of Stalin. But once he died, a new period was ushered in known as the "Khruschev thaw," which had broad implications for arts and letters. Among the more notable examples of writers of the *ocherk* in the Soviet Union during this period was Valentin Ovechkin. In the early 1950s he started to publish *ocherki* about collective farm life.[175] Ovechkin never lost sight of the socialist dream, and by the standards of, perhaps, the American experience, his *ocherki* may appear little different from the reportage of the 1920s and 1930s. But in their time his sketches provided a direct challenge to the prevailing literary ideology of "socialist realism," evidence that there can be degrees of resistance even if a work is not overtly iconoclastic. Ovechkin would take greater liberties with the form that approached, from a Western perspective, the fictional. But the practice was not new, as we saw with Kataev and Dostoevsky. Ovechkin's *ocherki* are based on his experiences as a collective farm manager, but he used fictional names. Received and perceived as journalistic sketches, they broke with the tradition of accounts that dealt with real life reflected in idealized heroes of socialist labor. Instead, he chose to write about real-life problems using pseudonyms. In Ovechkin's case this reveals an epistemological paradox very much at odds with prevailing journalistic paradigms in the United States, namely, that real-life problems conveyed with fictional names were more believable than the endless stream of real-life Soviet heroes idealized beyond credible belief.[176] But again, pseudonyms are not unknown in narrative literary journalism in the United States.

In 1953 the literary journal *Novy Mir* published an essay by the Soviet literary critic Vladimir Pomerantsev. In it he complained that there was little in the then contemporary practice of *ocherki* that was "sincere." In his view, the *ocherk* had become largely a rubber stamp for Soviet societal successes. The problem, Pomerantsev said, was that *ocherki* failed to acknowledge, much less address, societal problems and so lacked social "sincerity." In other words, such writing was part of a closed critical system of Soviet self-adulation. After taking to task failed examples that had become predominant during the period of Stalinist cultural hegemony, he praised the *ocherki* of Ovechkin for having the "sincerity" or integrity to report on the realities of collective farm life: "Ovechkin speaks of things which previously were not described. Before him, these topics were avoided, treated with silence. Some writers didn't see them at all; others considered these things to be under the jurisdiction of higher authorities and would not undertake to discuss them without their approval. But this writer took the topics and spoke about them so as to aid the higher authorities!" While Ovechkin's sketches may seem ideologically naïve today—his purpose, after all, was to "aid the higher authorities"—they were remarkable in their time for being willing to challenge the system at all. The challenge, of course, was on behalf of illustrating real-life problems of socialist construction. Indeed, Ovechkin's work, along with Pomerantsev's essay in *Novy Mir*, is considered among the groundbreaking instruments for the cultural "thaw."[177]

Ovechkin's international influence is reflected in the role he played as a mentor to the young Liu Binyan, one of China's most influential writers of *baogao wenxue* or *texie* starting in the 1950s, thus demonstrating once again the cosmopolitan cross-fertilization made possible by international communism. Liu's work eventually proved too subversive for the government. The result was that Liu was not permitted to return to China after he came to the United States in 1988 to teach and write. He spent the rest of his life in exile.[178] As with Ovechkin, Liu similarly took greater liberties with the form that approach, from a Western perspective, the fictional. The work that brought Liu fame in China, "At the Building Site of the Bridges," was based on a real event, used fictional names, and was published in a journal dedicated to printing short stories. Yet it was still perceived to be *baogao wenxue* or *texie,* in other words, a form of reportage literature.[179]

One of the beneficiaries of the cultural thaw in the Soviet Union was the Russian poet Anna Akhmatova, who turned, if only modestly, to the Russian and Soviet tradition of the sketch to insert a small *ocherk* in a collection of her poems titled "Requiem." The oldest poem dated back to 1935, a time when the Stalinist repression and secret "trials" were just beginning in earnest. They were poems she could not publish during the Stalin years, when she, widely regarded as one of Russia's greatest poets of the twentieth century (and by some one of the world's greatest),[180] was silenced by the state. During the purges in the late 1930s her third husband, the respected art historian Nikolai Punin, was arrested and died in prison. Lev Gumilev, her son by her first husband, Nikolai Gumilev (who was executed by the Bolsheviks), was also arrested and spent eighteen years in labor camps, although he survived to become one of the Soviet Union's and Russia's most notable ethnographers and historians.[181]

Akhmatova wrote the *ocherk* appended as an introduction to the group of poems in 1957, when it was safe to do so as a result of the cultural thaw. After all, this was the period when Alexander Solzhenitsyn began to publish. Akhmatova's miniature of an *ocherk* is called "Instead of a Preface," which is clearly ironic, given the name of the collective, "Requiem," because a requiem concludes a life. Now that she is old—she would die in 1965—and these poems, most of which she wrote during the years of repression, can be released to the public, they can only serve as a requiem for what has passed. Similarly, you cannot have a preface to what is now past when its purpose is to inaugurate a beginning.

In the *ocherk,* she recounts how she makes the rounds of prisons in Leningrad, presumably to visit, or get news of, either her husband or her son, although she does not specify (but to her readers it made little difference, given how ubiquitous the experience was). In making those rounds she meets others like herself. The *ocherk* is a brief anecdote and thus short enough to include here in its entirety. The "Yezhovian horror" Akhmatova speaks of is a reference to Nikolai Yezhov, the head of the Soviet secret police, who instituted the purges of the 1930s at the direction of Stalin.

INSTEAD OF A PREFACE

In the awful years of Yezhovian horror, I spent seventeen months standing in line in front of various prisons in Leningrad. One day someone "recognized" me [presumably because of her fame as a poet]. Then a woman with blue lips, who was standing behind me, and who, of course, had never heard my name, came out of the stupor which typified all of us, and whispered into my ear (everyone there spoke only in whispers):

—Can you describe this?

And I said:

—I can.

Then something like a fleeting smile passed over what had once been her face.[182]

The passage illustrates several points. First, and obviously, Akhmatova does not hesitate to draft for her literary purposes another genre, that of the *ocherk*, as offering its own kind of subversive revelation necessary for the introduction of the poems. Second, among the most unambiguous of Akhmatova's subversions is her simple assertion "I can," meaning that she can—and does in the *ocherk*—bear witness on behalf of the future regarding the Stalinist repression. That witness is in her poems, which she could not publish in Stalin's time. Third, the "fleeting smile" on what "had once been her face" of the woman asking the question reveals a subtle resistance against the authoritarian state, and in its fleetingness in a whispered exchange the gesture recalls what Sartre once observed, that even when someone's freedoms are constrained, one can always resist, at least internally.[183] The fleeting smile is just such a modest affirmation of resistance and freedom. Such are the results of the chronotopes of the inconclusive present. This, of course, is what Svetlana Alexievich would later capture in her "new reality," one not only linguistic but cultural as well.

Undoubtedly the most notable beneficiary of the cultural thaw if for no other reason than that he is a Nobel laureate, is Solzhenitsyn, whose *Gulag Archipelago* is an example of extended literary reportage writ on a large narrative and historical stage, a work that Solzhenitsyn characterizes in a subtitle as "An Experiment in Literary Investigation." In the "Author's Note" he insists, regarding the places, people, and events of which he writes, that "it all took place just as described here." But as a literary experiment his has at least as much in common with the reportage of Politkovskaya as with Alexievich's in the drafting of mixed rhetorical modalities. At times Solzhenitsyn's chapters, often first-person accounts of life in the Stalinist slave labor camps, engage largely in narra-description. For example:

And more than once, sitting on his cot in front of the table, propping his pudgy head on his short, pudgy arm, he would start to sing quietly in a sing-song voice and with lost, befogged eyes:

> *Forgotten and abandoned*
> *Since my young, early years,*
> *I was left a tiny orphan. . . .*

He could never get any further than that. At that point, he would break into explosive sobs. All that bursting strength which could not break through the walls that enclosed him he turned inward.[184]

Or, Solzhenitsyn describes how when he was a prisoner, "we were taken through the little emerald park in the Butyrki's interior courtyard, where the birds sang deafeningly, although they were probably only sparrows, and the green of the trees seemed unbearably bright to eyes no longer used to it. Never had my eyes seen the green of leaves with such intensity as they did that spring!"[185] Thus Solzhenitsyn savors a moment of intense personal inner freedom, and from the aesthetics of experience engages in an inherent resistance.

But at other times his is the stance of the polemicist engaging in vituperative accusations. Describing how six collective farmers were executed for cutting hay for their cows, Solzhenitsyn writes, "Even if Stalin had killed no others, I believe he deserved to be drawn and quartered just for the lives of those six Tsarskoye Selo peasants!"[186] Few probably would disagree with the assessment and condemnation of Stalin and his policies. But it is an assessment dismissing Stalin to his fate constatively instead of prompting it imaginatively through description of the differentiating qualities of each farmer. It is difficult to find fault with Solzhenitsyn, given the years he spent in Stalin's prisons. But in coming to his judgment of Stalin, he has placed his account in the distanced image of the absolute past, denying readers their own interpretive possibilities, their own moral outrage. And even in the two earlier examples we see polemics creeping in. When the prisoner bursts into explosive sobs and "turns inward," Solzhenitsyn adds to conclude the sentence "toward self-pity," thus tying up the meaning in a neat summation, instead of letting the reader decide imaginatively what the prisoner is turning inward toward. Similarly, when Solzhenitsyn is exhilarated by the green of spring, he adds, "And never in my life had I seen anything closer to God's paradise than that little Butyrki park, which never took more than thirty seconds to cross on the asphalt path."[187] Because he is on his way to be sentenced, we can, it is true, understand why he feels closer to God, and this also recalls Alexievich's invocation of the spiritual that is infused in so much Russian literature. Solzhenitsyn's deeply held Russian Orthodox faith is no secret. And undoubtedly it helped him survive, as it did Dostoevsky when the latter was imprisoned in Siberia a century earlier. But a polemic it still is, and thus it too provides the interpretation for the meaning of green in the courtyard in a tidy moral package: the open-ended present is denied.

In any event, Solzhenitsyn learned, too, that the ends justify the rhetorical means of production drafted in the interests of the moral enterprise. As he notes cynically of Gorky's *Belomor* in the preface to the first volume of *Gulag Archipelago*, in what is still another polemical diatribe, "Material for this book was also provided by *thirty-six* Soviet writers, headed by *Maxim Gorky*, authors of the disgraceful book on the White Sea Canal, which was the first in Russian literature to glorify slave labor."[188]

Such resistance to the ideological platitudes of communism would earn him, of course, exile from the Soviet Union.

We see in the late 1980s and early 1990s in the Soviet Union and Russia an emerging creative vision regarding cultural production described as *chernukha*, which derives from the Russian word for black, *chernyy*, meaning a black genre. In the final years of the Soviet experience it challenged the cultural status quo, the habits of seeing. And here the tradition of the *ocherk* comes full circle. As Aleksandr A. Genis notes, *chernukha* during the late Soviet period of the 1980s was often just a reinvention of the physiological sketch from 150 years earlier in Russia.[189] And yet that tradition was also very much part of a transnational exchange.

Of course, this period of Soviet decline and a renewed Russia is when Alexievich and Politkovskaya found their voices as authors of literary reportage. As noted, they provided the point of departure, but they are also the point of return. Not only are Alexievich and Politkovskaya practitioners of literary reportage as it evolved out of their own native traditions reaching back to the nineteenth century, but they are also heirs to the broader transnational European tradition. What their *ocherki*, or reportage literature, demonstrate is that if political ideology can co-opt the differences in the concrete metaphor of the inconclusive present, as such literature did for much of the Soviet period, the opposite is equally true. The phenomenal particular and what about it is unassimilable always has the potential to challenge established ideologies. This has happened repeatedly, such as, for example, in the Chinese experience. "What makes reportage literature fascinating," according to Charles Laughlin, "is precisely its ability to satisfy such different expectations, especially in that through its commitment to concrete experience it resists easy assimilation into the machines of propaganda. That is, although it is ironically a form of great importance and treasured by the Chinese Communist Party, it possesses within it more than other forms, such as fiction and poetry, the potential to critique the shortcomings of the socialist order it helped bring about."[190]

The same has been observed of the communist Polish reportage tradition during the Cold War period. Of it, Susan Greenberg writes, "The long, post-war years of communist censorship are commonly credited as a source of perverse inspiration for the writers of the former Soviet bloc, providing practice in the literary Game of disguising universal meanings in the detail of the text."[191] Diana Kuprel adds, "Reporters had to employ in their report-age sophisticated strategies of encoding in order to pass censorship," which readers then had to decipher by deploying "a highly critical sensibility."[192] The result was a resistance against and subversion of the existing political order. Still elsewhere, Sonja Merljak Zdovc has detected the similar circumstances in the Slovene tradition, strongly influenced by the communist experience when Slovenia was part of Tito's Yugoslavia: "Since journalists could not openly state their opinion of the political system, they wrapped it up in a feature story that had elements of short stories from the era of social realism. When painting the picture of poverty, they actually criticized the socialist authorities."[193] The "painting" of the aesthetics of experience provided the indictment.

Clearly, subversion is at the heart of Alexievich's "new reality," confronting what the Soviet authorities did not want to acknowledge: the impact of the Afghan war on the lives of Soviet citizens. As she notes of her interviews that became the basis of the book: "Every confession was like a portrait. They are not documents; they are images. I was trying to present a history of feelings, not the history of war [in Afghanistan] itself."[194] In the attempt to provide a history of feelings, we see her, whether consciously or not, embracing the "sentimental" of Shklovsky derived from the eighteenth-century meaning, one found in the details of the open-ended present that seeks to escape ten-dentiousness.

We know what happened to Politkovskaya because she insisted on report-ing on the phenomenal evidence of the atrocities committed by both sides in the Chechen war. She paid for her moral courage with her life when she was murdered in 2006.[195]

For our purposes, Alexievich clearly is much more a practitioner in the tradition of a narrative literary journalism similar to the American tradition (but again, not because she was influenced by the American). Politkovskaya, by contrast, is a sometime practitioner more rooted in the polemical discur-sive tradition to be found in the European feuilleton and the earlier physiol-ogy, a tradition that is much more rhetorically heterogeneous.

What can be detected, then, are two traditions that at times can be closely aligned. Narrative literary reportage and literary journalism are much the same when they both emphasize narrative and descriptive modalities and eschew digressive polemic. But while narrative literary journalism engages Bakhtin's inconclusive present, literary reportage historically has either done so or been co-opted by unambiguous ideology. The result poses an ongoing epistemological tension between two contraries: On one side are advocates of the form like Kisch and Politkovskaya who sought to bring the specular attempt to capture the inconclusive present in phenomena to epistemological closure. On the other are those like Alexievich who resisted such closure when embracing and emphasizing the inconclusive present over ideology. In this last, readers are permitted to draw their own conclusions—to engage in an imaginative dialogue—when presented with the evidence of the aesthetics of experience in the form of narra-description.

Another way to approach the "elasticity" of literary reportage is to recognize that rhetorically there are really many different literary reportages that can be deduced by modality and whether there is or is not unambiguous polemical intent (as opposed to subtle and ambiguous intent if one grants that all discourse to some extent always reflects ideology). Thus there can be (1) a polemical literary reportage that is discursive in nature; (2) a narra-descriptive literary reportage that is frozen in the tendentiousness of the distanced image of the absolute past; and (3) a narra-descriptive literary reportage that is much the same as narrative literary journalism, embracing the inconclusive or open-ended present that grants free interpretive possibilities to the author and reader. And yet the reality may all too often be one of degree among the three possibilities.

There is one consequence, however, to delineating the genre as one struggling between the open-ended present and the distanced image of the past, a consequence that may not sit well with some critics. A narra-descriptive literary reportage frozen in the tendentiousness of the distanced image of the absolute past seeks to foreclose free interpretive meanings and deny competing voices—the "performance" that engages readers in the "realizing" of a new reality and that encourages them in an act of imaginative self-efficacy. Such ersatz work is not a true "literary" journalism but rather an imitation designed to deny free interpretive possibilities.

So we can conclude that there is a qualitative difference when we are confronted by the distanced image of the past or the open-ended or inconclusive present. Because it is the differentiating qualities of experience in the latter that make the familiar unfamiliar. If the familiar only confirms the familiar in the distanced image of the absolute past, then all we are doing is preaching to the choir. And they are already among the converted.

5

Negotiating Cultural and
Personal Revelation

Aₗₑₓₐₙ𝒹ᵣₐ Fᵤₗₗₑᵣ's *Scribbling the Cat: Travels with an African Soldier* is a slender and ambitious volume, but at the same time a troubling one as the author attempts to navigate back and forth between a narrative literary journalism and what conventionally we would call memoir.[1] Thus she challenges our preconceptions of what constitutes genre. And one can legitimately ask the question: Is there any real difference between narrative literary journalism and memoir if both are fundamentally narra-descriptive, or chronotopic, in their referentiality to a phenomenal world? Moreover, one of the hallmarks of both a narrative literary journalism and memoir is that they are much more subjective discourses when compared to the conventional objectifying models of journalism dominant for so long in American practice. The result is that the boundaries between a narra-descriptive journalism and narra-descriptive memoir are not neatly delineated.

But within such a broadly ranging supra- or quantum genre, as it might be characterized, we can also detect modulations that distinguish by degree or emphasis between the two. Even a cursory glance at John Hersey's *Hiroshima* and Vladimir Nabokov's *Speak, Memory* reveals this.

My purpose is to examine this relationship, using *Scribbling the Cat* as a point of departure. From it I move on to explore how Linda Grant's *People on the Street* and Vladimir Nabokov's *Speak, Memory* successfully negotiate by degrees a narrative literary journalism in the first and memoir in the second. Then I return to Sara Davidson's "Real Property," discussed initially in chapter 3, to examine how she successfully engages in both. What we will find is that the two genres can overlap, and comfortably so. Also, to clarify, I do not suggest that all memoir is chronotopic. Just as there are different journalisms, there can also be different memoirs, often not much more than running accounts lacking in descriptive texture.

Inherently memoir's intention is personal revelation, given the author's subject, herself or himself as protagonist.[2] Inherently, as I suggested in the introduction, the intention of a narrative literary journalism (like any journalism) is cultural revelation, but a revelation very much personally inflected through a subjective voice when compared to more conventional models of journalism. This is where the concept of a narrative continuum or spectrum is helpful for understanding the relationship across such a range of discourses. Again, compared to more conventional mainstream models of journalism, the narra-descriptive version is in degree or emphasis much more personally inflected. But the same version compared to memoir is in degree or emphasis much more culturally inflected or revealing.

Herein lies the nexus of the issue involving the relationship between memoir and narra-descriptive journalism. You cannot have a stronger emphasis on the personal revelation of memoir without attaching some accouterments of cultural context; otherwise to do so would be to drift off into the ether of solipsism. Similarly, you cannot have the stronger emphasis on cultural revelation without the shaping consciousness of the author revealing herself or himself in a narra-descriptive journalism.[3] The issue then comes down to the degree of emphasis when it comes to deciding whether a work is more disposed toward personal revelation or cultural revelation. Fuller's *Scribbling the Cat* is, I would suggest, an attempt at both a narra-descriptive journalism and memoir. This results, however, in shortcomings which are instructive for such efforts.

The problem is that *Scribbling the Cat* betrays at times an unevenness, both structural and emotional. The reason is clear: Fuller the journalist quickly becomes implicated in something much larger within herself, something that remains unresolved, namely, how much to reveal of herself. *Scribbling the Cat* tells of Fuller's encounter and travels with a white former soldier from the long-extinct army of the breakaway British colony of Rhodesia, today's Zimbabwe. Hers is an attempt to come to terms with one of the losers of history. And that is why she is implicated. Because this is also a book about Fuller trying to come to terms with her past as a member of that tribe which became lost in history. She is white, was born in England in 1969, and came with her parents to Rhodesia when she was two years old. They came to farm, but eventually, after losing two farms to government appropriation in Zimbabwe after the white Rhodesian resistance collapsed, her parents moved the family to Malawi and then Zambia. Fuller was thirteen when they left Rhodesia, and like so many losers of history, she and her family scattered across the globe. Her parents remained in Zambia to operate a banana and fish-breeding farm. Fuller now lives in Wyoming and is divorced from her American husband. She has three children.[4]

The book was also the winner of the Lettre Ulysses Award in 2005. The selection committee demonstrated some courage in selecting a book that sympathetically portrayed such politically incorrect losers of history—especially Fuller's subject, and in a sense alter ego, the white former soldier and now Zambian farmer she calls "K," who from the age of seventeen was trained to be a killer in the notorious Rhodesian Light Infantry. In that regard, the committee defied what seems to be a strain of narrative literary journalism in recent years that reflects a politically correct social consciousness.

It is because the losers of history also have a voice that *Scribbling the Cat* has something in common with Mikhail Sholokhov's *Quiet Flows the Don*. This may appear an unseemly comparison; Fuller's slender volume is, to be sure, no four-volume Russian epic. Still, both Sholokhov and Fuller examine those who lost, and how they were scattered by that loss, geographically, psychically, spiritually, emotionally, until all they want is to return to some semblance of home despite the scars of their memories—Grigory Melekhov to the embrace of his small son, Fuller to her then husband and Montana home, and K, the trained-killer-turned-farmer, to starting a family again after the death of his son. For K it is the only antidote of promise to his past as he takes an uneasy comfort in his born-again Christianity, the unease surfacing when this former killing machine all too easily weeps from what appears to be a deep pool of guilt and regret.[5]

What we find in such complex, paradoxical portraits is that there is much to learn from the losers of history, and therein lies part of Fuller's promise and strength.

To some extent, *Scribbling the Cat* ("scribbling the cat" is, or rather was, white Rhodesian argot for "killing the cat," and reflects in part Fuller's intention in tracking down her tribe's and her own ghosts) is a continuation in theme of her first book, *Don't Let's Go to the Dogs Tonight: An African Childhood,* a critically acclaimed memoir of growing up in the old white Rhodesia while looking for terrorists under the bed, as well as her family's at times hilarious attempts to live a life that could never be normal during a time of civil war.[6] Fuller's style is reminiscent of a number of writers. They include Bruce Chatwin, Joan Didion, and Ernst Jünger. What they have in common in their narrative literary journalism is their skill at selecting details that beg for larger meaning, the resonance again of the particular in a contextual vacuum. It is the reader who will attempt to fill the vacuum.

For example, at the conclusion to the chapter where Fuller has met K for the first time—he has descended on her parents' farm to see her because he rarely gets to see a white woman, living as he does on his isolated banana plantation in the Zambian bush or *shateen*—Fuller writes: "I watched the pickup back out of the yard and, in a paste of mud, grind up the slick driveway. Mud splattered the side of the vehicle and flew out behind the back wheels in little red pellets. A cascade of egrets, rattled by the commotion, erupted out of the green grass and banked around to the fish ponds above the camp, their wings paper-white against the gray clouds."[7] End of chapter—and her introduction to K. So she teases the reader out of thought with phenomenal particulars lacking in elaborate or extended literary symbolism beyond being concrete metaphors; they are the meaningless detritus of phenomenal life that surrounds us. We yearn to decipher a meaning that ultimately may not be there. And beyond the concrete metaphors lie the immeasurable regions of the unassimilable that we faintly know exist in the phenomenal world, posing their threat of emerging in the future. It is a kind of foreshadowing, indirect and muted.

Moreover, Fuller's description "breathes" with a refreshing personification. It can be detected in the following examples: "the heat outside *sung* its stinging tune," or in the Sole Valley, where her parents have their farm, "the elevation rises just a few feet above *ennui*," or the "town of Sole has *metastasized* off the cluster of buildings that make up the border post between Zambia and Zimbabwe," and the "brilliant sunset that had *speared*, in slices of orange and *bleeding* red, through the mopane trees, had turned *sullen*." At the same time she engages in the opposite, investing emotional states with a sharp, deprived depersonalization. For example, she writes of her relationship with K, "there were pieces of me and pieces of him, and pieces of our history that were *barbed* together in a tangle in my head and I couldn't shake the feeling that in some inevitable way, I was responsible for K. And he for me."[8] Personification and its reverse, depersonification of emotional states, are hardly original. But here they are refreshing, given recent trends in narrative literary journalism to give the genre an ethnographic flavor, as if that granted respectability—more literal, and lacking in aesthetic resonance. I explore this issue more fully in the next chapter.

There is one possible exception to Fuller's emotionally edgy description: critics have noted that the description of K is unrealistically idealized.[9] On that I agree, but only up to a point. This is how he is introduced:

Even at first glance, K was more than ordinarily beautiful, but in a careless, superior way, like a dominant lion or an ancient fortress. . . . His lips

were full and sensual, suggesting a man of quick, intense emotion. His nose
was unequivocal—hard and ridged. . . . His thick hair was battleship gray,
trimmed and freshly washed. He had large, even, white teeth.

He looked bulletproof and he looked as if he were here on *purpose*, which
is a difficult trick to pull off in this wooly climate. He looked like he was his
own self-sufficient, debt-free, little nation. . . . As if he owned the ground
beneath his feet, and as if the sky balanced with ease on his shoulders.

He looked cathedral.

What is a man of your obvious beauty and talent doing in a place like this?[10]

So Fuller swoons in her reverie. I have added the elisions for a purpose,
because what emerges is what we might read in the historical romances that
construct our mythic Rhett Butlers. But I agree with the critics about the idealization only so far. Because they miss a point: despite the idealized description, K is all too imperfect. Beneath is a man who is terribly scarred—by war
and by having been trained as a killer at the age of seventeen to be merciless,
by the death of his five-year-old son from meningitis and his failed marriage,
and by his unrequited love for Fuller. Some may see his religion as a scar, too,
and others as a strength, because what is clear from the book is that it is about
the only thing holding him together. Fuller acknowledges what women often
have to acknowledge: that beneath the exteriors of men they idealize—those
who occupy the pages of historical romances—most are irredeemably flawed.
(In this regard, she and Sara Davidson have much in common, as we saw
in chapter 3.) Perhaps what the critics have not acknowledged are their own
failed expectations of men, failed because they were unreal from the outset.
The description of K, as it emerges, defies what we long to believe as reflected
in our habits of seeing.

Nor is this the only instance of turning conventional expectations and
assumptions on their head in Fuller's volume by making the familiar unfamiliar. We see it in the troubling first sentence of the book: "Because it is
the land that grew me, and because they are my people. . . . "[11] That might
be the sine qua non for Fuller's existence—at least in this book. It is her way
of saying that she sees herself thoroughly rooted in Africa and that she and
her white tribe are as much African as black Africans. In this regard, she
is staking a position little different from that of Americans of European
origin. From the perspective of white, liberal Americans, it is easy to suggest that whites in Rhodesia/Zimbabwe do not belong. But that undoes the
lie for Americans who need to examine their own relationship to the land
their forebears settled. The difference is that unlike many white Americans
today who can acknowledge abstractly the destruction of Native American
society by the founding white fathers and mothers, Fuller has the emotional
courage to say why she believes she belongs in Africa (even though family

circumstances landed her in Wyoming): this is the land that grew me. It is all she knows.

The ongoing tension between what constitutes a narrative literary journalism and what constitutes memoir is what makes the book so ambitious but also poses its biggest challenge. The challenge is reflected in Fuller's attempt to explore her own personal place as one of the losers of history. Thus we see her and K drawn to each other, and the book is in part a story about their unrequited love (or rather his unrequited love for her as it turns out). And unrequited love is in keeping with the theme of the losers of history. (Fuller makes clear, too, that the position of the white Rhodesians was morally wrong; she is no apologist for a lost cause.)

"What is harder to document are the nonfatal casualties of the war," Fuller announces, introducing what she will explore about the culture and land that made her.[12] She takes up the nonfatal casualties of the lost white tribe of Rhodesia—those politically incorrect losers of history whose existence it would be convenient to deny—so that she can demonstrate that they are casualties too, even if the wounds are self-inflicted, and for which it is difficult to have sympathy. In Fuller's account, what we detect is that the boundaries between personal revelation and cultural revelation are messy, imprecise, shifting, and, most important in Fuller's case, the two are indulging of each other. But after she has taken us into her confidence, there are consequences that can leave the reader wondering if she can be trusted.

> I had shaken loose the ghosts of K's past and he had allowed me into the deepest corners of his closet, not because I am a writer and I wanted to tell his story, but because he had believed himself in love with me, and because he had believed that in some very specific way I belonged to him. And in return, I had listened to every word K had spoken, and watched the nuance of his every move, not because I was in love with him, but because I had believed I wanted to write him into dry pages. It had been an idea based on a lie and on a hope neither of us could fulfill. It had been a broken contract from the start.[13]

Fuller could not have been more callous, something critics have noted.[14] She appears the mercenary journalist cruelly playing on K's emotions for her own ends and betraying him.[15] The lack of trust emerges when she spends an evening with Mapenga, one of K's former army colleagues. It is difficult to know what to make of this. The problem is that we cannot be sure what happened between her and Mapenga. All we know is that she gets drunk with him:

> My arms prickled and I felt suddenly dizzy, too full of the drunken night and of the slow, ponderous moon and the stars and of the heat-soaked day.

"The edge of the world," whispered Mapenga.

I rolled onto my back and Mapenga leaned over me. It was a moment before I could make out his face and then his lips were on mine. We kissed and it was some minutes before I felt the sharp edge of rock against my spine and turned my face away.[16]

Fuller engages in literary suggestion. Perhaps elsewhere this would not have posed a problem, but in this instance the account is part of the narrative climax that effectively ends the book. As a result, a furious K and Fuller will part company because he thinks she has had a sexual encounter with Mapenga. She denies it, but this exchange comes later, and given the nature of open-ended literary suggestion, one option is not to believe her. Her credibility is damaged further because what she tells K (her denial) is one thing, but she does not tell the reader outright that there was no sexual intimacy.

In the end, whether there was or not is less important. Rather something in the contract of personal confession has been withheld. Nor would it have been difficult to finesse the matter as part of that contract instead of leaving readers uncertain. To cite a hypothetical example: "I realized only later that I did it because I was drunk, I was confused, I was fed up with searching for something I couldn't find, that I had come to suspect I would never find. I did it because I was disappointed. I was disappointed in myself. I was disappointed in K. I wanted to lash out in my disappointment. I wanted to hurt him because I had permitted myself to be dominated by his history, my history." Some kind of self-reflection could have provided insight—personal revelation. Instead, all we know is that "we kissed and it was some minutes before I felt the sharp edge of rock against my spine and turned my face away." Hence the loaded statement. The next we know, she gets up and says she is going to bed. But she does not say she is doing so to escape Mapenga's advances.

What was lost, moreover, was the opportunity to confirm her father's prediction that gave the book its title. When she wants to visit K's farm for the first time, her father, because he knows K better, warns her, "Curiosity scribbled the cat." And still earlier, when she questions her father about his role in the Rhodesian war against black nationalists, he says, "Don't look back so much or you'll get wiped out on the tree in front of you." Which, in the end, is what happens. This is one of the risks one runs with this kind of writing: How much do you reveal of yourself? How much can you afford to reveal about yourself—to others and yourself? How deeply are you implicated by a double contract in which personal and cultural revelation vie with each other? Therein lies the challenge.

In examining the relationship between a narra-descriptive journalism and memoir, the issue, as I suggested, is how much to emphasize of personal revelation and how much of cultural revelation. We can detect this in the works of Grant, Nabokov, and Davidson, but with different—and successful—outcomes.

Grant, author of *People on the Street*, her account of modern-day Israel, and winner of the Lettre Ulysses Award the year after Fuller, makes it clear that she is using her personal life as a point of departure for a larger cultural examination, though one that will ultimately reflect back on her effort to understand who she is.[17] Grant is better known in the United Kingdom as a novelist (*The Cast Iron Shore, When I Lived in Modern Times, Still Here*). She is a nonbelieving Diaspora Jew who traveled to Tel Aviv in 2003 to write a novel only to set it aside when she discovered a remarkable society in the streets surrounding her. She began writing about daily life among Israeli Jews. Her purpose derived from personal reasons. She wanted to know "what a Jew is" in order to understand her own Jewishness.[18] Thus she recognizes what James Agee understood: that part of the integrity, authority, and authenticity of this kind of writing depends on recognizing one's relationship to what one is writing about.[19] But despite the strong personal motivation, Grant's account is not memoir, nor is it focused exclusively on personal revelation. While she uses her and her family's history—personal revelation—as points of departure, she is committed to what in the balance is more cultural revelation, and the result is her highly complex and textured tapestry of a heterogeneous or "polyglot" (many-voiced) Israeli society that is hardly homogeneous, as reflected in the cascade of vignettes she provides.

Grant makes clear that she is not trained as a journalist and thus can only approach her neighbors in her Tel Aviv community as a novelist. Hence she abjures opinions and political ideologies, turning instead with a keen eye for irony to the details that reveal the culture.[20] They are Wolfe's status details, as discussed in chapter 3. What Grant finds are endless complexities and contradictions irreducible to "opinions" and ideology. She discovers the different stories Israelis tell themselves in order to find a place in the universe and ultimately in Israel. And they are not stories of idealized Zionism. For example, her friend Michal "had two switches: first, the evil conniving corrupt politicians who ran the country, and the idiots who elect them, 'like retarded children the rest of the class has to wait to catch up until they finally understand that you cannot occupy another people forever and so brutally'; and second, shopping. 'You see this necklace? It's from a new store I found, you want to go there? I have a hair appointment at 11:30, just a blow job, but we could go after that, the prices are great.'"[21] That might make Michal seem to be an aging, consumer-oriented airhead except for what follows, her bitterness about what has happened to Israel. Her parents left South Africa in 1948, giving up their vineyards in Stellenbosch for the idealism of the kibbutz, only to see the early socialist values they worked so hard for betrayed by the political process. (The idealism includes, revealingly, an incident in which Michal as a young girl could not own a pretty blouse sent her by an aunt because everything on the kibbutz was communal property, and all the girls Michal's size got to wear it before she could in the interests of communal equality.)[22] Nor was the intention behind those early idealistic kibbutzim to disenfranchise Palestinians. Hence, one can imagine that Michal's self-indulgence with jewelry—her preoccupation with shopping—serves as a distraction from the betrayal of what she and her family had once cherished. But is that not what consumerism is about anyway? A distraction from our own dissatisfactions and disenfranchisements?

Or there is the Iraqi Jew Grant knows who spends all day frying chickpea balls in his falafel café on the block where Grant lives in Tel Aviv. He came with his parents to Israel in 1950 when he was seven,

> " . . . but my father never liked it here. Guess where he took us?"
> "America?"
> "No."
> "France?"
> "No."
> "Berlin?"
> "Tehran." He slapped the side of his head with his hand.[23]

And one can all but hear him moan, "Oy vey . . . Alas, woe." (Nevertheless, the café owner eventually returned to Israel.)

Grant's purpose, then, in narrating the different lives of different Israelis is to demonstrate that each Jew is in Israel because of his or her own story, yes, one often of displacement. But they are not there, contrary to what anti-Zionists say, because of some grand, sweeping ideology. Rather, they all, and Grant acknowledges that this includes the Palestinians, have their own individual reasons for why they are where they are.[24] In a telling observation, she said during her acceptance speech at the Lettre Ulysses Award in 2006 in Berlin, "I did not interview a single politician."[25] The reasons were clear. Politicians, enamored of flimsy sound bites, mouthing platitudes and bromides, do not provide insight into the human condition because they are ensnared in their own self-serving mythologies. She elaborates in her book: "In this part of the world opinions have become so debased a currency on the market place, there's such a glut of them, the inflation rate is so high, that they'll hardly buy you a Jaffa orange."[26] She is assaulting, then, Nietzsche's paler, cooler ideas, the *qualitas occulta*, by trying to return to the concrete metaphors of experience, as problematic as they may prove. It is all in the details and what they reveal. Grant focuses on the Israelis who live on the coastal plain, and especially on her one block in Tel Aviv. One place she was not interested in was Jerusalem. It weighed on her like a "lead helmet" because it was the city that the conventional news media focused their cameras on to capture the usual icons—and clichés—of confrontation between Jew and Arab: Israeli soldiers in helmets and suicide bombers in flowing robes.[27]

It was the Heraclitean details she wanted—what distinguishes, the Nietzschean differences—from everyday Israelis that would be suggestive of a larger story, though one not clearly and cleanly decipherable, about who Israelis really are: yes, "polyglot" and hardly homogeneous. It is in the coastal plain north and south of Tel Aviv that, as far as Grant is concerned, the real Israelis live. And if death is not quite imminent, nonetheless it lingers in the shadows so that efforts to live a normal life, going to a café with one's friends, becomes both a tragic act of dignity and an act of foolhardiness, eating a chocolate torte and drinking a latte in the midst of a figurative *danse macabre*.[28] Hence a new anti-myth to the stalwart myth of Zionism, the familiar made unfamiliar. Such is the strength of her cultural revelation, but one very much inflected by Grant's own personal revelations as a point of departure.

There is, too, the opposite when personal revelation must draw from the cultural or descend into the realm of solipsism. Here I turn to Nabokov's *Speak, Memory*, regarded as one of the outstanding English-language memoirs of the twentieth century.[29] That its intent and substance are personal revelation can be detected in the intimacy of the expressed authorial subjectivity. In the first chapter Nabokov writes, "Over and over again, my mind has made colossal efforts to distinguish the faintest of personal glimmers in the impersonal darkness on both sides of my life." In a moment of hyperbole he is speaking of what he can perceive of his pre-birth and post-death. Of course, that is not possible, and so with pre-birth and post-death like bookends, he is solely the center of his story. Elsewhere, his focus on the personal is reflected in his "quarrel with the Soviet dictatorship," though it is not about the lost family wealth but about the "nostalgia I have been cherishing all these years [which] is a hypotrophied sense of lost childhood, not sorrow for lost banknotes." So he lays plain his inner-directed ambition, that of excavating a more personal, not cultural, past. This can be detected, for example, in his characterization of the Russian Revolution as a "trite deus ex machina."[30] What a John Reed would see as "ten days that shook the world" Nabokov dismisses as a cliché, and here he has much in common with Viktor Shklovsky, as noted in the previous chapter. But culture is inescapable no matter how faint its outlines in the personal memoir—and here, of course, as applied to the chronotopic personal memoir. That Nabokov would be so dismissive of the Russian Revolution is one example. Despite the dismissal, the revolution is there, at some intersection of time and space, prompting and eliciting a response from him.

In another example, there is his memory of returning as a five-year-old in 1904 to Russia by train. At the border frontier between Germany and Russia, trains must be changed. His response is cultural. "An exciting sense of *rodina*, 'motherland,' was for the first time organically mingled with the comfortably creaking snow, the deep footprints across it, the red gloss of the engine stack, the birch logs piled high, under their private layer of transportable snow, on the red tender."[31] The description drawn from a childhood memory is clearly redolent of his Russianness. (Although originally Russian, Nabokov became a naturalized American. He was as fluent in English as he was in Russian; he learned to read English before he learned to read his native language because of his family's cosmopolitan background.)[32]

When the revolution does arrive, and "Lenin's gang," as Nabokov describes them dismissively, takes over, he and his family flee to Crimea. On the train ride, the cars are invaded by soldiers who are described as either "desert-ers" or "Red Heroes," and he cannot tell the difference.[33] Such contradictory interpretation, we see, is the ironic evidence of a society in upheaval. Therein lies the cultural context of journalism, even though Nabokov will turn back within himself in the act of personal revelation when he reveals that he resents the timing of the journey because he will be denied the opportunity to collect the pupae of butterflies. (Nabokov was a world-renowned lepidop-terist.) The shadows of culture linger around his personal revelation.

That his intention is personal revelation but one nonetheless implicated by culture can be detected in the irony of the conclusion to *Speak, Memory*. He, his wife Vera, and their son Dmitri are walking through the city streets of Saint-Nazaire, France, to the docks. Suddenly, as if described from Dmitri's childlike perspective, "There, in front of us, . . . it was most satisfying to make out among the jumbled angles of roofs and walls, a splendid ship's funnel, showing from behind the clothesline as something in a scrambled picture— Find What the Sailor Has Hidden—that the finder cannot unsee once it has been seen."[34]

So eyes open with childlike wonder in what becomes a children's game. End of book. And it marks their departure for the United States on the S.S. *Champlain*. The date is May 20, 1940. Nabokov does not say so, but he and his family are fleeing France before the German *Blitzkrieg* (that Niezschean *qualitas occulta* to which the Germans attached the ship of their fate). Clearly, playing a child's game amid such circumstances—war—is ironic, reflecting a kind of distraction (or escapism?). Or is the juxtaposition of the seemingly banal in war a triumph? But this is what a father does: He tries to protect his young son from war. While the orchestrations of culture cannot be escaped, their significance lies only in how they illuminate Nabokov's self-understanding. There is another irony Nabokov must have been aware of, intimating that there was no return to the past they were leaving. On returning to France, the *Champlain*, the rivet-and-steel ship of the Nabokov family's fate, was sunk by a mine. Nabokov does not mention it. But in the ship's destruction we detect the unassimilated sniffing at the periphery, reminding us just how temporary and fluid is chronotopic documentary.

Grant uses the personal as a point of embarkation for examining culture. Nabokov provides the context of culture, but only for the way it illuminates his own life. On these points, the predilections of both authors are clear. But then there is the possibility of both, as Sara Davidson demonstrates, because "Real Property" finely balances between the competing claims of narrative literary journalism and of memoir.

As we know from the discussion in chapter 3, Davidson's account is framed as a modern—better yet, postmodern—quest, and the quest myth is undone by an anti-myth as each goal in the quest descends from the sublime to the ridiculous. It would be easy to overlook that each stage of the quest is prompted by personal longing, given that the piece was included in Norman Sims's seminal collection *The Literary Journalists*.[35] But its inclusion does not exclude it as memoir. The stages of the quest are very much motivated by personal reasons. This is clear in the first stage of the quest, when Davidson the narrator goes in search of the "unscarred man" following her failed marriage. The next quest trial, to buy real estate, derives from its promise of permanency and rootedness, something Davidson is desperately seeking after the failure to find an unscarred man. Every stage of the quest is prompted by personal longing: listening to reggae, making trips to Israel, and taking up roller skating. This is why at the end of the piece she concludes, "I realized that I was thirty-five and I was still waiting, expecting to wake up from all of this."[36] Thus the personal revelation.

What she reflects on has always been, from the outset, a personal engagement with culture. What she arrives at is both personal and cultural revelation. Of the first, she realizes she may never be delivered from what she cannot wake up from, her own existential angst. Of the second, hers is a revelation regarding a generation adrift that finds the California Dream empty; they are implicated by something much larger. There the two genres sit neatly balanced in the creation of a supra- or quantum genre. But it is not a hybrid. If a hybrid, it is so only because of generic designations we impose. Rather, what we detect is simply a range of chronotopic or narra-descriptive documentary.

.   .   .

As these examples illustrate, the two generic approaches of a narra-descriptive journalism and a narra-descriptive memoir feed off each other because personal revelation and cultural revelation cannot be mutually exclusive. Personal revelation without cultural context will conclude in literary solipsism. Cultural revelation without personal context will conclude in an objectified journalism or sociological tract, appearing disembodied from the subjectivity that created it, the subjectivities that are its subject, and the subjectivities of the readers.

In a sense, *Scribbling the Cat* can be viewed as a transitional work for Fuller, and that may explain the unevenness in examining the personal and cultural. Chronologically it is sandwiched between her first book, *Don't Let's Go to the Dogs Tonight* (2001), and *The Legend of Colton H. Bryant* (2008). As noted, the first is securely grounded in memoir (her account of growing up in Rhodesia/Zimbabwe, Malawi, and Zambia), and the second is an account of the death of a roughneck in Wyoming's gas industry.[37] As an author, she is then taking her own journey, one negotiating between personal and cultural revelation.

In fairness, too, Fuller does to some extent redeem herself in the postscript chapter: "The Journey Is Now." But the redemption is incomplete because, among other things, it is after the fact—the fact of the accumulated chronotopes—in a postscript removed or disengaged from chronos in what amounts to a concluding digression. Again, it is the mistake Tolstoy made in providing a digression on what he meant by history at the end of *War and Peace,* when he concludes with a monologic commentary to explain his theory.[38] What Fuller reveals is that emotional confusion and the inability to reclaim or make sense of a history that left her and K losers are the joint revelation of the personal and cultural stories. And all you can do is try to move on like Grigory Melekhov in *Quiet Flows the Don* because that is all that is left. Fuller describes herself, K, and other members of her tribe, the lost white tribe of Rhodesia, as being like "clay pots fired in an oven that is overhot." The result is that "we . . . contain fatal cracks that we spend the rest of our lives itching to fill." That was why she and K "gravitated to each other, sure that the other held a secret balm—the magic glaze—that might make us whole."[39]

The problem is that the concluding chapter smells too much like a summary designed to neatly tie up loose ends. It runs the risk of being didactic. Granted, Fuller's is an ambitious effort that seeks to navigate back and forth between personal and cultural revelation in exploring the losers of history. But it illustrates some of the pitfalls an author can face when attempting to engage in both.

6

When Nature
Abhors a Vacuum

THERE is a descriptive passage in Adrian Nicole LeBlanc's *Random Family: Love, Drugs, Trouble, and Coming of Age in the Bronx* in which Coco and Iris, two poor Latinas, "skimmed the tattoo sketchbooks like two girls flipping through fashion magazines."[1] Thus the brief descriptive gestures of language reflect through irony the limited desires and ambitions of these urban, marginalized poor. While high fashion for some might be the couturier culture of Paris or Milan, here it is a tattoo. In the open-ended present, we can detect the familiar made unfamiliar.

And yet the passage also poses a problem precisely because it is so luminescent—or so illuminating of the human condition in its fundamental estrangement from the cultural construction of "high fashion." Because a problem for *Random Family* is often the absence of such descriptive details, resulting in an aesthetic vacuum as reflected in narrative summary. That said, *Random Family* is by no means guilty of a singular sin. I use it only as an example, because the problem can be detected in other examples of American narrative literary journalism, I would suggest, even though they are, like *Random Family,* critically acclaimed. This will be my focus in this last chapter, and it is necessary to understand if we are to better appreciate the prospects for the genre at the contemporary moment, in terms of both its promise and its limitations.

One cannot help but admire the decade-plus commitment of author LeBlanc in immersing herself in what was indeed a random family composed of Latino and Latina youth with little education and few opportunities for escaping their ghetto, often ensnared in a drug culture that provided the only means for material success. Two would go to jail for dealing drugs and one for accidentally killing his best friend. Meanwhile, sexual escape resulted in teenagers becoming unwed mothers, and not necessarily bad mothers, but often impoverished mothers of children from different fathers. Hence, and given the circumstances, we have the "random" family. The result is an examination of a culture in American life generally not accessible to mainstream—and particularly white—Americans.

As noted, the description can be effective. Another example is a scene in prison where, as an inmate prepares to leave the visitation cage that separates him from his wife and son, his wife calls out to him: " 'Look at your boy! Look at your boy!' The man to whom she called hopped, as if shaking off the visit. She shoved her son closer to the cage her husband was in. 'Say goodbye to your daddy. Look at your boy! Look at your boy!' She pressed the boy against what divided them."[2] The desperation of a mother to have the father acknowledge their son—in a prison—clearly reflects a poignant and painful emotional power.

Then there is a scene as the book draws to a conclusion where Cesar, who has now spent years weightlifting in prison, picks up his adolescent daughter like a barbell and places her across his shoulders, this in a moment of one random family's emotional intimacy—in a prison.[3] Again, we detect a poignant power. And the example serves to illustrate the familiar made unfamiliar. It is unlikely that most readers would have experienced such revealing familial intimacies under such circumstances.

But again this kind of description tends to be more the exception than the rule. While *Random Family* is certainly "narrative" in the conventional sense of reflecting a story's passage in time, the description is often isolated, marooned amid chronological summarizing. As the *Washington Post*'s critic John L. Jackson Jr. noted: "Each paragraph in *Random Family* seems rife with almost a lifetime's worth of change. Characters are getting killed, beaten, locked up and otherwise thwarted at every turn. Inundated by such misfortune, the reader finds his eyes beginning to glaze over."[4]

The use of the descriptive color that does exist is reminiscent of what is found in conventional feature writing: isolated instances designed to illustrate abstract and expository claims, as I noted in the first chapter. While *Random Family* is indeed a kind of "narrative journalism," it is not the kind of lushly descriptive narrative "literary" journalism we associate with a Tom Wolfe or a Joan Didion or a Truman Capote. This does not mean that there can never be summarizing narrative. There can be, as transition. But it must be used judiciously or the account will be reduced to one vast chronology, not unlike medieval chronicles: "On this day of Our Lord, a bridge washed out on the Cam. On the day after Saint Bartholomew's Feast, multitudes of crows descended on the forest. On Pentecost a severe hail storm trampled the barley," ad infinitum. What we detect is a constative discourse lacking the descriptive that teases us with imagined possibilities. The result is an endless list of constative transitions, instead of the descriptive details that help the reader realize a new reality, to cite Wolfgang Iser again: "Reading, then, is experienced as something which is happening—and happening is the hallmark of reality."[5]

To provide an example of narrative summary from *Random Family*: "There had been a shoot-out. The police hauled in Cesar, Mighty, and Rocco and questioned them separately. Rocco had, in fact, pulled the trigger, but Cesar lied to protect him, knowing that he'd receive less time as a juvenile. Mighty also lied and claimed to be the shooter. They were all responsible and Cesar shouldn't go down alone. Rocco and Mighty got shipped to Rikers and Cesar landed back at Spofford Hall."[6] We do not learn the descriptive details of the shoot-out, the dispute that prompted it, and who else was involved. Aside from the journalese—the three were "hauled in"—we know nothing of the arrests, or for that matter the trial. Similarly, they were "shipped" off to incarceration.

Or:

Back in the Bronx, Coco's cousin Jesus had finally been released from Rikers; Foxy had taken him in because his mother, Aida, had died while he was in prison and Jesus had nowhere else to go, but her generosity had consequences that spread all the way to Troy [New York]. Jesus had a temper when he got locked up, but when he came out, it was worse. He could get scary when he drank, and he seemed determined to catch up on all the fun he'd missed. But too much fun always led to trouble, and Jesus was on parole. He apparently got involved in a robbery and fled. Hector, however, got the brunt of the law's suspicion. Hector was staying indoors, trying to keep out of trouble, but it meant that he was always home when the detectives or Jesus's parole officer came to call. Meanwhile, Jesus crashed with Coco's older brother, Manuel, and his wife, Yasmin. Soon both men were partying and chasing girls, and Jesus had gotten Yasmin's sister pregnant. Manuel started getting mouthy with Yasmin, and Hector started following his brother's lead. At the end of her rope, Yasmin shipped Manuel's two kids up to Iris, but Iris quickly discovered that she couldn't handle them and passed them along to Coco. The boy was always trying to follow Coco into the bathroom; both children had rotten teeth and cried constantly from toothaches. Coco would try to distract them with hours of kick-the-can. They played outside even in the rain; she was afraid she would hurt them, otherwise. Foxy retrieved the children and brought them back to Yasmin. Coco was relieved, but worried and full of guilt.[7]

Both examples illustrate the observation made by Jackson: "Each paragraph in *Random Family* seems rife with almost a lifetime's worth of change. . . . Inundated by such misfortune, the reader finds his eyes beginning to glaze over." Fundamentally the examples are constative summaries, only reporting what happened, and not performative acts that invite the participation of the reader. Missing is Joaquín Martínez Pizarro's rhetoric of the scene, as discussed in chapter 1.

But as I indicated, LeBlanc is hardly alone in engaging in narrative summary. For example, Kerry Sheridan's *Bagpipe Brothers* is an account of the New York City Fire Department Band members who participated in rescue efforts on September 11, 2001, at the World Trade Center site. Again, we can detect examples of narrative summary:

> Outside Engine 69 and Ladder 28, the firefighters were growing agitated and resentful. The bosses were upstairs, their office door shut. No one knew what they were talking about in there. It would have been okay for the volunteers to stay and man the firehouses as long as the city firefighters were allowed to go. But being in the same vicinity as the volunteers, sitting there waiting for a bus that had been promised to arrive hours before, made the men aggressive and angry. "When are they gonna send us down there?" they asked each other. "Where's the bus, Chief?"[8]

What should be evident is the use of plural attribution in the second-to-last sentence to express a generalized experience, much as we saw in the example of the early Hemingway in chapter 2. Missing are the singular differences reflecting individual concrete metaphors. The last sentence of dialogue represents an intriguing rhetorical strategy because it seems to suggest the possibility of a singular response. But we do not know, given the previous attribution: "they asked each other."

In recent years, as newspapers have taken an increasing interest in more narrative approaches, narrative summary has often posed a problem. It can be detected in an account of a coal mine disaster and rescue published by the *Pittsburgh Post-Gazette* in 2002: "About a half-hour later, [Pennsylvania governor] Schweiker appeared live nationally on 'The Today Show' and announced that the [drill] bit had broken and the rescue, for the moment, had ceased. There were low moments for families huddled at the fire hall, but this was the worst."[9] What about the experience of miners' families could be described as the "worst" of the "low" at such a moment of high drama? We are told what happened but are not engaged in the performance. Elsewhere, during another moment of highly charged drama when a ventilation hole is successfully drilled down to where the miners are believed to have taken refuge underground, Bob Batz writes: "Nobody above ground knew for sure, but hopes soared. They were almost certain all nine were alive." Where is the evidence—the description—of the abstract soaring hopes? The "soaring hopes" are their own kind of Nietzschean paler, cooler idea: a platitude. Lacking is the rhetoric of the scene.

A 2001 article by Deb Kollars in the *Sacramento Bee* about a high school play similarly suffers: "As Juan took on the role of the confused and tender-hearted Marlow, it was a joy to watch. Fear, irritation, embarrassment, passion—he could do them all."[10] What is missing is a description of the confusion and tender-heartedness, as well as the fear, irritation, embarrassment, and passion. Instead the reader is left with what amounts to an abstract summary when told, "He could do them all." There is no sense of performative participation.

Still again:

> And yet, throughout, Sanders would pause and smile as another bit of dialogue survived intact or a set change happened without incident.
> "You guys are great," she would say over and over.
> Sanders took great joy in seeing her students on the stage. She kept thinking how far they had come.[11]

The particular moment and all that implies is missing. Kollars could have described Sanders waiting in anticipation to see if one specific difficult example of Shakespearean dialogue survived, then showing how the actor handled it and Sanders's reaction to it. Then her abstract "great joy," which undeniably is a paler, cooler idea because it, too, is a platitude (what in advertising is called "puffery") designed to create the illusion of greater particularity, could have been described when the dialogue survived, followed by her refrain, "You guys are great." A shift could follow to Sander'ss expressed thoughts as recovered by the reporter to give a sense of scenic immediacy—the "inconclusive present." Therein, the familiarity of desacralized myth—"great joy"—would be made less familiar by the distinguishing qualities reflected in and specific to those coordinates of time and space. But in the piece as published, those coordinates are taken for granted in the form of an abstract emotional mythology: "great joy."

In fairness, regarding Batz and Kollars, such writing is not entirely devoid of scene-by-scene construction. Here is one example, albeit minimalist, from Batz's piece:

> On his way to work that afternoon, he drove his red pickup truck to the take-out window at the East End Tavern, where his wife works as a cook.

He'd always stop by or call. That afternoon she leaned out the window and
asked if she could bring him home anything to eat that night, and he said no.
"I'm going to work now, hon," he told her.
She said, "I'll see you later."[12]

So we detect a stronger descriptive example of the inconclusive present, or
a moment located in time and space that has little meaning in itself until it
is connected with other scenes (and here again we detect what the modest
preposition "by" in Wolfe's "scene-by-scene construction" suggests about
location, affinity, and relationship in the construction of the narrative story).

What remains troubling is the extent to which one can sense the same
problems of narrative summary in other critically acclaimed book-length
works. We can detect it in Jonathan Harr's *A Civil Action* and in Thomas
Keneally's *Schindler's List*. To cite an example from *A Civil Action* (an account
of a lawsuit about the impact of toxic chemical pollution on families in
Woburn, Massachusetts):

> Schlichtmann, meanwhile, had been negotiating with Unifirst. At the first
> meeting the company's lawyer offered a hundred thousand dollars. Schlich-
> tmann set up a meeting at the Ritz-Carlton, just as he had done in the hotel
> fire case, and he brought in a groundwater expert from Princeton University.
> Unifirst's lawyer increased his offer to six hundred thousand. Schlichtmann
> wanted more. The negotiation stalled for a while, and then Schlichtmann
> organized another meeting at the Ritz. In the end, Unifirst offered to settle all
> claims for one million and fifty-thousand dollars. The company would pay
> four hundred thousand in cash immediately, and the balance in five years.[13]

Such writing may be serviceable as conventional feature writing. But what
Harr suspends is the rhetoric of the scene that engages in psychological
transport. The result is constative, and the passage recalls what Jackson said
of *Random Family*, that one is inundated.

To cite another example: "He tried not to think about money. His credit
cards were burdened with debt. Just recently he had attempted to use one
at a restaurant and it had been refused."[14] The passage refers again to Jan
Schlichtmann, the main protagonist in the book and the lawyer seeking the
settlement on behalf of the families of Woburn. Whatever the chronotopic
value of the incident, it is a value subordinated to the *qualitas occulta,* the
larger and broader abstract theme of his "credit cards burdened with debt."
The reader is being instructed what to think in a constative rhetoric instead
of a description. Such a description might (to use a hypothetical) show Schlichtmann walking into a Red Lobster, ordering the fish fry, sprinkling malt
vinegar on his chips, and then, when going to pay, having his MasterCard
with the hologram of the dove on it returned: "'I'm sorry,' the waitress said,

putting on her sincerest and most commiserating smile. 'But for some reason your card wasn't accepted.' Now the aftertaste of the fish and vinegar came back on Schlichtmann's palate, and he felt vaguely nauseated. 'I'm broke,' he recalled thinking." Such a "performative" text, to cite Iser again, encourages a more active reader response.[15]

Undoubtedly, too, *Schindler's List* is a compelling work and critically acclaimed; it won the Booker Prize in England (where it was titled *Schindler's Ark*), as well as Academy Awards for the movie version. One senses author Keneally, who said he approached the work as a novelist, struggling with the phenomenal details of the account of how Oscar Schindler rescued more than 1,100 Jews from the Holocaust.[16] Keneally does so by frequently embracing narrative summary. For example:

> As they reached the Appellplatz, prisoners were told to strip. They were lined up naked and run back and forth in front of the doctors. Blancke and Leon Gross, the collaborating Jewish physician, would make notations on the card, point at this prisoner, call on that one to verify his name. Back the prisoners would run, the physicians looking for signs of disease or muscular weakness. It was an odd and humiliating exercise. Men with dislocated backs (Pfefferberg, for example, whose back Hujar had thrown out with the blow of a whip handle); women with chronic diarrhea, red cabbage rubbed into their cheeks to give them color—all of them running for their lives and understanding it was so.[17]

What has gone largely missing is the one-of-a-kind particular—the concrete metaphor. Again we see pluralities such as "Men with dislocated backs. . . ." Curiously, Keneally gives Leopold Pfefferberg as an example. It was Pfefferberg who first interested the author in the story of Schindler and was keen on having him write the book. With a living witness, Keneally could have provided more of a description, not necessarily of Pfefferberg's nudity, but perhaps describing the humiliation he felt running naked with a dislocated back, and whether he was forced to hobble as he tried to ignore the pain. Or was there someone specific who could have been described as rubbing raw cabbage on her cheeks?

Then there is Schindler playing a game of cards with the camp commandant to win the freedom of the latter's maid, Helen Hirsch. "Out in her kitchen, Helen Hirsch did not know she had been saved over cards."[18] But what was she doing in the kitchen while her life was being saved? Peeling carrots? Peeling carrots is, after all, an everyday domestic chore—a banal activity much taken for granted. But when your fate is being decided while you peel carrots, a new unfamiliar is introduced. Hirsch survived the war and lived to see the book published (and to appear at the end of the movie). There was the potential to interview her on such details as part of the reporter's "immersion" process.

Thus, *Random Family* is not alone.

Possible reasons why daily journalists' efforts suffer include deadline pressures and a professional consciousness weaned on the inverted pyramid constantly drifting back to constative summary as part of their natural inclination, to recall Nietzsche. Other possible reasons for narrative summary when it comes to book-length efforts like *Random Family*, *A Civil Action*, and *Schindler's List* likely include the nature of the ambition to honor the obligation to a phenomenal referentiality, and what that implies when it comes to the overwhelming complexity of such epic efforts—epic in the sense of overwhelming evidence. Robert S. Boynton asked Harr, "Do you think of yourself as practicing immersion journalism?"[19] "Immersion journalism" has long been considered one of the prerequisites for the writer of a narrative literary journalism.[20] Harr acknowledged as much, but then added, revealingly, "Perhaps inundated or drowning journalism would be more accurate."[21] Harr began *A Civil Action* in 1986. While the book was a critical success, Boynton notes, "writing it nearly destroyed Harr's life."[22] Harr had a contract to deliver the completed book to the publisher in two years. But because of seemingly endless legal maneuverings and court hearings—the inconclusive present of phenomenal reality—it took eight years and five contract extensions to complete the book. As I noted in chapter 2, a consequence for Harr was that, in the aftermath of publishing *A Civil Action*, he said: "The next thing I want to try my hand at is fiction. It's exhausting to follow people around, and the facts of a real event sometimes don't occur in a way that lends itself to narrative elegance."[23] Thus he senses the attraction of the self-contained and sovereign world of fiction. (Despite his seeming ambivalence, he would go on to write nonfiction, including the acclaimed *The Lost Painting: The Quest for a Caravaggio Masterpiece*.)

Issues of taste, ethics, lack of information, faulty memories, and witnesses are among the more obvious reasons that account for such narrative summaries. Then there are the related limits of what we can know—the unassimilated. Such may contribute to the overall limits of the genre. Whatever the reasons, the end results are still narrative summaries lacking in more fully developed chronotopes, and what that means in terms of a diminished imaginative response by readers.

Also, while *Random Family*, *A Civil Action*, and *Schindler's List* were hailed by critics, critics tend to be intellectually sophisticated, since critiquing is what they do. What we do not know is how many readers actually failed to finish the books because, as Jackson said of *Random Families*, their "eyes glaze[d] over" from the barrage of constative summaries. Clearly those who are more literate (and who are capable of reading not only such works as narrative summaries but also more complex expository works such as literary criticism and discussions of quantum mechanics) can find such books worth the effort because, in a sense, they are better equipped or imaginatively enriched as readers to fill in the constative blanks. But who will put down such works because they lack the appeal of the more fully fleshed-out chronotope that excites the imagination with the possibilities of the dialogic? The issue is relevant, given the decline in reading abilities in the United States in recent years. The national testing service ACT found in 2006 that nearly half of high school seniors entering college could not read at the college level.[24] If you have a Ph.D., you are presumably more capable of negotiating constative reports, whether as news stories or as expository essays. Teachers can be blamed (especially because of the low expectations they have of students, as reflected in the epidemic of grade inflation), as can parents, the students, and society in general, as well as writers and editors who take readers for granted, thinking they can read at the level of the *New York Times,* the *New York Review of Books,* and the *New Yorker.*

The result of such narrative summaries is a contextual vacuum, and I would suggest that they have the capacity to evolve in either of two directions in the attempt to fill that vacuum. First, they can be expanded with the distinctive concrete metaphors of the chronotopes from which readers can negotiate their own meaning. In a sense, *Random Family* and other similar works may be a case of where less is more. In other words, the writer must select more judiciously from among the welter of summaries to provide a selection expanded to register a sense of descriptive or scenic place. That will be small comfort to authors who, like LeBlanc, Harr, and Keneally, have taken on projects of such magnitude.

Or, in the vacuum reflected in the summary, there can be the temptation to fill it with the "paler, cooler ideas" of our secular mythologies. In the absence of adequately developed chronotopes—in particular the description that furnishes space—the author is easily drawn into filling it with something. The result is, as noted, closer to traditional feature writing, in which an isolated scene serves to illustrate the abstract point. Such a digressiveness arises in *Random Family.* For example, "The pressure to buy things was always intense in the ghetto, but Christmas created a level of expectation that was unbearable, further compounded by the blues that came with every holiday." What we see is an expository (and constative) claim. Or, "The legal challenge was a lot like the challenge of demonstrating the impact of racism and poverty or substandard housing: How could you untangle the structural injustices from the self-inflicted damage?" Or, "Poverty pulled everybody down."[25] These are constative declarations directing how the reader should read, resulting in a monologic instead of scene-by-scene description that permits readers to interpret for themselves what poverty means.

LeBlanc reveals her purpose in her "Author's Note" at the end of the book: "I could not have written intimately about this particular American experience of class injustice had the many people in this book not opened their lives to me."[26] There it is: the neat homilitic summation, the polemic about class injustice. Like others, LeBlanc could not resist the temptation of the kind of monologic that, again, ensnared Tolstoy. It is not that one does not necessarily address ideological concerns such as class injustice in a descriptive journalism. Rather, it is how one does so. Why is such a descriptive approach more persuasive? Because the reader is empowered to draw his or her own interpretations.

Also, part of the effectiveness of a text is what will still be readable seventy years from now. Suggestive description is more likely to be relevant in the future because of the one common denominator between our present and that future: the "common sense-appeal of the shared common senses" we can reasonably expect our grandchildren to have. Except for the occasional archaism, we can still relate to James Boswell's description of Samuel Johnson more than two centuries ago: "He wore a full suit of plain brown clothes, with twisted-hair button of the same colour; a large bushy, greyish wig, a plain shirt, black worsted stockings, and silver buckles. Upon this tour, when journeying, he wore boots, and a very wide brown cloth greatcoat, with pockets which might have almost held the two volumes of his folio dictionary; and he carried in his hand a large English oak stick."[27] In contrast, polemical narrative journalism from the more recent 1930s can seem quaintly outdated. Agnes Smedley, for example, writes of the communist takeover of the town of Shangpo in China, "In such a way did the Red Army reach into the hearts of the masses and start the long work of creating that which the peasants always seemed to have longed for."[28] The problem with such polemics is that they do not age well because they are constrained by the distanced image of the ideological past.

We can also detect a relationship between polemic and traditional ethnographic study that has implications for a narra-descriptive journalism. In recent years there has been an increasing identification of texts of narrative journalism and a narrra-descriptive journalism with ethnography and related social sciences. The *Post*'s Jackson applauds the "ethnographic research" by LeBlanc.[29] *Newsweek*'s critic characterized *Random Family* as "literary anthropology."[30] The earliest reference (1957) I have so far found to a narrative literary journalism serving as a kind of ethnography, although the word is not used, is in relation to Lafcadio Hearn's work: "Hearn's sketches are just about the only picture we have of Negro life in a border city in the post–Civil War period. They form an invaluable record of the customs, folkways, and family organization of the urban Negro; they form also a case study of the process of acculturation at a vital transitional point in American Negro history."[31] The observation is ethnographic in all but name. The comparison of narra-descriptive journalism with ethnography has also been raised in the scholarship.[32]

But in suggesting that such texts have ethnographic value there is a risk, because we are invoking sociological positivism. Indeed, for purposes of library classification *Random Family* is categorized as social science.[33] Such a characterization reflects efforts to grant the form a social-scientific legitimacy. After all, such writing has had difficulty finding literary legitimacy. But a social-scientific legitimacy is shortsighted precisely because any scientized effort must have as its goal the elimination of ambiguity. And ambiguity is at the heart of scene-by-scene construction that "teases us out of thought," leading us to irony and paradox, and to the familiar made unfamiliar. As the novelist Linda Grant observed of writing *People on the Street*: "Now this was my dilemma as a writer. I did not think that literature should make a statement. In fact, I thought the exact opposite: that it should create ambiguity, doubt, discomfort, confusion." The initial result will be "chaos," out of which will eventually emerge deeper insights but not easy answers, she suggests.[34]

A writer, then, must choose between a polemic, whether overtly political or one that claims a positivist foundation for its argument like the ethnographic; or to engage a rhetoric that will leave much to the reader's imagination. If it is both, the focus becomes fuzzy. This accounts for my ambivalence about *Random Family* because of the richness of the examples of LeBlanc's marooned description. The examples draw too much attention to themselves, as if seeking to escape (as the inconclusive present must) the bonds of the homily or polemic that reflects the distanced image of the past lacking in polyphony.

It may not have been LeBlanc's intention to pursue a literary purpose in her project, for the ambiguity of the inconclusive present has been corralled and restrained in the clear and unambiguous service of the social cause. But what we see is that expectations of readers have been raised by indulging the inconclusive present—the rhetoric of the scene—only to have those expectations undercut with the screed. When LeBlanc says, "Poverty pulled everybody down," she is unambiguous in characterizing—reporting on—her subjects as "poor" in what is a constative statement. And that is the problem with traditional ethnography. It attempts to announce unambiguously what to value and how much, and that is at odds with the purpose of a narrative journalism aspiring to be literary. The problem is that once you have elicited an imaginative response from the chronotopes, the introduction of an ethnographic label, that someone is "poor," reduces that person once again to the Other. Such a strategy defeats the purpose of a narra-descriptive or chronotopic journalism when it beckons with its call to explore the open-ended or inconclusive present in phenomenal experience.

Nor am I the only one to detect this issue of a confused or fuzzy focus in the work. So did the *Post's* critic, Jackson. Except that he approached *Random Family* from a different direction. He is an anthropologist, and the author of *Harlemworld: Doing Race and Class in Contemporary Black America.* For him there was too much of an emphasis on dramatic narrative and not enough on what I would call the homilies and polemics of the "ethnographic" ambition. LeBlanc's approach, Jackson said, "mandates that she eschew any substantive discussion of the macro-structural forces (deindustrialization, suburbanization, institutionalized social inequalities, international market forces, revitalizing empowerment zone regulations, etc.) that provide important contextual clues for making sense of places like the South Bronx, places that seem to become hothouses for illicit underground economies and the overly fragile social relationships they spawn."[35] In the "macro-structural," the global view, lies the promise of the discursive homily, the moral corrective. What Jackson does not appreciate is that there can be a substantial dialogic, polyvocal, that teases us out of thought with a performative reality we can participate in by means of psychological transport. What he calls for is constative in nature. Hence conventional ethnography. Does this mean that one of us is right and the other wrong? No, it means that we have both detected from very different epistemological approaches conflicting ambitions in *Random Family,* in which the reader is caught between the rhetoric of the scene and the rhetoric of the polemic. Neither predominates.

The problem of narrative summary that invites into the vacuum discursive expressions helps us better understand what succeeds and does not succeed in a narra-descriptive journalism. Again, *Random Family* is a compelling work in its time and place. But given that the "common sense-appeal of the shared common senses" is underdeveloped—that it is not sustained with "scene-by-scene construction" introducing us to the inconclusive present—one cannot be confident that it will be such a compelling read forty or seventy years from now. That is unfortunate for the decade spent in trying to explore what is undoubtedly an important cultural phenomenon, one in which tattoos serving for high fashion provided the promise of a more lasting dialogic.

Conclusion

This volume began as a series of independent queries regarding the nature and identity of what is often called literary journalism, narrative in disposition, which I prefer to characterize as a narrative literary journalism, or a narra-descriptive journalism. For that matter, it could be characterized as a chronotopic journalism. To conclude, I will provide a summary of the issues involved. But, I also want to consider what my findings could mean, very tentatively, for the future. This is because no one would dispute the changing nature of our media as they have moved toward convergence in cyberspace. Moreover, what are the potential implications of a narra-descriptive journalism for improving the capacity of the news system to deal with compelling societal issues?

My summary:

1. *Why is a more traditional narrative model in the form of a narrative literary journalism desirable in journalism practice after a century in which it was largely (but not entirely) submerged beneath dominant professional practices?*

It has been suggested that all text is narrative.[1] What we have to bear in mind, however, is that there is text that seeks to move beyond or escape narrative. Perhaps it can never entirely do so. But we can detect this movement away from narrative in the dominant models of print journalism in the twentieth century as well as into the beginning of the present, the hard news story and the feature story, as well as variations in between. Their level of abstraction is designed to disengage the reader cognitively from experience. The virtue of a narra-descriptive journalism is that it engages the reader in the way the human mind is constructed to do so, by means of storytelling, starting somewhere with a beginning complication (albeit tentative given the fluidity of experience), followed by a middle of progressing actions (again albeit tentative), and concluding with some kind of resolution (and again tentative given that there are no true conclusions in the world of experience). The issue, however, is not so much the rhetorical structure, which is at least as old as Aristotle's *Poetics,* but rather that it is more cognitively efficient for sorting through the flood of information we are exposed to every day in order to make some sense of the contingencies and seeming contingencies to which we are also exposed. Moreover, it permits readers greater participation in the making of their own meaning, thus empowering them in a way that the older conventional models of journalism cannot.

2. *What makes a narrative literary journalism's referentiality to phenomena different from that of other related genres, particularly conventional fictions on the one hand and dominant journalism practices on the other?*

The problem is that "real life" in the form of the phenomenal world is not as simple as some critics would suggest. Aside from the way we interpret phenomena as shaped and molded by language and culture and their ongoing negotiation, the phenomenal world we detect or sense is always one of a kind. Therein lies part of the distinctive nature of a narra-descriptive journalism. It can never be entirely severed from its location at the unique intersection of one time and one place in space, or what could be viewed as a version of the Bakhtian chronotope. This is in contrast to conventional fictions, which, because they deny such a distinctive time and location, exist *only* in the realm of allegory. They are self-contained, occupying their own "sovereign worlds" free of phenomenal referentiality. The greater degree of abstraction associated with the more traditional models of journalism also tends to diminish the value of the chronotopic concrete metaphor. Moreover, and despite the claims of the concrete metaphor to one time and place, humans cannot perceive the full nature of any particular phenomenon. Therein lies the paradox: What seems so concrete is ultimately incomplete. Thus, in a narra-descriptive journalism there is always the potential for what was once unassimilated to emerge into consciousness and be assimilated later into those earlier accounts and interpretations. Hence, one of the virtues of such a journalism is that the beginnings of Aristotle's prescription are always tentative, as are its middle actions and conclusions. So we detect the narrative of the inconclusive present, carnivalesque in nature, in which the familiar is so often made unfamiliar by what earlier we could not recognize among our conventional assumptions.

3. *Given the emphasis on the referential to the phenomenal particular, or material world, what are the consequences in a narra-descriptive journalism for the mediated social realities we create for ourselves as a community?*

This may well be the most important legacy of the New Journalism, that variation on a narra-descriptive journalism that emerged in the 1960s and

1970s, which has rarely been equaled, although I would not suggest that there have not been more recent successful examples. But I would argue that the phenomenon of the New Journalism still has lessons to offer. Specifically, much of the New Journalism was engaged in the demythification of secular myth, or the cultural and by extension personal assumptions that a society and its individuals tend to take for granted, as, for example, in the entitlement implicit in the idealized assumption of the American Dream. Such a journalism served as an important corrective for the social blinders a society had donned, and, moreover, demonstrates how a society can engage in a healthy self-critique. It is, of course, the distinctive chronotopes of the carnivalesque that contribute to making the familiar unfamiliar, thus resulting in the reader having to make new meaning.

4. *Any comparative study must acknowledge the development of the similar European tradition of literary reportage, or reportage literature, given its widespread historical practice. How is the kind of narrative literary journalism I explore similar to and different from the literary reportage tradition of European origin?*

What we can detect is that a broader literary reportage, or reportage literature tradition, is by comparison more "elastic," particularly when examined in light of the international proletarian writers' movement, which had a worldwide presence in the 1920s and 1930s. This is detected in the seminal German and Russian traditions, and their influence beyond. But given that so much of it was polemical, does that disqualify it as literary, if by "literary" we mean that it is not constructed in Bakhtin's "distanced image of the absolute past" but instead draws on the carnivalesque of his "open-ended" or "inconclusive present"? Undoubtedly this question will attract advocates on both sides of the issue, but to ignore it would be to suggest that all such works are qualitatively the same. Clearly they are not.

5. *How does a narrative literary journalism—fundamentally a narra-descriptive journalism drawn from the aesthetics of experience—differ from similar narra-descriptive memoir?*

One of the hallmarks of a narra-descriptive journalism is that it is a much more subjective form (inflected with a more personal voice) than the more objectifying conventional models of journalism dominant in American practice even if the subjectivity is merely reflected in the shaping consciousness of the author selecting descriptive details. But there are consequences. This is because an increasing reflexivity ultimately results in memoir, as consciousness shifts from an outward focus on cultural revelation to an inward focus on personal revelation. The result is that each must to some extent partake of the other on a spectrum or continuum in which personal revelation may be emphasized more than the cultural, or the cultural may be emphasized more than the personal. Neither is mutually exclusive. And there are those examples that balance relatively evenly between the two extremes of solipsism and objectification in what ultimately constitutes a kind of quantum or supra-genre, documentary and chronotopic in nature.

6. *Granted that a narrative literary journalism is richly textured with literary tropes, why do many recent examples, often critically acclaimed, fall short?*

There has been a discouraging propensity in those examples to engage in narrative summary—to remove the descriptive. Without the common sense-appeal of the shared common senses reflected in the descriptive, the result is largely a cognitive vacuum and a constative discourse. What can be detected is that if there is an attempt to fill the vacuum, it can be filled either with the inconclusive present of the chronotope or with varieties of Nietzsche's *qualitas occulta*—polemics. The virtue of the former, of course, is that it offers more potential for individually constructed meaning by means of the imagined images, with new possibilities of meaning emerging when the familiar is made unfamiliar.

What I have examined is past, and of course we always examine the past in order to try to understand, as problematic as it may prove, what may follow. And here I offer some speculations. But I emphasize that they are only speculations. I am cautioned by the example of Frederic Hudson, who, in his 1873 *Journalism in the United States, from 1691–1872*, predicted that someday our newspapers would be delivered by hot air balloons.[2] He demonstrates an incapacity to imagine a world without paper news, in which the news would someday "fly," in a manner of speaking, through the air on radio waves in a very different manner from that of hot air balloons. Thus we detect the frailties of our predictions.

One clearly cannot ignore the rapid changes in contemporary electronic media, and this book raises the question as to what applications there might be in the world of convergent media. (As Brian Boyd has pointed out as only one of many critics, narrative is not constrained to just the printed text.)[3] But one must note that the vaunted convergence of media such as text, graphics, sound, and video in cyberspace has not necessarily been a homogenizing convergence or metamorphosis. Rather, what we detect are media in closer proximity to one another. To some extent such a "convergence" has long been going on. One can see it in the placement of block prints next to text in illustrated weeklies such as *Leslie's* and *Harper's* starting in the 1850s. We see this phenomenon evolve into the old *Look, Life,* and *Saturday Evening Post* magazines. A venerable practitioner is *National Geographic.* Of course, within such constellations of media the reader has even greater freedom to construct very much his or her own narrative.

This is why the approach I have taken may have possibilities for application to interactive multimedia efforts. The experience will be different from solely alphabetic text, to be sure. But still there is no reason why it cannot be applied. Most obviously, the narrative approach—how we naturally inquire into the phenomenal world around us—is still relevant. We need stories to make sense of what in the flood of information we do not understand. In the case of a journalism, central to that is how our senses respond to the concrete metaphor represented as located in a singular time and space. For that reason, it can never escape fully into allegory, or, in other words, deny its referentiality. Consider James Agee's *Let Us Now Praise Famous Men*. While the printed text can be read independently of the accompanying photographs, it can still be viewed as an early attempt at "converging" media, as I noted in chapter 2. If we examine the photographs taken by Walker Evans that accompany the text, what can be detected are the possibilities. The photographs are presented without identification and pagination. The second photograph in succession is of a man sitting, dressed in overalls, presumably one of the tenant farmers Agee writes about. Because the photographs were taken by Evans as part of the Farm Security Administration's efforts to document the Great Depression in rural America, the man in the photograph can be identified as Floyd Burroughs of Hale County, Alabama. His pseudonym in the book is "George Gudger."[4] Similarly, the twenty-eighth photograph in succession shows another tenant farmer in denim overalls. In real life he was Frank Tengle, whose pseudonym in the book is "Fred Ricketts."[5] In examining the two photographs in the construction of a narrative, one can complement Agee's description of denim overalls, where he notes "the coldness of sweat when they are young, and their stiffness; their sweetness to the skin and pleasure of sweating when they are old, the thin metal buttons of the fly."[6] Those worn by Tengle/Ricketts, because of their dark color, look almost new (given the way denim loses color after repeated washings), with all that implies about stiff new denim that clings coldly with sweat to flesh. Those worn by Burroughs/Gudger look well worn, faded, soft, and more absorbent of sweat. One can compare the photographs to the rest of the description. For that matter, the printed text complements the photographs in a mutual interpretive synergy.

To take a more contemporary example, one from cyberspace, there is "Baptism by Fire," published by the *New York Times* online in 2014 using alphabetic text, photos, diagrams, and video to reconstruct a rookie firefighter's first fire call in New York City. With the text serving as the point of access into the larger mixed-media story, one again detects narrative possibilities of interpretation. Certainly the subject derives from the carni-valesque of experience—or the unique and distinctive contingencies that arise. There is much here that cannot be controlled in advance. We also detect efforts to seek out the unfamiliar, when, for example, author N. R. Kleinfield observes: "The thing about the vast majority of first fires is they are both memorable and unmemorable. For the firefighter, the memory is permanent. But to the outside world, they tend to be ordinary fires." So he explores the unfamiliar most readers (in the larger sense of reading or interpreting differ-ent media) would not know. For the young probationary firefighter, Jordan Sullivan, the rescue of an infant in a bedroom filled with black smoke is not just another fire department rescue reported in a conventional news story, fundamentally constative. "Two Children Saved in Apartment Fire," a con-ventional headline might read. In fact, the hard news story of the event, the constative account of the fire, was not published in the *Times*. Rather, readers were invited to participate in the performance of a more traditional narra-tive, with Aristotle's tentative "beginning" that arouses tentative expectations in the "middle," which arrives at the tentative "conclusion." The online article contains photographs and diagrams of the apartment building, as well as of the apartment showing the route Sullivan followed, groping his way amid smoke, searching for children the mother said had not escaped. The article has links to video, which includes interviews with Sullivan after the fire, and one of a training exercise in a smoke-filled room to illustrate the challenges a firefighter faces in searching for bodies under such conditions. Between these and the alphabetic text, the story unfolds. As the narrative proceeds, Sullivan crawls into a bedroom (crawling because the smoke is thicker higher up). Reaching out in the smoke with his left hand, he feels the leg of a baby's crib. He reaches over, searching, and places his hand on blankets, and then a soggy diaper. It is the soggy diaper of an unconscious infant. Certainly this is an instance of the inconclusive present that makes the familiar of rescue unfamiliar. It challenges or breaks through secular mythologies, associating the banal of a baby's wet diaper with an apartment aflame and filled with blinding smoke. Communally, there are the television commercials we are exposed to showing the secular mythology of a happy baby in a dry diaper. If we have been parents, there are our own memories of making a baby happy when we put on a clean diaper. Then there are the secular mythologies of conventional news in the construction or rescue, whose headline might again read, "Two Children Saved in Apartment Fire." Part of the challenge of the inconclusive present, too, is that in the *Times* account the rescue has not yet been completed, because in that moment of Sullivan's touching a soggy diaper one cannot conclude that the infant is alive.[7]

The infant is saved in the end. But of course, the story has the potential to continue, since no story of the phenomenal chronotope ever concludes. And the *Times* story intentionally continues when it invites firefighters to send in their accounts of their first fires. Seven accounts were published from as far away as Texas and California.[8]

I would note, however, that the written text could be read by itself without the accompaniment of the photos, diagrams, and video.[9] While these embellish, the written text tells the tale. This raises the question, are the pictures, diagrams, and video necessary? Or do they largely serve the function of extended expository digression, consistent with the conventional feature story tradition in newspapering, and thus designed to explain rather than result in the psychological transport of a narrative performance? This is not intended as a criticism. Instead, it is to raise the question whether there can be truly chronotopic narrative without disrupting to some extent the narrative journey and the influence it casts over the imagination. Because to what extent is the psychological transport lost in shifting among media? There is an earlier analogue. Newspapers, at least for much of the twentieth century, had what were called "jumps." This meant that stories continued on inside pages. And the prevailing philosophy was that jumps proved disruptive, causing a major share of readers not to continue reading on the inside page.

Moreover, the use of different media involves, in effect, mental multitasking as a reader switches, for example, from print to video. As one groundbreaking Stanford University study revealed, "People who are regularly bombarded with several streams of electronic information do not pay attention, control their memory, or switch from one job to another as well as those who prefer to complete one task at a time."[10] Thus they are more apt to lose their train of thought, and with it the psychological transport. Obviously this has potential implications for multimedia narratives. This is true especially if the literary Darwinists are correct in their assessment that the brain developed the linearity of storytelling as a means of survival. What potentially gets lost is a survival skill rooted in how humans evolved.

Still another interpretation, given the dominant role of text in the *Times* story, is that one medium among the array will have to provide a singular and dominating continuity to which the others are adjuncts. There is no reason why it has to be written text. But that also raises the specter that a more sensorially accessible media of graphic images could result in the diminishing role of such text. After all, as newspaper studies have shown, pictures capture the eye first, then headlines.[11] The question then is what is lost cognitively if the image dominates and reading abilities decline.

Yet, given that a "reader" is still focused on the telling of one journalistic story derived from the intersection of one time and place, research may yet show an efficacy to such various efforts. We shall have to await the future to see if such concerns will be addressed and resolved. What we should not expect is that newspapers will be delivered by lighter-than-air balloons.

To what extent such a narra-descriptive journalism—however reflected by different media—can improve on the capacity of the news system to deal with compelling societal issues yet must be determined, if it can be. There are those who will decry the limitations of the kind of narrative I discuss in this volume, such as Rodney Benson: "In its search for melodrama, personalized narrative journalism can give short shrift to structural complexities, power dynamics, and diverse perspectives such as those characterizing immigration." He offers his comments in an examination of Sonia Nazario's *Enrique's Journey.* He also notes, "Long-form narrative has become the sacred totem of American journalism."[12] He does not provide a basis for the claim and so has constructed a straw man for what he perceives as the failings of such work. As noted in the previous chapter, the anthropologist John L. Jackson also criticized a narrative approach. But if works of narra-descriptive journalism lack in expository analysis, it should be borne in mind that Benson and Jackson are highly literate intellectuals who can successfully navigate the abstractions of expository accounts. One of the lessons of this volume, I hope, is that there is no one politically correct form of journalism, or for that matter no one correct form of discourse for inquiry. What those who are eager to find fault with in a narra-descriptive journalism should bear in mind is that in an era of declining reading capabilities,[13] as I discussed in the previous chapter, narra-descriptive journalism provides a compelling means to get those disinclined to read to take up the practice of reading the more cognitively accessible story form, and as a consequence be introduced to the kinds of issues that then benefit, in the evolution of cognitive abilities, from other, more sophisticated and evolved expository examinations written by Ph.D.s. Not everybody has a Ph.D., and it is elitist to expect everyone to read at such a level. A fundamental point to this book is that narrative is the way the mind naturally inquires into the phenomenal world. If you are an intellectual and forget that, you forget a lot of potential readers. Moreover, the more "real" readings are perceived, as in narra-descriptive journalism or documentary, the more cognitive impact the work has. Of course, given this book, I would be foolish to say that there is not a place for analytical exposition. But at the same time, one only creates an elite of readers if we banish narra-descriptive discourse.

The proof is in the "story." As Kathy Roberts Forde and Matthew W. Ross have ably demonstrated, there is the influential role "Hiroshima," the *New Yorker* article, played in creating a national conversation, along with radio reporting on its publication that included readings of the account over the air. The phenomenon generated a national discussion among Americans about the horrific destructiveness of atomic warfare. In fact, as Forde and Ross note, the Truman administration did not want Americans to know how terrible the destruction had been at Hiroshima and Nagasaki.[14] While the national discussion among Americans might be difficult to imagine in print today, nonetheless Forde's and Ross's examination suggests the potential possibilities for creating national conversations on compelling issues, social or otherwise, in the form of mixed media in cyberspace. Whatever the shortcomings of such mixed efforts, it would be a story journalism composed of diverse media that draw on the referential instability of the aesthetics of experience so that new interpretations can challenge our secular myths. (And one perceives the kind of secular myth the Truman administration was attempting to cultivate and sustain among Americans in 1946.) Thus civic engagement could be nurtured, as John J. Pauly observed.[15]

There cannot, of course, truly be a conclusion to an ongoing discussion. At best, I hope I have provided some critical perspectives that help to demonstrate why a narra-descriptive journalism is distinctive, compelling, and even profound, and ultimately worthy of continued examination. This is because—if for no other reason—it is a discourse directed at trying to recover the illusion of experience from unique times and places, and in doing so it reveals to us existential consequences we cannot ignore for fear that they could come back to haunt us, much like photos of the piles of bones from the battle of Verdun in 1916, as I noted in the introduction. It is, of course, an illusion to think we can recover those experiences in a mediation. But from accounts of phenomenal consequences refusing to repudiate their referential origins, there is much they can still teach, given their open-ended and inconclusive nature.

Notes

Introduction

1. Peter Dear, *Discipline and Experience: The Mathematical Way in the Scientific Revolution* (Chicago: University of Chicago Press, 1995), 25.

2. Norman Sims, "The Problem and the Promise of Literary Journalism Studies," *Literary Journalism Studies* 1.1 (Spring 2009): 8.

3. John C. Hartsock, *A History of American Literary Journalism: The Emergence of a Modern Narrative Form* (Amherst: University of Massachusetts Press, 2000), 247.

4. Ibid., 9.

5. Tom Wolfe, "The New Journalism," in *The New Journalism*, ed. Tom Wolfe and E. E. Johnson (New York: Harper and Row, 1973), 9.

6. Ibid., 8–9, 41–46.

7. See the mission statement of the journal *Literary Journalism Studies*, www.literary journalismstudies.org; also John C. Hartsock, "Literary Reportage: The 'Other' Literary Journalism," *Genre: Forms of Discourse and Culture* 42 (Spring–Summer 2009): 113–34.

8. On the idea of a narrative literary journalism as a kind of "quantum narrative," see my article "'Literary Journalism' as an Epistemological Moving Object within a Larger 'Quantum' Narrative," *Journal of Communication Inquiry* 23 (October 1999): 432–47.

9. Hartsock, *History of American Literary Journalism*, 13.

10. Wolfe, "New Journalism," 29.

11. Hartsock, *History of American Literary Journalism*, 51, 69, 241–48.

12. Charles A. Laughlin, *Chinese Reportage: The Aesthetics of Historical Experience* (Durham: Duke University Press, 2002), 1.

13. Tom Leddy, "The Nature of Everyday Aesthetics," in *The Aesthetics of Everyday Life*, ed. Andrew Light and Jonathan M. Smith (New York: Columbia University Press, 2005), 4, 7.

14. Joseph H. Kupfer, *Experience as Art: Aesthetics in Everyday Life* (Albany: State University of New York Press, 1983), 191–93.

15. Ibid.

16. Mark Edmundson, "Theory's Battle against the Poets," *Harper's*, August 1995, 31.

17. Wolfe, "New Journalism" 7–9, 22, 32–33, 37–41; Hartsock, *History of American Literary Journalism,* 118.

18. Wolfe, "New Journalism," 22.

19. Hartsock, *History of American Literary Journalism,* 82–83.

20. See my more complete discussion in "The Critical Marginalization of American Literary Journalism," *Critical Studies in Mass Communication* 15 (1998): 61–84.

21. James Agee and Walker Evans, *Let Us Now Praise Famous Men: Three Tenant Families* (1941; repr., Boston: Houghton Mifflin, 1969), 239.

1. Telling News Naturally

1. Jon Franklin, "Frightening Journey through Tunnels of the Brain," in *The Best of Pulitzer Prize News Writing*, ed. William David Sloan, Valarie McCrary, and Johanna Cleary (Columbus: Publishing Horizons, 1986), 74.

2. I use this spelling for clarity. Undoubtedly old-timers will be disappointed because it replaces "lede." The spelling "lede," for the beginning of a news story, was coined in the news business in the nineteenth century to distinguish it from "lead," as in the soft, malleable metal used for casting type (also, "leading" is the amount of space between lines of type). Because "lede" is the more unfamiliar spelling, I have favored "lead."

3. Hayden White, *The Content of the Form: Narrative Discourse and Historical Representation* (Baltimore: Johns Hopkins University Press, 1987), 1.

4. Timothy C. Brock, Jeffrey J. Strange, and Melanie C. Green, "Power beyond Reckoning," in *Narrative Impact: Social and Cognitive Foundations*, ed. Timothy C. Brock, Jeffrey J. Strange, and Melanie C. Green (New York: Psychology Press, 2002), 1.

5. In speaking of "story" in the traditional narrative sense, I should make a distinction. When it comes to discussing "story" in journalism, the term is not so easily identified. When I was a newspaper reporter, we talked of hard news or breaking news as "hard news stories." But they were clearly on the model of the summary lead, inverted pyramid type of documentary account I discuss in this chapter, and in many ways rhetorically operate in opposition to traditional narrative. Or they were conventional feature stories. Read on, and the reader will see what I mean.

6. John C. Hartsock, *A History of American Literary Journalism: The Emergence of a Modern Narrative Form* (Amherst: University of Massachusetts Press, 2000), 55–59, 229–40. Also see David T. Z. Mindich, *Just the Facts: How Objectivity Came to Define American Journalism* (New York: New York University Press, 1998), which provides a fuller, more nuanced account. Where the hard news story stands today is difficult to assess. It is alive and well in the *New York Times*, as well as in small papers like my hometown *Cortland Standard*. But given the decline of the daily newspaper in recent years and the rise of digital news, it remains to be seen if the traditional hard news story has much of a future.

7. See Gérard Genette, "Frontiers of Narrative," in *Figures of Literary Discourse*, trans. Alan Sheridan (New York: Columbia University Press, 1982), 127; and Robert Scholes, "Language, Narrative, and Anti-narrative," in *On Narrative*, ed., W. J. T. Mitchell (Chicago: University of Chicago Press, 1981), 205.

8. One can detect here in the emphasis on "narrative" and "descriptive" the old modes of discourse articulated by the Scottish rhetorician Alexander Bain in 1866, modes that included persuasion, exposition, narration, and description, which would haunt at least a half century of freshman composition courses when they started to be introduced in the late nineteenth century. But by doing so, the four modes entered more broadly into English vernacular culture and are now all but taken for granted. See Robert J. Connors, "The Rise and Fall of the Modes of Discourse," *College Composition and Communication* 32.4 (December 1981): 441–55. For "setting," see Alison Booth and Kelly J. Mays, *The Norton Introduction to Literature*, 10th ed. (New York: Norton, 2010), ix–xi. One can detect in the emphasis on

narrative and descriptive Mikhail Bakhtin's concept of the "chronotope," which I explore more fully in the next chapter.

9. Louis L. Snyder and Richard B. Morris, eds., *A Treasury of Great Reporting: "Literature under Pressure" from the Sixteenth Century to Our Own Time*, preface by Herbert Bayard Swope (New York: Simon and Schuster, 1962), xxix; Fred Fedler, *Reporting for the Media*, 6th ed. (New York: Harcourt Brace College Publishers, 1997), 159–61.

10. Hartsock, *History of American Literary Journalism*, 124.

11. For the complication-resolution model, see Jon Franklin, *Writing for Story: Craft Secrets of Dramatic Nonfiction by a Two-Time Pulitzer Prize Winner* (New York: Plume, 1986), 25.

12. Hans Robert Jauss, *Toward an Aesthetic of Reception*, trans. Timothy Bahti (Minneapolis: University of Minnesota Press, 1982), 23; Aristotle, *Poetics* 1450b27.

13. Diana Sugg, "Cruelest Mystery: Death before Life," *Baltimore Sun*, March 24, 2002. Sections of this chapter, e.g., the discussion of Sugg, are derived in part from my article " 'It Was a Dark and Stormy Night,': Newspaper Reporters Rediscover the Art of Narrative literary Journalism and Their Own Epistemological Hertitage," *Prose Studies* 29.2 (August 2007): 247–84.

14. Nor would I suggest that this is the only difference between human interest feature writing and a narra-descriptive journalism. But it is a significant difference.

15. Tom Wolfe, "The New Journalism," in *The New Journalism*, ed. Tom Wolfe and E. E. Johnson (New York: Harper and Row, 1973), 31.

16. George Orwell, *Homage to Catalonia* (1938; repr., New York: Harcourt Brace Jovanovich, 1980), 46.

17. Ernst Jünger, *The Storm of Steel: From the Diary of a German Storm-Troop Officer on the Western Front*, trans. Basil Creighton (1929; repr., New York: Howard Fertig, 1975), 22.

18. Hartsock, *History of American Literary Journalism*, 35–36, 137–38.

19. I initially explored this in the *History* (ibid., 247).

20. Cathy N. Davidson, "Ideology and Genre: The Rise of the Novel in America," *Proceedings of the American Antiquarian Society* 96 (1986): 303.

21. Walter Benjamin, "On Some Motifs in Baudelaire," in *Illuminations*, ed. Hannah Arendt, trans. Harry Zohn (New York: Schocken, 1969), 159.

22. Ibid.

23. Wolfgang Iser, *The Act of Reading: A Theory of Aesthetic Response* (Baltimore: Johns Hopkins University Press, 1978), 68.

24. *The Compact Edition of the Oxford English Dictionary*, vol. 1 (Oxford: Oxford University Press, 1971), s.v. "constative."

25. Iser, *Act of Reading*, 61.

26. Jauss, *Toward an Aesthetic of Reception*, 21.

27. Hartsock, *History of American Literary Journalism*, 68.

28. Quoted in Joaquín Martínez Pizarro, *A Rhetoric of the Scene: Dramatic Narrative in the Early Middle Ages* (Toronto: University of Toronto Press, 1989).

29. Ibid., 10, 13.

30. Jauss, *Toward an Aesthetic of Reception*, 21, 23.

31. Edward O. Wilson, "The Power of Story," *American Educator* 26 (Spring 2002): 10.

32. Brian Boyd, *On the Origin of Stories: Evolution, Cognition, and Fiction* (Cambridge: Harvard University Press, 2009), 181, 131.

33. Arthur C. Graesser, Brent Olde, and Bianca Klettke, "How Does the Mind Construct and Represent Stories?" in *Narrative Impact: Social and Cognitive Foundations*, ed. Timothy C. Brock, Jeffrey J. Strange, and Melanie C. Green (New York: Psychology Press, 2002), 240.

34. Melanie C. Green, "Transportation into Narrative Worlds: The Role of Prior Knowledge and Perceived Realism," *Discourse Processes* 38.2 (2004): 247, 257, 260, 262.

35. Ibid., 248.

36. Raymond A. Mar, William M. Kelley, Todd F. Heatherton, and C. Neil Macrae, "Detecting Agency from the Biological Motion of Veridical vs. Animated Agents," *Social Cognitive and Affective Neuroscience* 2.3 (2007): 204.

37. For psychological transport, see also Richard J. Gerrig, *Experiencing Narrative Worlds: On the Psychological Activities of Reading* (New Haven: Yale University Press, 1993), 136. See also Green, "Transportation into Narrative Worlds."

38. Jeremy Hsu, "The Secrets of Storytelling: Our Love for Telling Tales Reveals the Workings of the Mind," *Scientific American Mind* 19.4 (August 2008): 41–51.

39. Hartsock, *History of American Literary Journalism*, 61–69, 151.

40. *Oxford American Dictionary* (New York: Oxford University Press, 1980).

41. Hartsock, *History of American Literary Journalism*, 66, 191–97.

42. Hartsock, "It Was a Dark and Stormy Night".

43. Readership Institute, Impact Study, Media Management Center, Northwestern University, 2000, www.readership.org.

44. Clark, Martire, and Bartolomeo, Inc., "Leveraging Newspaper Assets: Highlights," report prepared for the American Society of Newspaper Editors and the Newspaper Association of America, October 14, 1998, http://files.asne.org.

45. Ronald Weber, "Some Sort of Artistic Excitement," in *The Reporter as Artist: A Look at the New Journalism Controversy*, ed. Ronald Weber (New York: Hastings House, 1974), 20.

46. Michael Schudson, *Discovering the News: A Social History of American Newspapers* (New York: Basic Books, 1978), 71–72, 74.

47. Mateus Yuri Passos, Érica Masiero Nering, and Juliano Mauricio de Carvalho, "The Chudnovsky Case: How Literary Journalism Can Open the 'Black Box' of Science," *Literary Journalism Studies* 2.2 (Fall 2010): 27–45.

48. Jay Rosen, "The Action of the Idea: Public Journalism in Built Form," in *The Idea of Public Journalism*, ed. Theodore L. Glasser (New York: Guilford Press, 1999), 22.

49. John J. Pauly, "Journalism and the Sociology of Public Life," in *The Idea of Public Journalism*, ed. Theodore L. Glasser (New York: Guilford Press, 1999), 148.

50. John J. Pauly, "Literary Journalism and the Drama of Civic Life," *Literary Journalism Studies* 3.2 (Fall 2011): 82.

2. Telling the Leaves from the Forest

1. Ernest Hemingway, "Italy 1927," *New Republic*, May 18, 1927, 351.

2. Mary McCarthy, "Settling the Colonel's Hash," reprinted in *Literary Journalism in the Twentieth Century*, ed. Norman Sims (New York: Oxford University Press, 1990), 252.

3. Tom Wolfe, "The New Journalism," in *The New Journalism*, ed. Tom Wolfe and E. E. Johnson (New York: Harper and Row, 1973), 33.

4. Stephen Greenblatt, *The Swerve: How the World Became Modern* (New York: Norton, 2011), 254.

5. Sestri is known more formally as Sestri Levante and is located on the Italian Riviera not far from Portofino. Comune Sestri Levante, www.comune.sestri-levante.ge.it.

6. An approximate consensus as a community, inherently interpretive, is similar to the idea of an "interpretive community" articulated by, among others, Stanley Fish. See his *Is There a Text in This Classroom? The Authority of Interpretive Communities* (Cambridge:

Harvard University Press, 1980). For the "context of experience of aesthetic perception," see Hans Robert Jauss, *Toward an Aesthetic of Reception*, trans. Timothy Bahti (Minneapolis: University of Minnesota Press, 1982), 23.

7. I pick up here where I left off in my earlier history by exploring more deeply the place of Nietzschean literary aesthetics for understanding the genre, as well as Bakhtin's concept of the novel of the inconclusive present.

8. Joseph Childers and Gary Hentzi, general eds., *Columbia Dictionary of Modern Literary and Cultural Criticism* (New York: Columbia University Press, 1995), 74.

9. Friedrich Nietzsche, "On Truth and Falsity in Their Ultramoral Sense," in *Early Greek Philosophy and Other Essays* (1911), trans. Maximilian A. Mügge (New York: Russell and Russell, 1964), 181.

10. Ibid, 179, 181, emphasis added.

11. Mas'ud Zavarzadeh, *The Mythopoeic Reality: The Postwar American Nonfiction Novel* (Urbana: University of Illinois Press, 1976), 226.

12. This was thoughtfully explored in Darrel Mansell's "Unsettling the Colonel's Hash: 'Fact' in Autobiography," in Sims, *Literary Journalism in the Twentieth Century*, 261–80.

13. McCarthy, "Settling the Colonel's Hash," 250.

14. Ibid., 253. McCarthy's usage of "centrifugal" and "centripetal" should not be confused with Ma'sud Zavarzadeh's use of the terms in his later examination of the "nonfiction novel." See Zavarzadeh, *Mythopoeic Reality*, 226. Their meanings are almost opposite. The differences arise because both are engaged in metaphor making, and what that implies about how they explain their metaphors.

15. Mikhail M. Bakhtin, *The Dialogic Imagination*, ed. Michael Holquist, trans. Caryl Emerson and Michael Holquist (Austin: University of Texas Press, 1981), 84, 85.

16. See, for example, Nele Bemong et al., eds. *Bakhtin's Theory of the Literary Chronotope: Reflections, Applications, Perspectives* (Ghent: Academia Press, 2010).

17. Bakhtin, *Dialogic Imagination*, 84; Bemong et al., *Bakhtin's Theory*.

18. Bakhtin, *Dialogic Imagination*, 253.

19. Wolfgang Iser, *The Act of Reading: A Theory of Aesthetic Response* (Baltimore: Johns Hopkins University Press, 1978), 140.

20. Bakhtin, *Dialogic Imagination*, 254.

21. Bakhtin takes a similar if slightly different position: "All the novel's abstract elements—philosophical and social generalizations, ideas, analyses of cause and effect—gravitate toward the chronotope and through it take on flesh and blood" (*Dialogic Imagination*, 250).

22. Paula Bock, "In Her Mother's Shoes," *Seattle Times*, December 1, 2002.

23. While *Les Misérables* references historical events, they are backdrops for fictional or invented protagonists.

24. See, among other accounts, George Plimpton, "Capote's Long Ride," *New Yorker*, October 1, 1997, 62–70; Kevin Helliker, "Capote Classic 'In Cold Blood' Tainted by Long-Lost Files," *Wall Street Journal*, February 8, 2013.

25. This is explored by Lennard J. Davis in *Factual Fictions: The Origins of the English Novel* (Philadelphia: University of Pennsylvania Press, 1996), 151–61. I also explore the issue in my *A History of American Literary Journalism: The Emergence of a Modern Narrative Form* (Amherst: University of Massachusetts Press, 2000), 81–90, 111–20.

26. It is a minor literary classic of the regional school of writers if inclusion in *The Oxford Companion to American Literature* serves as the basis for the claim. See James D. Hart, *Oxford Companion to American Literature*, rev. Phillip W. Leininger, 6th ed. (New

York: Oxford University Press, 1995), 710, s.v. "Westcott, Edward Noyes," the novel's author. By today's standards *David Harum* would be considered local color. And by those same standards the prose would appear to be overwrought, and the dialect renders the dialogue nearly indecipherable in the attempt to demonstrate the vernacular of small-town upstate New York life.

27. Edward Noyes Westcott, *David Harum: A Story of American Life* (New York: D. Appleton and Company, 1898–99). On the aphorism, see *Bartlett's Familiar Quotations*, 14th ed. (Boston: Little, Brown, 1968), 811; and Westcott, *David Harum*, 184.

28. Arthur T. Vance, *The Real David Harum* (New York: Baker and Taylor, 1902).

29. Full disclosure: the author and his wife are the current owners of the house and have been closely involved in its preservation.

30. Westcott, *David Harum*, 205.

31. The same occurred when the Cortland Overall Company placed the real-life photo of David Hannum on its stationery and invoices, identifying him as the fictional "David Harum." Moreover, around the time of the radio soap opera in the 1940s, as best can be dated, a print of a photograph was distributed with the caption "David Harum's homestead as it looked 76 years ago." The photograph shows a wintry scene with David Hannum and his son Frankie in a horse-drawn sled in front of the house, which existed then and still exists in time and space. The photograph has been tentatively dated to 1869. All references to David Hannum / David Harum memorabilia are in the collection of the author, although much can be found online, especially postcards, the original book, and Will Rogers memorabilia on eBay.

32. Robert C. Schank and Tamara R. Berman, "The Persuasive Role of Stories in Knowledge and Action," in *Narrative Impact: Social and Cognitive Foundations*, ed. Melanie C. Green, Jeffrey J. Strange, and Timothy C. Brock (New York: Psychology Press, 2002), 292.

33. Hartsock, *History of American Literary Journalism*, 101–4.

34. Victor Shklovsky, "Art as Technique," in *Russian Formalist Criticism: Four Essays*, ed. and trans. Lee T. Lemon and Marion J. Reis (Lincoln: University of Nebraska Press, 1965), 12.

35. Ibid., 3.

36. Ibid., 12, 11.

37. Ernst Jünger, *The Storm of Steel: From the Diary of a German Storm-Troop Officer on the Western Front*, trans. Basil Creighton (1929; repr., New York: Howard Fertig, 1975), 106.

38. Bruce Chatwin, "Ernst Jünger: An Aesthete at War," in *What Am I Doing Here* (New York: Viking, 1989), 301.

39. Marcus Paul Bullock, *The Violent Eye: Ernst Jünger's Visions and Revisions on the European Right* (Detroit: Wayne State University Press, 1992), 126.

40. Jünger, *Storm of Steel*, 22–23, emphasis added.

41. See Gaye Tuchman, "Making News by Doing Work: Routinizing the Unexpected," in *A Social Meaning of News*, ed. Dan Berkowitz (Thousand Oaks, CA: Sage, 1997), 171–92. I find Tuchman's typology of journalistic genres too rigid and simplistic, however. It is based on interviews at one newspaper and one radio station in the United States. As anyone who has ever worked in multiple newsrooms will know, those genres cannot be so neatly delineated. For example, "hard" news and "spot" news were not necessarily different in newsrooms I worked in. Tuchman tries to address this in a graphic table, but the result is still an attempt at discrete classification attended, ironically, by the evidence of when discrete classification does not work (see 171–83).

42. James Agee and Walker Evans, *Let Us Now Praise Famous Men: Three Tenant Families* (1941; repr., Boston: Houghton Mifflin, 1969).

43. Hartsock, *History of American Literary Journalism,* 185; William Stott, *Documentary Expression and Thirties America* (New York: Oxford University Press, 1973), 238, 240.

44. Marie Majerová, "Als Egonek den Roman zum Tod verurteilte," in *Kisch-Kalendar,* ed. Franz Carl Weiskopf ([East] Berlin: Aufbau-Verlag, 1955), 185–86; translation in the text by Lydia Fetler Hartsock and John C. Hartsock.

45. Quoted ibid., 185–86.

46. Paul Ashdown, "James Agee," in *A Sourcebook of American Literary Journalism: Representative Writers in an Emerging Genre,* ed. Thomas B. Connery (New York: Greenwood Press, 1992), 202.

47. Agee and Evans, *Let Us Now,* 265–66.

48. Ibid., 266.

49. Ibid., l–li.

50. Ibid., 33.

51. Ibid., xlvii.

52. See, for example, Shelley Fisher Fishkin's examination in *From Fact to Fiction: Journalism and Imaginative Writing in America* (Baltimore: Johns Hopkins University Press, 1985), 137–39.

53. Ernest Hemingway, "A Silent, Ghastly Procession," *Toronto Daily Star,* October 20, 1922, reprinted in *By-Line: Ernest Hemingway: Selected Articles and Dispatches of Four Decades,* ed. William White (New York: Charles Scribner's Sons, 1967), 51.

54. Ibid.

55. Ernest Hemingway, *The Short Stories of Ernest Hemingway* (New York: Charles Scribner's Sons, 1966), 97.

56. A synonym for tasting of alum is astringency, which is natural to dry red wines because it is the quality that makes them feel dry, or that makes the mouth pucker from dryness. But there are any number of causes for astringency. See *Roget's International Thesaurus,* 3rd ed. (New York: Thomas Y. Crowell, 1962), s.v. "astringency"; Jancis Robinson, ed., *Oxford Companion to Wine,* 2nd ed. (Oxford: Oxford University Press, 1999), s.v. "astringency," "mouthfeel," "bentonite."

57. Mary Poovey, *A History of the Modern Fact* (Chicago: University of Chicago Press, 1998), 40.

58. This recalls Derrida's concept of linguistic excess. The difference is that there is not only a linguistic excess but also a phenomenal excess, and as we will see, it is the relationship between these two that poses the quandary in quantum physics. The only question, then, is which comes first, which is ultimately a chicken-and-egg question. See Jacques Derrida, *Writing and Difference,* trans. Alan Bass (London: Routledge, 1978), 75.

59. Poovey, *History of the Modern Fact,* 15, emphasis added.

60. Charles R. Berger and Steven H. Chaffee, eds., *Handbook of Communication Science* (Beverley Hills: Sage, 1987), 17, emphasis added.

61. This question is explored in my article "The Critical Marginalization of American Literary Journalism," *Critical Studies in Mass Communication* 15 (1998): 61–84.

62. Iser, *Act of Reading,* 125.

63. David Herman, *Storytelling and the Sciences of the Mind* (Cambridge: MIT Press, 2013), 98.

64. Jauss, *Toward an Aesthetic of Reception,* 53.

65. Lee Smolin, *The Life of the Cosmos* (New York: Oxford University Press, 1997), 250.

66. Ibid., 251, 249.

67. Samuel Johnson, *A Journey to the Western Islands of Scotland* (1775), and James Boswell, *The Journal of a Tour to the Hebrides with Samuel Johnson LL.D.* (1786), ed. and intro. Peter Levi (New York: Penguin, 1984), 141.

68. Ibid., 139. I initially explore this in *History of American Literary Journalism*, 53.

69. For Boswell's account of the visit to MacKinnon's cave, see his *Journal of a Tour to the Hebrides with Samuel Johnson LL.D.* (1786).

70. See, for example, Thomas B. Connery, "A Third Way to Tell the Story: American Literary Journalism at the Turn of the Century," in Sims, *Literary Journalism in the Twentieth Century*, 3–20; Ronald Weber, "Some Sort of Artistic Excitement," in *The Reporter as Artist: A Look at the New Journalism Controversy*, ed. Ronald Weber (New York: Hastings House, 1974), 18–20, 21; Dan Wakefield, "The Personal Voice and the Impersonal Eye," in Weber, *The Reporter as Artist*, 41–44, 46; Herbert Gold, "On Epidemic First-Personism," in Weber, *The Reporter as Artist*, 283–87; Dwight Macdonald, "Parajournalism, or Tom Wolfe's Magic Writing Machine," in Weber, *The Reporter as Artist*, 223, 227; Thomas Powers, "Cry Wolfe," *Commonweal* 102 (1975): 497, 499; Alfred Kazin, "The Imagination of Fact," in *Bright Book of Life* (Boston: Little, Brown, 1973), 240.

71. Mark Edmundson, "Theory's Battle against the Poets," *Harper's* 291 (August 1995): 31.

72. John Keats, "Ode on a Grecian Urn" (1819), in *The Complete Poetry and Selected Prose of John Keats*, ed. Harold Edgar Briggs (New York: Modern Library, 1915), 295.

73. Werner Heisenberg, *Physics and Philosophy: The Revolution in Modern Science,* World Perspectives, vol. 19, ed. Ruth Nanda Anshen (New York: Harper and Brothers, 1958), 179; Werner Heisenberg, *Physics and Beyond: Encounters and Conversations,* World Perspectives, vol. 42, ed. Ruth Nanda Anshen, trans. Arnold J. Pomerans (New York: Harper and Row, 1971), 135.

74. Ronald Weber, *The Literature of Fact: Literary Nonfiction in American Writing* (Athens: Ohio University Press, 1980), 1.

75. John Hersey, *Hiroshima* (1946; New York: Bantam, 1986).

76. Ernest Hemingway, *Death in the Afternoon* (New York: Charles Scribner's Sons, 1932), 192.

77. Schank and Berman, "Persuasive Role of Stories in Knowledge and Action," 292.

78. Brian Boyd, *On the Origin of Stories: Evolution, Cognition, and Fiction* (Cambridge: Harvard University Press, 2009), 166.

79. Iser, *Act of Reading*, 70.

80. For "iconic," see David L. Ulin, "What Happened Here?," *Columbia Journalism Review*, February 25, 2010, www.cjr.org.

81. Joan Didion, "Some Dreamers of the Golden Dream," in *Slouching Towards Bethlehem* (New York: Farrar, Straus and Giroux, 1968), 22, 23, 26.

82. Robert S. Boynton, *The New New Journalism* (New York: Vintage, 2005), 126.

83. Donald Rayfield, *Anton Chekhov: A Life* (New York: Henry Holt, 1998), 203; Ernest J. Simmons, *Chekhov: A Biography* (Chicago: University of Chicago Press, 1970), 190. Over the years I have heard many variations on this axiom, including that the gun was, no less, a cannon (this from an undergraduate literature class). Chekhov was known to repeat the axiom in many different variations.

84. As I noted in *A History of American Literary Journalism*, David Bromwich makes a not dissimilar observation about the seemingly contingent in rearticulating a viewpoint of Irving Howe: "The detail we call irrelevant or gratuitous has a way of seeming peculiarly

right, so that we think it belongs just where it occurs, though strictly speaking it lacks any formal and dramatic warrant." Arguably, however, the lingering uncertainty of the paternity of Miller's child has a significant formal or dramatic warrant, given its location in the conclusion. Or, arguably, if it does seem "peculiarly right," as Bromwich says, it seems so because it tries to mimic precisely what, in part, makes documentary forms so distinctive: that there is always a lingering and unpredictable unassimilated. See my *History of American Literary Journalism*, 174. For David Bromwich, see "What Novels Are For," *New York Times Book Review,* October 30, 1994, 7.

85. Plimpton, "Capote's Long Ride," 61–70; Truman Capote, *In Cold Blood: A True Account of a Multiple Murder and Its Consequences* (New York: Signet, 1965), 341–43.

86. For the superiority of fiction over nonfiction or narrative documentary (as I would prefer), see, for example, Boyd, *On the Origin,* 381–83; Herman, *Storytelling,* 7; and Keith Oatley, "Why Fiction May Be Twice as True as Fact: Fiction as Cognitive and Emotional Simulation," *Review of General Psychology* 3.2 (June 1999): 101–17.

87. Oatley, "Why Fiction," 101–17.

88. Boyd, *On the Origin,* 382–83.

89. Ibid., 129.

90. John Tooby and Leda Cosmides, "Does Beauty Build Adapted Minds? Toward an Evolutionary Theory of Aesthetics, Fiction and the Arts," *SubStance* 94/95 (2001): 12.

91. Boyd, *On the Origin,* 195.

92. Iser, *Act of Reading,* 140.

93. George R. Potts, Mark F. St. John, and Donald Kirson, "Incorporating New Information into Existing World Knowledge," *Cognitive Psychology* 21 (1989): 331.

94. Richard J. Gerrig, *Experiencing Narrative Worlds: On the Psychological Activities of Reading* (New Haven: Yale University Press, 1993), 136. See also Melanie C. Green and Timothy C. Brock, "In the Mind's Eye: Transportation-Imagery Model of Narrative Persuasion," in *Narrative Impact: Social and Cognitive Foundations,* ed. Timothy C. Brock, Jeffrey J. Strange, and Melanie C. Green (New York: Psychology Press, 2002), 317.

95. I initially explored this in chapter 1. See Melanie C. Green, "Transportation into Narrative Worlds: The Role of Prior Knowledge and Perceived Realism," *Discourse Processes* 38.2 (2004): 257, 260, 262; Raymond A. Mar, William M. Kelley, Todd F. Heatherton, and C. Neil Macrae, "Detecting Agency from the Biological Motion of Veridical vs. Animated Agents," *Social Cognitive and Affective Neuroscience* 2.3 (2007): 204.

96. Schank and Berman, "Pervasive Role of Stories in Knowledge and Action," 301–3.

97. Potts, St. John, and Kirson, *Incorporating New Information,* 331.

98. Dorrit Cohn, *The Distinction of Fiction* (Baltimore: Johns Hopkins University Press, 1999), 15.

99. Herman, *Storytelling,* 104.

100. Ibid., 132.

101. Ibid., 142. See also Gerrig, *Experiencing Narrative Worlds,* 136.

102. Gerrig, *Experiencing Narrative Worlds,* 224. See also Green, "Transportation into Narrative Worlds," 257, 260, 262.

103. Herman, *Storytelling,* 132.

104. Oatley, "Why Fiction," 7.

105. Dale Maharidge and Michael Williamson, *And Their Children After Them* (New York: Pantheon, 1989).

106. Hersey, *Hiroshima,* 21.

107. Jauss, *Toward an Aesthetic of Reception,* 53.

108. Hartsock, *History of American Literary Journalism,* 41–51.

109. Mikhail Bakhtin, *Problems of Dostoevsky's Poetics,* trans. R. W. Rotsel ([Ann Arbor]: Ardis, 1973), 88–89.

110. Bakhtin, *Dialogic Imagination,* 39.

111. Iser, *Act of Reading,* 369.

112. Agee, *Let Us Now,* 266.

113. I explore this question, but only in a very preliminary fashion, in my *History,* 42.

114. Hemingway, "Italy," 353.

115. Peter Dear, *Discipline and Experience: The Mathematical Way in the Scientific Revolution* (Chicago: University of Chicago Press, 1995), 25, emphasis added.

3. The Death of the Dream of Paradise

1. Tom Wolfe, *The Right Stuff* (New York: Bantam, 1980), 4.

2. See, from *The Reporter as Artist: A Look at the New Journalism Controversy,* ed. Ronald Weber (New York: Hastings House, 1974), Ronald Weber, "Some Sort of Artistic Excitement," 18–20, 21; Dan Wakefield, "The Personal Voice and the Impersonal Eye," 41–44; Herbert Gold, "On Epidemic First-Personism," 283–87; and Dwight Macdonald, "Parajournalism, Or Tom Wolfe's Magic Writing Machine," 223, 227; also Thomas Powers, "Cry Wolfe," *Commonweal* 102 (1975): 497, 499; Alfred Kazin, "The Imagination of Fact," in *Bright Book of Life: American Novelists and Storytellers from Hemingway to Mailer* (Boston: Little, Brown, 1973), 240.

3. Mircea Eliade, *Myths, Dreams and Mysteries: The Encounter between Contemporary Faiths and Archaic Realities,* ed. Ruth Nanden Anshen, trans. Philip Mairet (New York: Harper and Row, 1960), 28.

4. Mircea Eliade, *Myth and Reality,* trans. Willard Trask (New York: Harper and Row, 1963), 6.

5. Michel de Certeau, *The Writing of History,* trans. Tom Conley (New York: Columbia University Press, 1988), 1–3.

6. Eliade, *Myth and Reality,* 191.

7. Ibid., 2.

8. Roland Barthes, *Mythologies,* trans. Annette Lavers (New York: Noonday Press, 1972), 109–11, 116–26, 114–15, emphasis added.

9. A. Bartlett Giamatti, *Take Time for Paradise: Americans and Their Games* (New York: Summit Books, 1989), 95, 93, 36, 42–43.

10. Eliade, *Myth and Reality,* 191, 5.

11. Giamatti, *Take Time,* 71.

12. James W. Carey, ed., *Media, Myths, and Narratives: Television and the Press* (Thousand Oaks, CA: Sage, 1988).

13. Jack Lule, *Daily News, Eternal Stories: The Mythological Role of Journalism* (New York: Guilford Press, 2001).

14. N. R. Kleinfield, "U.S. Attacked: Hijacked Jets Destroy Twin Towers and Hit Pentagon in Day of Terror," *New York Times,* September 12, 2001.

15. Cornelius Ryan, *The Last Battle* (New York: Simon and Schuster, 1966), 386–87; Albert Speer, *Inside the Third Reich: Memoirs,* trans. Richard Winston and Clara Winston (New York: Macmillan, 1970), 463.

16. Serge Schmemann, "U.S. Attacked: President Vows to Exact Punishment for Evil," *New York Times,* September 12, 2001.

17. Stanley Cohen and Jock Young, "Effects and Consequences," in *The Manufacture of*

News: Social Problems, Deviance and the Mass Media, ed. Stanley Cohen and Jock Young, rev. ed. (London: Constable, 1981), 431.

18. S. Elizabeth Bird and Robert W. Dardenne, "Myth, Chronicle, and Story: Exploring the Narrative Qualities of News," in *Media, Myths, and Narratives: Television and the Press*, ed. James W. Carey (Newbury Park, CA: Sage, 1988), 81.

19. Clifford Geertz, "Common Sense as a Cultural System," in *Local Knowledge: Further Essays in Interpretive Anthropology* (New York: Basic Books, 1983), 76, 93.

20. Ernst Jünger, *The Storm of Steel: From the Diary of a German Storm-Troop Officer on the Western Front*, trans. Basil Creighton (1929; repr., New York: Howard Fertig, 1975), 23.

21. Bird and Dardenne, "Myth, Chronicle, and Story," 71.

22. Barthes, *Mythologies*, 117–18.

23. James W. Carey, "A Cultural Approach to Communication," in *Communication as Culture: Essays on Media and Society*, ed. James W. Carey (Boston: Unwin Hyman, 1989), 19. Originally published with the same title in *Communication* 2.1 (1975).

24. Tom Wolfe, "The New Journalism," in *The New Journalism*, ed. Tom Wolfe and E. E. Johnson (New York: Harper and Row, 1973), 31–32.

25. Wolfe, *Right Stuff*, 2.

26. Eliade, *Myth and Reality*, 186.

27. Norman Sims, "The Literary Journalists," in *The Literary Journalists*, ed. Norman Sims (New York: Ballantine, 1984), 22, emphasis added.

28. Ibid.

29. Tracy Kidder, *House* (Boston: Houghton Mifflin, 1985), 329.

30. Eliade, *Dreams*, 28.

31. Wolfe, "New Journalism," 40.

32. Barthes, *Mythologies*, 135.

33. Wolfe, *Right Stuff*, 1.

34. Ibid., 3, 4.

35. Ibid., 3.

36. Joseph Brodsky, "On 'September 1, 1939' by W. H. Auden," in *Less Than One: Selected Essays* (New York: Farrar Straus Giroux, 1986), 317.

37. Wolfe, *Right Stuff*, 3, 6.

38. M. C. Howatson, ed., *The Oxford Companion to Classical Literature*, 2nd ed. (Oxford: Oxford University Press, 1990), 177, s.v. "Daedalus."

39. Tom Wolfe, *The Electric Kool-Aid Acid Test* (New York: Bantam, 1969). For references to ingesting LSD in beverages like orange juice and Kool-Aid, see 61, 68–87, and 244.

40. Tom Wolfe, "The Kandy-Kolored Tangerine-Flake Streamline Baby," in *The Kandy-Kolored Tangerine-Flake Streamline Baby* (New York: Farrar, Straus and Giroux, 1966), xiii–xiv.

41. The idea of the American Dream is credited to the popular historian James Truslow Adams: "But there has been also the American dream, that dream of a land in which life should be better and richer and fuller for every man, with opportunity for each according to ability or achievement. It is a difficult dream for the European upper classes to interpret adequately, and too many of us ourselves have grown weary and mistrustful of it. It is not a dream of motor cars and high wages merely, but a dream of social order in which each man and each woman shall be able to attain to the fullest stature of which they are innately capable, and be recognized by others for what they are, regardless of the fortuitous circumstances of birth or position." James Truslow Adams, *The Epic of America* (Boston: Little, Brown, 1931), 214–15.

42. Wolfe, "Kandy-Colored," 61–64.

43. John C. Hartsock, *A History of American Literary Journalism: The Emergence of a Modern Narrative Form* (Amherst: University of Massachusetts Press, 2000), 61–69, 151.

44. Alan Trachtenberg, "Experiments in Another Country: Stephen Crane's City Sketches," *Southern Review* 10 (April 1974): 273.

45. Linda Hutcheon, *The Politics of Postmodernism* (New York: Routledge, 1989), 89–91, 94. Hutcheon emphasizes the postmodern contrast between earlier and more contemporary representation. To me it is logical to extend that to the contrast between representation in secular myth and the more (relatively) contemporary representations by narrative literary journalists. This provides one more measure for the postmodern nature of the New Journalism. I would like to thank Holly E. Schreiber for bringing to my attention what I see as Hutcheon's important contribution to understanding postmodern parody.

46. Ibid., 99, 101.

47. Truman Capote, *In Cold Blood: A True Account of a Multiple Murder and Its Consequences* (New York: Signet, 1965), 28–30, 35–36.

48. Paul de Man, "Criticism and Crisis," in *Blindness and Insight* (Minneapolis: University of Minnesota Press, 1983), 12.

49. See, among other accounts, George Plimpton, "Capote's Long Ride," *New Yorker,* October 1, 1997, 62–70; Kevin Helliker, "Capote Classic 'In Cold Blood' Tainted by Long-Lost Files," *Wall Street Journal,* February 8, 2013.

50. Capote, *In Cold Blood,* 6.

51. Joan Didion, "Some Dreamers of the Golden Dream," in *Slouching Towards Bethlehem* (New York: Farrar, Straus and Giroux, 1968), 3.

52. Ibid., 4.

53. Ibid., 15.

54. Ibid., 17.

55. Giamatti, *Take Time,* 36.

56. Ibid., 42–43.

57. Didion, "Some Dreamers of the Golden Dream," 21.

58. Ibid., 24.

59. Ibid., 28.

60. In 2006 Lucille Miller's daughter published in the *Los Angeles Times* an account of the day she learned her father had died. See Debra J. Miller, "A Mother's Crime," *Los Angeles Times,* April 2, 2006. According to the article, Lucille Miller served seven years of a life sentence in prison and died in 1986.

61. Sara Davidson, "Real Property," in *Real Property* (Garden City, NY: Doubleday, 1980), 16.

62. Ibid., 19, 35.

63. Ibid., 36.

64. Ibid., 39–40.

65. Ibid., 15.

66. See Kevin Kerrane and Ben Yagoda, eds., *The Art of Fact: A Historical Anthology of Literary Journalism* (New York: Scribner, 1997), 302; Edd Applegate, *Literary Journalism: A Biographical Dictionary of Writers and Editors* (Westport, CT: Greenwood, 1996), 260–63; Arthur J. Kaul, ed., *American Literary Journalists, 1945–1995,* 1st series, *Dictionary of Literary Biography* 185 (Detroit: Gale Research, 1997); and Hartsock, *History of American Literary Journalism,* 200.

67. Eliade, *Myth and Reality,* 2.

68. Ibid., 123. But here, the source sings the lyrics incorrectly. The correct lyrics, originally sung by Scott MacKenzie, are, "If you're going to San Francisco . . ."

69. Michael Herr, *Dispatches* (New York: Vintage, 1991), 185, 83, 7.

70. Ibid., 137.

71. Ibid., 5, 8.

72. Jünger, *Storm of Steel,* 22–23.

73. Sims, "Literary Journalists," 21–25.

4. The "Elasticity" of Literary Reportage

1. See Kevin Kerrane and Ben Yagoda, eds., *The Art of Fact: A Historical Anthology of Literary Journalism* (New York: Scribner, 1997), 11, 536–48.

2. I initially explored this subject in my article "Literary Reportage: The 'Other' Literary Journalism" in *Genre: Forms of Discourse and Culture.* 42 (Spring/Summer 2009): 113–34.

3. Tom Wolfe, "The New Journalism," in *The New Journalism,* ed. Tom Wolfe and E. E. Johnson (New York: Harper and Row, 1973), 9.

4. Edd Applegate, ed., *Literary Journalism: A Biographical Dictionary of Writers and Editors* (Westport, CT: Greenwood Press, 1996), xvi.

5. Gay Talese, *Fame and Obscurity* (New York: Ivy Books, 1993), vii.

6. Richard Goldstein, *Reporting the Counterculture* (Boston: Unwin Hyman, 1989), xvii.

7. John C. Hartsock, *A History of American Literary Journalism: The Emergence of a Modern Narrative Form* (Amherst: University of Massachusetts Press, 2000), 81–117.

8. See *Webster's Seventh New Collegiate Dictionary,* s.v. "reportage."

9. Lettre Ulysses Award, 2006, www.lettre-ulysses-award.org.

10. *Granta,* April 29, 2007, www.granta.com.

11. Rudolph G. Wagner, *Inside a Service Trade: Studies in Contemporary Chinese Prose,* Harvard-Yenching Institute Monograph series 34 (Cambridge: Council on East Asian Studies, Harvard University, 1992), 376.

12. Peter Monteath, "The Spanish Civil War and the Aesthetics of Reportage," in *Literature and War,* ed. David Bevan (Amsterdam: Rodopi, 1990), 81.

13. See the Norwegian-themed issue of *Literary Journalism Studies* 5.1 (Spring 2013); also see Juan Orlando Pérez González, "Revolution Is Such a Beautiful Word! Literary Journalism in Castro's Cuba" *Literary Journalism Studies* 4.2 (Fall 2012): 1–28; and Sonja Merljak Zdovc, "Literary Journalism: The Intersection of Literature and Journalism," *Acta Neophilologica* 37.1–2 (2004): 17–22.

14. Lettre Ulysses Award, 2005, www.lettre-ulysses-award.org.

15. Lettre Ulysses Award, 2003, www.lettre-ulysses-award.org.

16. Harold B. Segel, *Egon Erwin Kisch: The Raging Reporter* (West Lafayette, IN: Purdue University Press, 1992), 74.

17. Charles A. Laughlin, *Chinese Reportage: The Aesthetics of Historical Experience* (Durham: Duke University Press, 2002), 1.

18. Wagner, *Inside a Service Trade,* 348–49.

19. *Cihai* (Thesaurus), one-volume ed. (Shanghai: Shanghai cishu chubanshe, 1979), 679, cited by Yingjin Zhang, "Narrative, Ideology, Subjectivity: Defining a Subjective Discourse in Chinese Reportage," in *Politics, Ideology, and Literary Discourse in Modern China,* ed. Liu Kang and Xiaobing Kang (Durham: Duke University Press, 1992), 214.

20. On *ocherk,* see Kenneth Katzner, ed., *English-Russian Russian-English Dictionary* (New York: John Wiley and Sons, 1984); on see also *The Great Soviet Encyclopedia,* 3rd ed. (1970–1979), s.v. "Sketch, literary," http://encyclopedia2.thefreedictionary.com.

21. Isabel Hilton, "Commentary—A Prize for the Underrated Genre of Literary Reportage," *New Statesman,* October 13, 2003, www.newstatesman.com.

22. John C. Hartsock, "Chapter Title: 'Murder or Execution?,'" *DoubleTake* (Spring–Summer 2007): 107–8.

23. In the text, I will continue to use the spelling "Alexievich" because this is the preferred spelling on her website. See www.alexievich.info/indexEN.html. Also, all of her later works use this spelling. But in citations of her works I use the spelling under which the work was originally published in English.

24. Svetlana Alexiyevich, "Boys in Zinc," trans. Arch Tait, *Granta* (Autumn 1990): 145–61; Alexievich, *Zinky Boys,* trans. Julia and Robin Whitby (New York: Norton, 1992). Alexievich, *Voices from Chernobyl,* trans. Keith Gessen (Normal, OK Dalkey Archive Press, 2005). Besides inclusion in Kerrane and Yagoda, *The Art of Fact,* "Boys in Zinc" was also reprinted in *The Granta Book of Reportage* in 1993. I use the original *Granta* version.

25. Anna Politkovskaya, *A Dirty War: A Russian Reporter in Chechnya,* ed. and trans. John Crowfoot (London: Harvill Press, 2001).

26. S[vetlana] Alexiyevich, *War's Unwomanly Face,* trans. Keith Hammond and Lyudmila Lezhneva (Moscow: Progress Publishers, 1988).

27. Alexiyevich, "Boys in Zinc," 151.

28. Ibid., 150.

29. William E. Harkins, *Dictionary of Russian Literature* (New York: Philosophical Library, 1956), 360.

30. Alexievich, *Zinky Boys,* 181.

31. Alexiyevich, "Boys in Zinc," 146.

32. Joseph Brodsky, "On 'September 1, 1939' by W. H. Auden," in *Less Than One: Selected Essays* (New York: Farrar Straus Giroux, 1986), 317.

33. Alexiyevich, "Boys in Zinc," 146.

34. Ibid., 152, 153.

35. Ibid., 156–57.

36. Ibid., 157.

37. Ibid., 157–58.

38. S. Elizabeth Bird and Robert W. Dardenne, "Myth, Chronicle, and Story: Exploring the Narrative Qualities of News," in *Media, Myths, and Narratives: Television and the Press,* ed. James W. Carey (Newbury Park, CA: Sage, 1988), 71.

39. Elizabeth A. Warner, "Russian Peasant Beliefs and Practices Concerning Death and the Supernatural Collected in Novosokol'niki Region, Pskov Province, Russia, 1995," pt. 2, "Death in Natural Circumstances," *Folklore* 111.2 (2000): 259; *Handbook of Burial Rites* (Toronto: Mount Pleasant Group of Cemeteries, 1985), 19.

40. Warner, "Russian Peasant Beliefs," 264; "A Question about Open Coffins," Orthodox Christian Information Center, http://orthodoxinfo.com; also witnessed by the author on numerous occasions.

41. It might be worth noting that Dovnar's kneeling before her husband is another curious detail that echoes an older tradition. It is one drawn from Russian wedding culture. In the tradition, which goes back to the nineteenth century, the bride demonstrates her obedience to her husband by getting down on her knees and prostrating herself at his feet. It recalls the passage in the Epistle to the Ephesians, traditionally recited at Russian Orthodox

weddings, which admonishes "the wife see that she reverence her husband." Of course, this can justifiably prompt protests from feminists. But again we detect the turning to an older mythos, that of Tamara's great-grandmothers, in a challenge to Soviet secular myths. See Henry Neville Hutchinson, *Marriage Customs in Many Lands* (London: Seeley Co., 1897), 199; "Wedding Traditions in Russian Orthodox Church, Judaism and Islam," www.english .pravda.ru; Ephesians 5:33 (King James version).

42. Alexiyevich, "Boys in Zinc," 151.

43. Alexievich, *Zinky Boys*, 2.

44. Ibid., 1–10.

45. Karyakin was the first notable Soviet man of letters to publicly call for the restoration of citizenship to Russian novelist and Nobel laureate Alexander Solzhenitsyn, who was exiled from the Soviet Union in 1974 and stripped of his citizenship.

46. Capote, *In Cold Blood*, 9.

47. Alexievich, "Boys in Zinc," 160–61.

48. Alexievich, *Zinky Boys*, 3–5.

49. Harkins, *Dictionary of Russian Literature*, 314, s.v. "Pushkin, Alexander Sergeyevich."

50. Alexievich, *Zinky Boys*, 6. In most translations "Valla" is translated as "Bela."

51. Ibid.

52. Ibid., 7.

53. Ibid., 10.

54. Ibid., 8.

55. John Keats, "Ode on a Grecian Urn," in *The Complete Poetry and Selected Prose of John Keats*, ed. Harold Edgar Briggs (1819; repr., New York: Modern Library, 1915), 295.

56. Nicholas Berdyaev, *Dostoevsky*, trans. Donald Atwater (New York: New American Library, 1974), 9.

57. Alexievich, *Zinky Boys*, 8.

58. Matthew 24:4–5.

59. Ibid., 9.

60. Berdyaev, *Dostoevsky*, 188–212.

61. Kerrane and Yagoda, *Art of Fact*, 536–48.

62. Politkovskaya, *A Dirty War*, 13, 102, 244.

63. Ibid., 312.

64. Ibid., 313–14.

65. John C. Hartsock, "'It Was a Dark and Stormy Night': Newspaper Reporters Rediscover the Art of Narrative Literary Journalism and Their Own Epistemological Heritage," *Prose Studies* 29.2 (August 2007): 263.

66. Hartsock, *History of American Literary Journalism*, 13.

67. Wagner, *Inside a Service Trade*, 360.

68. Laughlin, *Chinese Reportage*, 13, 17–44.

69. *Physiology of Petersburg* (Fiziologia Peterburga) is the correct title of the original 1845 edition published in St Petersburg. The translation I use here is Nikolai Nekrasov, ed., *Petersburg: The Physiology of a City*, trans. Thomas Gaiton Marullo (Evanston: Northwestern University Press, 2009). It contains selections from the original. For "physiological sketch," see Alexander Grigorevich Tseitlin, *Stanovlenie Realisma v Russkoi Literature: Ruskii Fiziologicheski Ocherk* (The formation of realism in Russian literature: The Russian physiological sketch) (Moscow: Izdatelstvo "Nayuka," 1965), 91–94, 159–65, 302–8.

70. Kenneth A. Lantz, "Physiological Sketch," in *The Dostoevsky Encyclopedia* (Westport, CT: Greenwood, 2004), 317–18.

71. Martina Lauster, *Sketches of the Nineteenth Century: European Journalism and Its Physiologies, 1830–50* (Baskingstoke, Hampshire: Palgrave Macmillan, 2007), 1–9, 140–43.

72. In the typologies, too, one detects the echo of "characters" popular in the seventeenth century, with antecedents going back to classical Greece.

73. Nekrasov, *Petersburg,* 51–70, 71–99, 101–30, 131–57.

74. Nikolai Nekrasov, "The Petersburg Corners," ibid., 142–45.

75. Nekrasov, *Petersburg,* 151–251.

76. Ivan Turgenev, *A Hunter's Sketches,* ed. O. Gorchakov (1852; repr., Moscow: Foreign Languages Publishing House, n.d.), 451.

77. Hartsock, *History of American Literary Journalism,* 127–28.

78. Turgenev, *Hunter's Sketches,* 453–55.

79. Leo Tolstoy, *The Sebastopol Sketches,* trans. David McDuff (New York: Penguin Classics, 1986).

80. Fyodor Dostoevsky, *Notes from a Dead House,* trans. L. Navrozov and Y. Guralsky (1862; repr., Moscow: Foreign Languages Publishing House, n.d.).

81. Anton Chekhov, *The Island: A Journey to Sakhalin,* trans. Luba and Michael Terpak (1895; repr., New York: Washington Square Press, 1967).

82. Maxim Gorky, *Through Russia,* trans. C. J. Hogarth (1921; repr. London: J. M. Dent and Sons, 1959); Maxim Gorky, "How I Learnt to Write," trans. Julius Katzer, *On Literature* (Moscow: Foreign Languages Publishing House, [1960?]), 62–66; Charles A. Moser, ed., *The Cambridge History of Russian Literature* (Cambridge: Cambridge University Press, 1989), 372.

83. Maxim Gorky, "The Ninth of January," in *Selected Short Stories by Maxim Gorky* (New York: Frederick Ungar Publishing Co., 1959), 168–94. This, however, was not a fictional short story despite the volume's title.

84. Vladimir Arsenyev, jacket notes, *Dersu Uzala,* trans. V. Schneerson (1923; repr., Moscow: Foreign Languages Publishing House, n.d.).

85. Gleb Struve, *Russian Literature under Lenin and Stalin: 1917–1953* (Norman: University of Oklahoma Press, 1971), 217. *Dersu Uzala* is perhaps better known in the West because of the 1975 Academy Award–winning Soviet-Japanese film production of the same name directed by Akira Kurosawa.

86. Siegfried Kracauer, *The Salaried Masses: Duty and Distraction in Weimar Germany,* trans. Quintin Hoare (1930; repr., London: Verso, 1998), 32.

87. Wagner, *Inside a Service Trade,* 311–15.

88. Danica Kozlová and Jiři Tomáš, *Egon Erwin Kisch: Journalist and Fighter,* trans. John Newton (Prague: International Organization of Journalists, 1985), 18–21; Segel, *Egon Erwin Kisch,* 12–16.

89. Kozlová and Tomáš, *Egon Erwin Kisch,* 20.

90. Paul Harvey and J. E. Heseltine, eds., *The Oxford Companion to French Literature* (Oxford: Clarendon Press, 1969), 272, 632.

91. Segel, *Egon Erwin Kisch,* xi.

92. Marie Majerová, "Als Egonek den Roman Zum Tod Verurteilte," in *Kisch-Kalendar,* ed. Franz Carl Weiskopf ([East] Berlin: Aufbau-Verlag, 1955), 185–86; translation in the text is by Lydia Fetler Hartsock and John C. Hartsock.

93. John Carey, ed., *The Faber Book of Reportage* (London: Faber and Faber, 1987); John Carey, ed., *Eyewitness to History* (New York: Avon, 1990).

94. Karl Breul, *New Cassell's German Dictionary,* ed. and rev. Harold T. Betteridge (New York: Funk and Wagnalls, 1958).

95. "*Stern* und Gruner + Jahr stiften neuen Preis," *Stern* 25, October 2004, www.stern.de.

96. Frank Berberich, interview by John C. Hartsock, Berlin, May 23, 2006.

97. Laughlin, *Chinese Reportage*, 12.

98. Hartsock, *History of American Literary Journalism*, 67–69.

99. See. by Egon Erwin Kisch, *Zaren, Popen, Bolschewiken* (1927; repr., Berlin: Aufbau-Verlag, 1977); *Paradies Amerika* (1929; repr., Berlin: Aufbau Verlag, 1994); *Changing Asia*, trans. Rita Reil (New York: Alfred A. Knopf, 1935); *Secret China,* trans. Michael Davidson (London: John Lane, 1935); and *Australian Landfall,* trans. John Fisher (1937; repr., London: Secker and Warburg, 1969).

100. Barbara Foley, *Radical Presentations: Politics and Form in U.S. Proletarian Fiction, 1921–1941* (Durham: Duke University Press, 1993), 65. See also Michael Denning, *The Cultural Front: The Laboring of American Culture in the Twentieth Century* (New York: Verso, 1996), xi–xx.

101. See, for example, all in *New Masses,* Ernest Hemingway, "Fascism Is a Lie," June 22, 1937, 4; John Dos Passos, "The Unemployed Report," February 13, 1934, 11–12; Edna St. Vincent Millay, "Justice Denied in Massachusetts," August 25, 1936, 4; Muriel Rukeyser, "Barcelona on the Barricades," September 1, 1936, 1–12; Sinclair Lewis, "Christmas 1935," December 17, 1936, 1–5; Theodore Dreiser, "Like the Good Deed," December 15, 1936, 1–10; Upton Sinclair, "Let Us Educate and Explain," September 8, 1936, 11–17; Sherwood Anderson, "Belief in Man," December 15, 1936, 30.

102. Joseph North, *No Men Are Strangers* (New York: International Publishers, 1958), 105.

103. Joseph North, "Reportage," in *American Writers' Congress,* ed. Henry Hart (New York: International, 1935), 121.

104. Xiao Qian, "Shang'ai xinwen gogzkuo, ji Xiao Qian tongzhi dui Zhongguo shehui-kexueyuan xinwen yanjiusheng de yici jianghua" [Beloved newspaper work: Comrade Xiao Qian's talk to researchers in journalism at the Chinese Academy of Social Sciences], *Xinwen yanjiu xiliao* 4.74 (1979), quoted in Wagner, *Inside a Service Trade*, 348.

105. Kisch, *Secret China*; Wagner, *Inside a Service Trade*, 327.

106. "Wuchan jieji wenxue yundong xin de qingshi ji women de renwu" [New trends in the proletarian literary movement and our tasks], *Wenhua douzheng* [Cultural Struggle] 1.1 (August 1930): 152, quoted in Laughlin, *Chinese Reportage*, 17.

107. Kawaguchi Ko, "Deguo de xinxing wenxue" [A newly emerging literature in Germany], trans. Feng Xuanzhang, *Tuohuangzhe* 1.2 (1930): 732, quoted in Wagner, *Inside a Service Trade*, 348.

108. Wagner, *Inside a Service Trade*, 348.

109. "Für Egon Erwin Kisch zum 50. Geburstag," *Internationale Literatur* 4 (April 1935): 3–30.

110. Wagner, *Inside a Service Trade*, 327.

111. Theodor Balk, "Egon Erwin Kisch and His Reportage: On the 50th Year of a Noted Revolutionary Reporter", *International Literature* 4 (April 1935): 67.

112. Lee Gutkind, speech, Ithaca College, Ithaca, NY, February 1, 2005.

113. Kisch, *Asia*, 91–94, 240–58.

114. Wagner, *Inside a Service Trade,* 341–45.

115. Kisch, *Asia*, 186, 258.

116. Segel, *Egon Erwin Kisch*, 38–43.

117. North, "Reportage,"121.

118. Segel, *Egon Erwin Kisch*, 32–34.

119. Wagner, *Inside a Service Trade*, 359.

120. Larissa Reisner, *Hamburg at the Barricades*, trans. and ed. Richard Chappell (London: Pluto, 1977); Cathy Porter, *Larissa Reisner* (London: Virago, 1988), 58–59, 190–91.

121. Egon Erwin Kisch, "John Reed, ein Reporter auf der Barikade," *Mein Leben für die Zeitung 1926–1947,* Journalistische Texte 2 ([East] Berlin: Aufbau-Verlag, 1983), 91–92, quoted in Segel, *Egon Erwin Kisch*, 34.

122. Egon Erwin Kisch, "Bekanntschaft mit Maxim Gorki," *Die Rote Fahne*, March 22, 1928, quoted in Wagner, *Inside a Service Trade*, 359.

123. William Stott, *Documentary Expression and Thirties America* (New York: Oxford University Press, 1973), 54–55.

124. Wagner, *Inside a Service Trade*, 346–47.

125. Struve, *Russian Literature*, 197, 215.

126. Dmitry V. Kharitonov, "Literature of Fact as a Fact of Literature," *Literary Journalism Studies.* under review (emphasis added).

127. Ibid., 211–17.

128. Marc Slonim, *Soviet Russian Literature: Writers and Problems, 1911–1977*, 2nd rev. ed. (New York: Oxford University Press, 1977), 172.

129. Segel, *Egon Erwin Kisch*, 37.

130. Wolfgang Kasack, *Dictionary of Russian Literature since 1917,* trans. Maria Carlson and Jane T. Hedges (New York: Columbia University Press, 1988), 423–24; Struve, *Russian Literature*, 211–17, 265; Slonim, *Soviet Russian Literature*, 172.

131. [Sergei Tretyakov], *A Chinese Testament: The Autobiography of Tan Shih-Hua as Told to S. Tretyakov* (1930; repr., New York: Simon and Schuster, 1934), v.

132. Devin Fore, preface to "The Writer and the Socialist Village: Sergei Tret'iakov," trans. Devin Fore, *October* 118, special issue, "Soviet Factography" (Fall 2006): 64.

133. Walter Benjamin, "The Author as Producer," in *Reflections: Essays, Aphorisms, Autobiographical Writings*, ed. and intro. Peter Demetz, trans. Edmund Jephcott (New York: Schocken Books, 1986), 223–24.

134. Fore, preface, 64.

135. Sergei Tret'iakov, "The Writer and the Socialist Village," trans. Devin Fore, *October* 118, special issue: "Soviet Factography" (Fall 2006), 69.

136. Wolfe, "New Journalism," 9, 40–41.

137. Benjamin, "Author as Producer," 221.

138. I use Harriet Borland's translation from her *Soviet Literary Theory and Practice during the First Five-Year Plan 1928–32* (1950; rpt. New York: Greenwood Press, 1969), 62.

139. Maxim Gorky, "O Literature" in *O Literature*, ed. N. F. Belchikov, 3rd ed., enl. (Moscow: Soviet Writer, 1937), 58.

140. Maxim Gorky, L. Auerbach, and S. G. Firin, eds., *Belomor* (New York: Harrison Smith and Robert Haas, 1935).

141. Ibid., 165.

142. Valentin Kataev, *Time Forward!,* trans. Charles Malamuth (New York: Farrar and Rhinehart, 1933).

143. The problem is that their individual contributions are not identified in *Belomor*. Instead, Kataev and Shklovsky (spelled "Schklovsky") are identified in the English translation as part of a collective of thirty-four authors on the verso page facing the title page. See Gorky, Auerbach, and Firin, *Belomor*, n.p.

144. Mary A. Nichols, *Writers at Work: Russian Production Novels and the Construction of Soviet Culture* (Lewisburg, PA: Bucknell University Press, 2010), 197.

145. Struve, *Russian Literature*, 246; Slonim, *Soviet Russian Literature*, 244; Nichols, *Writers at Work*, 197.

146. Nichols, *Writers at Work*, 197, 201–207.

147. Ibid., 217.

148. Hartsock, *History of American Literary Journalism*, 119.

149. Borland, *Soviet Literary Theory and Practice*, 47, 48–49, 55–56, 76.

150. Ibid., 38.

151. Kasack, *Dictionary of Russian Literature*, 161.

152. Kataev, *Time Forward!*, 336, 337.

153. Ibid., 338.

154. Struve, *Russian Literature*, 247; Slonim, *Soviet Russian Literature*, 244; Borland, *Soviet Literary Theory*, 88.

155. Slonim, *Soviet Russian Literature*, 244.

156. Hartsock, *History of American Literary Journalism*, 111–20.

157. Slonim, *Soviet Russian Literature*, 244.

158. Struve, *Russian Literature*, 269.

159. Granville Hicks et al., eds., *Proletarian Literature in the United States* (New York: International Publishers, 1935), 62, 213.

160. Richard Sheldon, introduction to Victor Shklovsky, *A Sentimental Journey*, trans. Richard Sheldon (Ithaca: Cornell University Press, 1970), xv, xxiv.

161. Ibid., xx, v.

162. Ibid., 60, 139.

163. Ibid., 146.

164. Ibid., 124.

165. Ibid., 73.

166. Ibid., 153.

167. Ibid., 74, 149.

168. John Reed, *Ten Days That Shook the World* (1919; repr., New York: Modern Library, 1935), 2, 313.

169. Mikhail Bakhtin, *Problems of Dostoevsky's Poetics*, trans. R. W. Rotsel ([Ann Arbor]: Ardis, 1973), 45–46, 57–60, 150.

170. Robert E. Humphrey, "John Reed," in *A Sourcebook of American Literary Journalism: Representative Writers of an Emerging Genre*, ed. Thomas B. Connery (New York: Greenwood Press, 1992), 159.

171. David C. Duke, *John Reed* (Boston: Twayne, 1987), 30.

172. Duke, *John Reed*, 35.

173. A. J. P. Taylor, introduction to *Ten Days That Shook the World* (1919; rpt. London: Penguin, 1977), x. See also Daniel W. Lehman, *Matters of Fact: Reading Nonfiction Over the Edge* (Columbus: Ohio State University Press, 1997), 90.

174. Nikolai Chuzhak, "A Writer's Handbook," trans. Devin Fore, *October* 118, special issue: "Soviet Factography" (Fall 2006): 91, 86, 82.

175. Valentin Ovechkin, *Collective Farm Sidelights* (Moscow: Foreign Languages Publishing House, n.d.).

176. Wagner, *Inside a Service Trade*, 249.

177. Vladimir Pomerantsev, "On Sincerity in Literature," *Novy Mir* (December 1953), www.sovlit.com.

178. Liu Binyan, *A Higher Kind of Loyalty*, trans. Zhu Hong (New York: Pantheon Books), 279–80.

179. Wagner, *Inside a Service Trade*, 47–48.
180. Joseph Brodsky, introduction to *Poems by Anna Akhmatova*, trans. Lynn Coffin (New York: W. W. Norton, 1983), xxx; Solomon Volkov, *Conversations with Joseph Brodsky*, trans. Marian Schwartz (New York: Free Press, 1998), 257–58; Tomas Venclova, "Poetry and Remembrance," review of *The Akhmatova Journals*, vol. 1, *1938–41*, *Washington Post Book World*, April 4, 1994, 2.
181. "Lev Gumilev," *Russipedia*, http://russiapedia.rt.com.
182. Anna Akhmatova, "Requiem: Instead of a Preface," in *Poems*, trans. Lyn Coffin (New York: W. W. Norton, 1983), 82.
183. Jean Paul Sartre, "The Republic of Silence," in *The Republic of Silence*, ed. A. J. Liebling (New York: Harcourt, Brace, 1947), 491–500.
184. Alexander I. Solzhenitsyn, *The Gulag Archipelago: 1918–1956*, vol. 1–2 (New York: Harper and Row, 1973), 201.
185. Ibid., 274–75.
186. Ibid., 437.
187. Ibid., 275.
188. Ibid., xii. Solzhenitsyn cites thirty-six. The English translation identifies thirty-four.
189. Alexander Genis, "Perestroika as a Shift in Literary Paradigm," in *Russian Postmodernism: New Perspectives on Post-Soviet Culture*, ed. Mikhail N. Epstein, Alexander A. Genis, and Slobodanka M. Vladiv-Glover, Studies in Slavic Literature, Culture, and Society, vol. 3 (New York: Berghahn Books, 1999), 91–92.
190. Laughlin, *Chinese Reportage*, 7.
191. Susan Greenberg, "Kapuściński and Beyond: The Polish School of Reportage," in *Global Literary Journalism: Exploring the Journalistic Imagination*, ed. Richard Lance Keeble and John Tulloch (New York: Peter Lang, 2012), 129. I find Greenberg's assessment especially useful because it goes beyond the contributions of Ryszard Kapuściński to the genre and provides insight into the more contemporary Polish experience, which has been little explored but which is indeed a very rich tradition.
192. Diana Kuprel, "Literary Reportage: Between and Beyond Art and Fact," in *History of the Literary Cultures of East-Central Europe: Junctures and Disjunctures in the 19th and 20th Centuries*, ed. Marcel Cornis-Pope and John Neubauer, vol. 1 (Amsterdam: John Benjamins, 2004), 385.
193. Sonja Merljak Zdovc, "Literary Journalism: The Intersection of Literature and Journalism," *Acta Neophilologica* 37, nos. 1–2 (2004): 17–22. See also Leonora Flis, *Factual Fictions: Narrative Truth and the Contemporary American Documentary Novel* (Newcastle upon Tyne: Cambridge Scholars, 2010), 165.
194. Alexiyevich, "Boys in Zinc," 537.
195. Hartsock, "Chapter Title: 'Murder or Execution?'" 107–8.

5. Negotiating Cultural and Personal Revelation

1. Alexandra Fuller, *Scribbling the Cat: Travels with an African Soldier* (New York: Penguin, 2004).
2. A contemporary dictionary definition will reveal this; see, for example, *Oxford American Dictionary* (1980). Elsewhere it is described as a "literature of personal revelation." See Joseph T. Shipley, ed., *Dictionary of World Literature* (Paterson, NJ: Littlefield, Adams, 1962), 32.
3. For that matter, we cannot entirely exclude the shaping consciousness from all journal-

isms; although subjectivity may appear to be entirely missing from a hard news, objectified account, it is still there, discreetly camouflaged and marked by its absence, because inevitably the writing of hard news still reflects a shaping consciousness.

4. Alexandra Fuller, "Alexandra Fuller on Loneliness after Divorce: 'Falling' Author Explains How Not to Feel Alone," *Huffington Post,* January 25, 2013, www.huffingtonpost .com.

5. Fuller, *Scribbling the Cat,* 27, 59.

6. Alexandra Fuller, *Don't Let's Go to the Dogs Tonight: An African Childhood* (New York: Random House, 2003).

7. Fuller, *Scribbling the Cat,* 29.

8. Ibid., 100, 3, 4, 171, 73, all emphasis added.

9. Leonora Todaro, "Bulletproof Hunk: Fuller and K Take a Road Trip—But Does She Blaller His Skop?," review of *Scribbling the Cat: Travels with an African Soldier,* by Alexandra Fuller, *Village Voice,* May 25, 2004. www.villagevoice.com; Laura Miller, "The Infantryman," review of *Scribbling the Cat: Travels with an African Soldier,* by Alexandra Fuller, *New York Times,* May 9, 2004.

10. Fuller, *Scribbling the Cat,* 20.

11. Ibid., 3.

12. Ibid., 29.

13. Ibid., 238.

14. Todaro, "Bulletproof Hunk"; Miller, "Infantryman."

15. The issue of betrayal is one ably explored by Kathy Roberts Forde in her examination of Janet Malcolm's legal travails resulting from an article Malcolm published in the *New Yorker* about the Freud critic Jeffrey Masson. Robert Alexander takes up the issue in a similar examination. See Kathy Roberts Forde, *Literary Journalism on Trial: Masson v. New Yorker and the First Amendment* (Amherst: University of Massachusetts Press, 2008), 139–43; Robert Alexander, "'My Story Is Always Escaping into Other People': Subjectivity, Objectivity, and the Double in American Literary Journalism," *Literary Journalism Studies* 1.1 (Spring 2009): 57–66.

16. Fuller, *Scribbling the Cat,* 234.

17. John C. Hartsock, "'Lettre' from Berlin," *DoubleTake* 2.1 (2007): 106–11.

18. Linda Grant, *The People on the Street: A Writer's View of Israel* (London: Virago, 2006), 5–6, 19, 208.

19. James Agee and Walker Evans, *Let Us Now Praise Famous Men: Three Tenant Families* (1941; repr., Boston: Houghton Mifflin, 1969), 239.

20. Grant, *People on the Street,* 191.

21. Ibid., 57.

22. Ibid., 58.

23. Ibid., 3.

24. Ibid., 191, 197.

25. Linda Grant, acceptance speech, Lettre Ulysses Award, Berlin, September 30, 2006 (quotation from my notes of the event, which I attended; I have been unable to find the speech published or online).

26. Grant, *People on the Street,* 6.

27. Ibid., 64.

28. Ibid., 1.

29. Jenny Stringer, ed., *The Oxford Companion to Twentieth-Century Literature in English* (Oxford: Oxford University Press, 1996), 477, s.v. "Nabokov, Vladimir."

30. Vladimir Nabokov, *Speak, Memory: An Autobiography Revisited* (New York: G. P. Putnam's Sons, 1966), 20, 73, 229.

31. Ibid., 96.

32. Ibid., 79.

33. Ibid., 242.

34. Ibid., 309–10.

35. Norman Sims, "Literary Journalists," in *The Literary Journalists,* ed. Norman Sims (New York: Ballantine, 1984), 187–212.

36. Sara Davidson, "Real Property," in *Real Property* (Garden City, NY: Doubleday, 1980), 8, 35, 36, 40.

37. Fuller, *Let's Not Go to the Dogs Tonight;* Alexandra Fuller, *The Legend of Colton H. Bryant* (New York: Penguin, 2008).

38. This is the point raised by Mikhail Bakhtin, in his *Problems of Dostoevsky's Poetics,* trans. R. W. Rotsel ([Ann Arbor]: Ardis, 1973), 45–46, 57–60, 150. See also Caryl Emerson, "The Tolstoy Connection in Bakhtin," *PMLA* 100.1 (January 1985): 68–80.

39. Fuller, *Scribbling the Cat,* 250.

6. When Nature Abhors a Vacuum

1. Adrian Nicole LeBlanc, *Random Family: Love, Drugs, Trouble, and Coming of Age in the Bronx* (New York: Scribner, 2003), 183.

2. Ibid., 193–94.

3. Ibid., 403.

4. John L. Jackson Jr., "Numb with Pain," review of *Random Family*, by Adrian Nicole LeBlanc, *Washington Post*, February 12, 2003.

5. Wolfgang Iser, *The Act of Reading: A Theory of Aesthetic Response* (Baltimore: Johns Hopkins University Press, 1978), 365.

6. LeBlanc, *Random Family*, 85.

7. Ibid., 274–75.

8. Kerry Sheridan, *Bagpipe Brothers* (New Brunswick, NJ: Rivergate Books, 2006), 67.

9. Bob Batz et al., "'All Nine Alive': The Story of the Quecreek Mine Rescue," *Pittsburgh Post-Gazette*, August 4, 2002.

10. Deb Kollars, "Staging a Comeback: Burbank Looks to Make Bright Lights Shine Again," four-part series, *Sacramento Bee*, December 16–19, 2001.

11. Ibid.

12. Batz, "All Nine Alive."

13. Jonathan Harr, *A Civil Action* (New York: Vintage, 1996), 146.

14. Ibid., 218.

15. Iser, Act of Reading, 61, 68.

16. Thomas Keneally, *Schindler's List* (1982; New York: Touchstone, 1992), 10.

17. Ibid., 260.

18. Ibid., 280.

19. Robert S. Boynton, *The New New Journalism* (New York: Vintage, 2005), 114.

20. Norman Sims, ed., *Literary Journalism in the Twentieth Century* (New York: Oxford University Press, 1990), 1–12.

21. Boynton, *New New Journalism*, 114.

22. Ibid., 103.

23. Ibid., 126.

24. "Reading Between the Lines: What the ACT Reveals about College Readiness in Reading," www.act.org/research/policymakers/pdf/reading_report.pdf.

25. LeBlanc, *Random Family*, 178, 290, 147.

26. Ibid., 405.

27. James Boswell, *The Journal of a Tour to the Hebrides with Samuel Johnson LL.D.*, and Samuel Johnson, *A Journey to the Western Islands of Scotland*, ed. and intro. Peter Levi (New York: Penguin, 1984), 165.

28. Agnes Smedley, "The Fall of Shangpo," in *Proletarian Literature in the United States*, ed. Granville Hicks et al. (New York: International Publishers, 1935), 251.

29. Jackson, "Numb with Pain."

30. Michael J. Agovino, "I Wanted to Be Here All of the Time," *Newsweek*, February 10, 2003, 68.

31. John Ball, introduction to Lafcadio Hearn, *Children of the Levee*, ed. O. W. Frost (Lexington: University of Kentucky Press, 1957), 7–8.

32. Bruce Gillespie, "Building Bridges between Literary Journalism and Alternative Ethnographic Forms: Opportunities and Challenges," *Literary Journalism Studies* 4.2 (Fall 2012): 67–79. Nevertheless, the alternative ethnographic forms described in the article read more like a narrative literary journalism, in my view. What we can detect is that ethnographers who practice alternative, more subjective forms of ethnography are benefiting from the premise behind narrative literary journalism.

33. LeBlanc, *Random Family*, back cover.

34. Linda Grant, *The People on the Street: A Writer's View of Israel* (London: Virago, 2006), 191.

35. Jackson, "Numb with Pain."

Conclusion

1. Brian Boyd, *On the Origin of Stories: Evolution, Cognition, and Fiction* (Cambridge: Harvard University Press, 2009), 159.

2. Frederic Hudson, *Journalism in the United States, from 1691–1872* (New York: Harper and Brothers, 1873), 714.

3. Ibid.

4. Library of Congress, Prints and Photographs Division, FSA/OWI Collection, LC-USF342-T0-008138-A. See also www.getty.edu/art/gettyguide artObjectDetails?artobj=52190.

5. Library of Congress, Prints and Photographs Division, FSA/OWI Collection, LC-USF342-T01-008154-A. See also www.getty.edu/art/gettyguide/artObjectDetails?artobj =52143.

6. James Agee, *Let Us Now Praise Famous Men* (Boston: Houghton Mifflin, 1941), 265–66.

7. N. R. Kleinfield, "Baptism by Fire: A New York Firefighter Confronts His First Test," *New York Times*, June 20, 2014, www.nytimes.com.

8. "First Fires: The Fears and Rewards," *New York Times*, www.nytimes.com.

9. The issue is more complicated than it appears. The online version of Kleinfield's "Baptism by Fire" was published on June 20, 2014. The print newspaper version was published two days later on June 22. It is understandable that the written text would be more likely to suffice for a print version. But the larger issue is whether, as I note later, one medium among the array will have to provide a dominating continuity (one might characterize it

as a dominating media rhetoric) to which the others are adjuncts when it comes to online multimedia projects. Given the inherent visceral appeal of graphic images, especially video, this has implications for static and abstract alphabetic text.

10. Adam Gorlick, "Media Multitaskers Pay Mental Price, Stanford Study Shows," *Stanford Report,* August 24, 2009, http://news.stanford.edu. See also Eyal Ophir, Clifford Nass, and Anthony D. Wagner, "Cognitive Control in Media Multitaskers," *Proceedings of the National Academy of Sciences* 106.37 (September 15, 2009): 15583.

11. This is a complex issue well beyond the scope of this book. In 1991 the Poynter Institute conducted its first eye-tracking test on newspaper readers, which concluded that the movement of the eyes was attracted first to bold graphic elements, specifically photographs and headlines in that order, before they arrived at reading the text of an article. Poynter conducted another eye-tracking study in 2007 in which readers read both newspapers and online news. Here it appeared that online alphabetic text fared better. Newspaper readers read less of their articles while those reading online news read more. However, the second study acknowledged that online readers engaged in more scanning of the electronic text, instead of giving it a close reading. In narra-descriptive journalism, where the detail of concrete metaphor is a critical source of meaning, scanning is less likely to do it justice. Also, the problem with an eye-tracking study is that it can only track the movement of the eyes, but it cannot measure what meanings were derived in the reading process. Scanning without absorbing may account for why it appeared online readers were reading more of the text. One has to take into consideration the qualitative differences in the nature of reading. Also, the readers in the second study read online news derived from traditional newspaper sources, news organs historically based in print. But if news reporting were unencumbered by such a traditional approach, would the result be very different, with an emphasis placed more on the visual appeal of bold graphics, especially if such reports were inaugurated with video as the dominant medium? Printed text is static and movement occurs only in the imaginations of the brain, not visually on the screen. For the Poynter studies, see Paul Martin Lester, *Visual Communication: Images with Messages* (Boston: Wadsworth, 2014), 49–50.

12. Rodney Benson, "Why Narrative Is Not Enough: Immigration and Genres of Journalism," in *Reporting at the Southern Borders: Journalism and Public Debates on Immigration in the US and the EU,* ed. Giovanna Dell'Orto and Vicki L. Birchfield, Routledge Studies in Global Information, Politics and Society (New York: Routledge, 2013), 73. In fairness, Benson is criticizing what he sees as the inadequacy of a more traditional narrative aproach. But he provides no evidence that such an approach has been presented as preferred. His sweeping claim regarding traditional narrative does not stand up to scrutiny and strikes me as a straw-man argument. Moreover, by dismissing narrative, he at the least inscribes a more critically complex rhetorical model as the desired model. This is what I object to.

13. "Reading between the Lines: What the ACT Reveals about College Readiness in Reading," www.act.org.

14. Kathy Roberts Forde and Matthew W. Ross, "Radio and Civic Courage in the Communications Circuit of John Hersey's 'Hiroshima,'" *Literary Journalism Studies* 3.2 (Fall 2011): 31–38, esp. 35.

15. John J. Pauly, "Journalism and the Sociology of Public Life," in *The Idea of Public Journalism,* ed. Theodore L. Glasser (New York: Guilford Press, 1999), 148; John J. Pauly, "Literary Journalism and the Drama of Civic Life," *Literary Journalism Studies* 3.2 (Fall 2011): 82.

Index

JOHN C. HARTSOCK is the author of the critically acclaimed *A History of American Literary Journalism: The Emergence of a Modern Narrative Form* (University of Massachusetts Press, 2000), recipient of two history awards for outstanding scholarship in the field from the Association for Education in Journalism and Mass Communication and from the American Journalism Historians Association. Hartsock was the founding editor of *Literary Journalism Studies*, the journal of the International Association for Literary Journalism Studies. He has lectured widely on the subject of narrative/literary journalism, and his articles have appeared in *Prose Studies, Genre, Points of Entry, Journal of Communication Inquiry,* and *Critical Studies in Mass Communication*. Hartsock is also the author of *Seasons of a Finger Lakes Winery* (2011), recipient of a first-place Gourmand Award in Paris for excellence in wine writing. He teaches at the State University of New York at Cortland.